D1533727

HITLER'S INTERPRETER

THE MACMILLAN COMPANY
NEW YORK · BOSTON · CHICAGO
DALLAS · ATLANTA · SAN FRANCISCO

MACMILLAN AND CO., LIMITED
LONDON · BOMBAY · CALCUTTA
MADRAS · MELBOURNE

THE MACMILLAN COMPANY
OF CANADA, LIMITED
TORONTO

HITLER'S INTERPRETER

by

DR PAUL SCHMIDT

Edited by R. H. C. Steed

NEW YORK

THE MACMILLAN COMPANY

1951

RICHMOND COLLEGE LIBRARY

Copyright, 1950, 1951, by
International Press Alliance Corporation

All rights reserved—no part of this book may be reproduced in any form without permission in writing from the publisher, except by a reviewer who wishes to quote brief passages in connection with a review written for inclusion in magazine or newspaper.

PRINTED IN THE UNITED STATES OF AMERICA

First Printing

The material from *The Ciano Diaries: 1939-1943* is quoted by permission of the publishers, Doubleday & Company, Inc. Copyright, 1945-1946, by Doubleday & Company, Inc.

CONTENTS

Editor's Preface

ALTHOUGH we inevitably think of Paul Schmidt as "Hitler's Interpreter", he had in fact been interpreting for a whole series of German Chancellors and Foreign Ministers during the decade before Hitler and Ribbentrop entered the international scene.

The first half of the German edition of Dr. Schmidt's book is devoted to his reminiscences of that earlier period. I decided, in preparing a book of reasonable size and closely sustained interest for the ordinary British reader, to leave out the pre-Hitlerian part altogether. Frankly, in the space at our disposal, it is Hitler we are interested in—not Mueller, Marx, Luther, Curtius, Brüning, or even Stresemann.

Looking back down Schmidt's vista of German history since the end of the first World War, I was surprised to find how much it was still dominated by the figure of Hitler. He bulks across the threshold, still almost too near to be in focus, lurid in the glow of the gigantic disaster he unleashed. And when we look beyond him at his immediate predecessors they appear, in contrast, as grey, mundane figures, clearly-defined, fully-explained, and unexciting except to the student.

There is however a danger that, plunging straight into the Hitler epoch, the reader may be mesmerised by the magnitude and speed of events into believing that Germany's restoration and German history between the two wars began with Hitler. How far this was from being the case is shown by Schmidt's notes in the full German edition on all the private meetings and international conferences at which Hitler's predecessors fought the way upwards for Germany from defeat to equality of rights. The milestones tell their own tale: end of the Ruhr occupation (1925); Locarno Pact (1925); restoration of civil aviation (1926); Germany's entry into the League as a Great Power (1926); end of the Rhineland occupation (1930); end of reparations (1932); three-Power statement on German equality (1932).

9

I should like to salvage one anecdote in particular from Schmidt's pre-Hitler reminiscences because it shows with what tact and caution the German statesmen of the early '20's had to tread. The scene was the London conference in 1924 on reparations, which the French were determined to restrict to that one subject, while the Germans wished to bring up proposals for ending the Ruhr occupation. The German Chancellor, Marx—who could not face the prospect of returning to Germany without something with which to appease German nationalist sentiment—had taken great pains to wrap up a reference to the Ruhr in the most unobtrusive manner possible in a statement at the conference on the Dawes report.

But, at the crucial moment, the unfortunate German interpreter, carried away by patriotic feelings, had said with too much emphasis in his French translation: "And, of course, the question of the Ruhr must also be discussed."

The effect on the French Prime Minister, Herriot, was disastrous. He was as scared of returning to Paris and confessing that the Ruhr had been discussed as Marx was of returning to Berlin and admitting that it had not. Herriot at once stopped the translation and indignantly declared that, if the word "Ruhr" were as much as mentioned again, he would leave at once. The interpreter was withdrawn in disgrace by the German delegation—a convenient scapegoat.

It was at this delicate juncture that Schmidt, then aged 24 and a junior member of the German Foreign Office interpreting staff, was called on to take over. Stresemann, in a clandestine meeting with Herriot at the R.A.C. in Pall Mall, put his case so persuasively that Herriot promised to use all his influence in Paris in favour of calling off the Ruhr occupation. And he kept his word. Thus was created the bond of confidence and esteem between Herriot and Stresemann—later continued between Briand and Stresemann—which was a major factor in Germany's restoration to European equality.

Schmidt saw in this a proof that between *hommes de bonne volonté*, men of good will, regardless of nationality, even the greatest difficulties could be overcome. Twenty years of unique experience of diplomacy in its most intimate top-level aspect confirmed this opinion, and added to it the conviction that "the real enemies of mankind are the fanatics, in whatever camp they may be."

Schmidt is at pains to make it clear that he places the Nazis in that category—especially Hitler and Ribbentrop. He is damning and often contemptuous in his judgments of the men for whom he worked so loyally for so long—and has been criticised on that account. He claims that he was never a Nazi sympathiser, that he merely did his job as a civil servant and expert technician, that he made no secret of his independent outlook and that this was duly noted against him in his dossier.

This account of himself seems to be borne out by the impression he made, among others, on Sir Nevile Henderson, British Ambassador in Berlin until the outbreak of war. He certainly showed considerable courage of a negative kind in that, despite his very special position, he resisted pressure to join the Nazi Party until 1943. On the other hand, he makes no concession to the view that the German people as a whole were in any way responsible for Hitler. He attributes the triumph of the nationalist extremist in Germany to the economic crisis of 1930-1932 and to what he describes as the mistakes on the part of the Allies in making their concessions to Germany too late and too grudgingly. I think Schmidt might fairly be described as an enlightened, cosmopolitanised German nationalist, and find it a little hard on him that we have to hand him down to posterity as "Hitler's Interpreter" and not, perhaps more aptly, as "Stresemann's Interpreter"—a title to which he has at least an equal claim.

A final word on the subject of editing. I have deleted or condensed a passage here and there which would have no particular interest for the English reader, writing in a connecting sentence where necessary so as to maintain the continuity without the distraction of "editor's notes."

R.H.C. STEED.

CHAPTER I

(1935)

THE first time I interpreted for Hitler was on March 25, 1935, when Sir John Simon and Mr. Anthony Eden came to Berlin for talks on the European crisis caused by German re-armament. Simon was then Foreign Secretary, and Eden Lord Privy Seal. Also present were von Neurath, German Foreign Minister, and Ribbentrop, at that time Special Commissioner for Disarmament Questions.

I was surprised when I received the order to attend. It was true that I was senior interpreter at the German Foreign Office, and had worked for practically every German Chancellor and Foreign Minister in the ten years up to the advent of the Hitler Government in January 1933. But then things had changed. Germany had dropped out of the small, man-to-man international discussions, and had adopted the method of notes, memoranda and public pronouncements.

Furthermore, Hitler disliked the German Foreign Office and everyone connected with it. In the previous conversations between him and foreigners the interpreting had been done by Ribbentrop, Baldur von Schirach or some other National Socialist. Our Foreign Office officials were horrified when they heard that Hitler would not even allow State Secretary von Bulow to be present at these highly important discussions with Simon and Eden. In an attempt to ensure that at least one member of the Foreign Office should attend, in addition to von Neurath, they decided to put me forward as interpreter. On being told that I had done good work at Geneva for a long time, Hitler remarked: "If he was at Geneva he's bound to be no good—but so far as I'm concerned we can give him a trial."

The developments leading up to this Anglo-German meeting had been just as unexpected as the conference itself. Both France and England had been watching developments in

Germany with growing concern. The British Government was extremely uneasy about German armaments, particularly about the growth of the German air force. "England's boundary is on the Rhine," Baldwin had stated in the House of Commons in July 1934, and in November he had quite frankly admitted that German rearmament gave definite grounds for general concern. But while France, adhering to her established policy, endeavoured to protect herself against Germany by a comprehensive system of security pacts, the British Government indicated that it desired to arrive at a clarification of German intentions by discussion. This idea found expression in a joint Anglo-French communiqué of February 3rd, 1935: "Great Britain and France are agreed that nothing would contribute more to the re-establishment of confidence and the prospect of peace between the nations than a general settlement freely concluded between Germany and the other Powers."

The German reply to this Anglo-French initiative was given in mid-February in a Note which stated: "The German Government welcomes the spirit of frankness expressed in the communications of His Britannic Majesty's Government and the French Government. It would therefore be glad . . . if His Britannic Majesty's Government were willing to enter into an exchange of views with the German Government." I was not a little astonished at Hitler's sudden change to a peaceful tone as I translated the Note into English.

With surprising speed and readiness the British Government then offered to send the Foreign Minister to Berlin at the beginning of March. But another unexpected development occurred : shortly before Simon's visit was due the British Government issued a White Paper in order to justify its own rearmament to Parliament. Our Languages Service translated from the official text: "Germany is not only rearming openly on a large scale despite the provisions of Part V of the Treaty of Versailles, but has also given notice of withdrawal from the League of Nations and the Disarmament Conference. . . . The action of His Majesty's Government does not, of course, imply condonation of a breach of the Treaty of Versailles." The White Paper continued that if German rearmament progressed uncontrolled at its present pace, it would increase the uneasiness of Germany's neighbours, and therefore endanger peace. Moreover, the spirit in which the people of Germany, more especially her youth, were being organised gave grounds for the uneasiness which had indisputably arisen.

The National Socialist press was indignant. The visit was postponed because Hitler had a cold. Our Foreign Office maintained, rightly or wrongly, that this really was the truth and not a diplomatic lie.

Events now followed one another apace. On March 6th, France introduced two years military service. On March 7th, the Franco-Belgian military agreement of 1921 was extended. On March 16th, Hitler replied with conscription for Germany. The military equality, which was accorded to Germany in December 1932 by negotiated agreement "in a system of security for all nations," became an actual fact as a result of a unilateral decision taken by the Reich outside any security system. My Foreign Office friends commented that this could have been achieved more quickly and smoothly by negotiation, as in the case of the evacuation of the Rhineland and of reparations. In the light of my experience of the negotiations conducted by Stresemann and Brüning I agreed that the method pursued by those two statesmen would have attained the objective quicker, had it not been for the adverse effects of German developments before and after 1933. That it would have been cheaper, Germany and the whole world knows only too well.

Not more than two days later, on March 18th, the British Government protested: "His Majesty's Government in the United Kingdom feel bound to convey to the German Government their protest against the announcement made by the latter on March 16th of the decision to adopt conscription and to increase the peace-time basis of the German army to 36 divisions.

"Following upon the announcement of a German Air Force, such a declaration is a further example of unilateral action, which, apart from the issue of principle, is calculated seriously to increase uneasiness in Europe. . . .

"They (His Majesty's Government) wish to be assured that the German Government still desires the visit to take place, within the terms of reference previously agreed."

I was at that time working in the Languages Section of the Foreign Office, where we promptly translated this and the subsequent flow of documents for Hitler's benefit. The last sentence, about Simon's visit, really astonished us, for we never expected that the English would, after this indignant protest, politely ask in the same breath whether they could come to Berlin.

"As far as I am concerned," François-Poncet, then French Ambassador in Berlin, writes in his Memoirs, "I suggested immediately after March 16th that the Powers should at once recall their ambassadors, and by speedily concluding the Eastern and the Danubian Pacts, forthwith set up a common defensive front against Germany. England should naturally let it be known that any negotiations would now be superfluous, and that Sir John Simon had therefore finally given up his plan of a visit to Berlin. My suggestion was regarded as too drastic, and was therefore not considered."

It was not until March 21st that M. François-Poncet handed us the French protest, which I translated for Hitler as follows: "These decisions (conscription, 36 divisions, creation of an Air Force) clearly conflict with Germany's obligations under the treaties she has signed. They also conflict with the statement of December 11th, 1932 (Equality of rights within a security system). . . . The Government of the Reich has deliberately transgressed the fundamental principles of international law. . . . The Government of the French Republic considers it to be its duty to make the most emphatic protest, with full reservations for the future."

Half an hour later, our future allies, the Italians, put in an appearance. The Italian Ambassador, in a Note which we had to translate very quickly, spoke only of reserving all rights for future action. In his last sentence he stated that the Italian Government could accept no *fait accompli* resulting from a "unilateral decision annulling international undertakings." A mere comparison of the text of these three Notes showed me that Germany's isolation had begun to loosen. Cracks were apparent in the united front. It was with this thought in my mind that, two days later, I sat as interpreter between Hitler and Simon in the Reich's Chancellery.

Hitler welcomed Neurath and myself quite pleasantly on the morning of March 25th in his office in the extension which had been completed under Brüning. It was the first time I ever saw Hitler in the flesh—I had never attended any of his public meetings. I was surprised to find that he was only of medium height—photographs and newsreels always made him appear tall.

Sir John Simon and Anthony Eden were shown in. There were friendly smiles and handshakes all round, despite the very recent protests and the warning that "unilateral action had seriously aggravated anxiety abroad." Hitler's smile was especially friendly—for the very good reason that the presence of the English guests was a triumph for him.

"I believe that National Socialism has saved Germany, and thereby perhaps all Europe, from the most terrible catastrophe of all times . . . We have experienced Bolshevism in our own country . . . We are only safe against the Bolshevists if we have armaments which they respect." He spoke occasionally with some passion, but never went beyond the limits of what I had heard in the more excited moments of other international discussions.

His phraseology was perfectly conventional. He expressed himself clearly and adroitly, was clearly very sure of his arguments, was easily understood, and not difficult to translate into English. He appeared to have everything he wanted to say very clear in his own mind. On the table before him lay a fresh writing block, which remained unused throughout the negotiations. He had no notes with him.

I watched him closely when, from time to time, he paused to think over what he was about to say, so that I had an opportunity to look up from my note-book. He had clear blue eyes which gazed penetratingly at the person to whom he was speaking. As the discussion proceeded, he addressed his remarks increasingly to me—I have often noticed, while interpreting, this tendency in a speaker to turn instinctively to the man who understands what he is saying. In the case of Hitler, I felt that although he looked at me, he did not see me. His mind was busy with his own thoughts, and he was unaware of his surroundings. When he spoke about a matter 'of special importance his face became very expressive; his nostrils quivered as he described the dangers of Bolshevism for Europe. He emphasised his words with jerky, energetic gestures of the right hand, sometimes clenching his fist.

He was certainly not the raging demagogue I had half expected to see. That morning, and during all these conversations with the Englishmen, he impressed me as a man who advanced his arguments intelligently and skilfully, observing all the conventions of such political discussions, as though he had done nothing else for years. The only unusual thing about him was the length at which he spoke. During the whole morning session he was practically the only speaker, Simon and Eden only occasionally interjecting a remark or asking a question. From time to time Hitler seemed to become faintly aware that their interest was flagging, they did not, of course, understand much of what he was saying. He would then, at intervals of fifteen or twenty minutes, call on me to translate.

Simon, with his large brown eyes, looked at Hitler with by no means unsympathetic interest as he listened to him. His face naturally expressed a certain paternal benevolence. I had noticed it in Geneva when I heard him stating his country's views in his well-modulated voice with all the clarity of an English jurist though perhaps with too much emphasis on the purely formal aspects. Watching him now, as he listened attentively to Hitler, I had the feeling that his expression of paternal understanding was deepening. Perhaps he was pleasantly surprised to find, instead of the wild Nazi of British propaganda, a man who was emotional and emphatic, but not unreasonable or ill-natured. In later years, when foreign visitors spoke to me almost with enthusiasm of the impression Hitler made on them, I often suspected that this effect was produced by a reaction against the somewhat crude anti-Hitler propaganda.

On the other hand, I occasionally noticed a rather more sceptical expression flit over the face of Eden, who understood enough German to be able to follow Hitler more or less. Some of Eden's questions and observations showed he had considerable doubts about Hitler and what he was saying. "There are actually no indications," he once observed, "that the Russians have any aggressive plans against Germany." And in a slightly sarcastic tone he asked: "On what are your fears actually based?"

"I have rather more experience in these matters than is general in England," Hitler parried, and added heatedly, throwing out his chin: "I began my political career just when the Bolshevists were launching their first attack in Germany." Then he went off again into a monologue on Bolshevists individually and in general which, with translation, lasted until lunch.

This first meeting, lasting from 10.15 a.m. until two o'clock, passed off in a very pleasant atmosphere. Such at least was Hitler's impression. "We have made good contact with each other," he said to one of his trusties, as he left his office. Turning to me and shaking me by the hand he added: "You did your job splendidly. I had no idea that interpreting could be done like that. Hitherto I have always had to stop after each sentence for it to be translated."

"You were in good form today," Eden said when I met him in the hall; we knew each other from many a difficult session at Geneva.

The Englishmen lunched with Neurath, after which the discussion was resumed. On the German side, Neurath and Ribbentrop remained silent. Simon opened the session by advancing, in a very mild and friendly way, the British reservations regarding Germany's unilateral denunciation of the Treaty of Versailles, while Eden reverted to German fears of Russia's aggressive intentions. "Here the Eastern Pact could be of great service," he stated, thereby indicating the subject for the first part of the afternoon session. He briefly outlined the nature of such a treaty. Germany, Poland, Soviet Russia, Czecho-Slovakia, Finland, Esthonia, Latvia and Lithuania were envisaged as signatories. The Treaty States should pledge themselves to mutual assistance in the event of one of the partners attacking another.

At the mention of Lithuania, Hitler for the first time showed anger. "We will have nothing whatever to do with Lithuania," he exclaimed with flashing eyes, suddenly seeming to be a different person. I was often to see such unexpected outbursts in the future. Almost without transition, he would suddenly fly into a rage; his voice would become hoarse, he would roll his *r*'s and clench his fists, while his eyes blazed. "In no circumstances shall we make a pact with a State which stamps upon the German minority in Memel," he shouted. Then the storm subsided as suddenly as it had begun, and Hitler was again the quiet, polished negotiator he had been before the Lithuanian squall. His excitement was explained by the fact that for months 126 citizens of Memel had been on trial for conspiracy before a Kovno court-martial, and the case was now nearing its end.

Speaking more quietly, Hitler refused an Eastern Pact on further and more weighty grounds. "Between National Socialism and Bolshevism," he stated emphatically, "any association is completely out of the question." He added with almost passionate excitement: "Hundreds of my party comrades have been murdered by Bolshevists. German soldiers and civilians have fallen in the fight against Bolshevist risings. Between Bolshevists and ourselves there will always be these dead, who will prevent any common participation in a pact or other agreement." Moreover, there was a third objection to the Eastern Pact—Germany's justifiable mistrust of all collective agreements. "They do not prevent war, but encourage it and promote its extension." Bilateral treaties were preferable, and Germany was prepared to conclude such non-aggression pacts with all her neighbours. "Except Lithuania, of course," he said vehemently, but added more quietly: "As long as the Memel question remains unsettled."

Eden put in another word for the Eastern Pact, asking whether this could not be combined with a system of bilateral non-aggression pacts or agreements of mutual assistance. But Hitler rejected this suggestion too, saying that one could not have two different groups of members within the framework of a general agreement. He was wholly averse to the idea of mutual assistance. Significantly, he suggested instead that the individual countries should confine themselves to an undertaking not to assist an aggressor. "That would localise wars instead of making them more general," he said with apparent logic—but it was the logic of a man whose plan was to deal with his opponents one by one, and wanted to 'avoid that anyone should stand in his way. At that time the motive behind his argument was not evident; it was later to be revealed by his actions.

By some adroit questions, Simon passed from the Eastern to
the Danubian Pact, which was to be directed against interference
in the internal affairs of the Danubian States. This proposal
was based on a French scheme which aimed at preventing the
Anschluss of Austria and Germany and putting a barrier of
treaties against an extension of the Reich's influence over the
Balkans. I had been told at our Foreign Office that Hitler was
particularly opposed to this idea for obvious reasons, and I
therefore expected that he would give the English an emphatic
"No." But to my surprise he did not do so. "Fundamentally,
Germany has no objection to such a Pact," I heard him say, in
seeming agreement. I did, however, prick up my ears at the
word "fundamentally." At Geneva, when a delegate agreed
en principe, one knew that he would oppose the proposal in practice. Was Hitler using this old international device? His
very next words confirmed my surmise, as he observed, almost
casually: "But it would have to be stated quite clearly how
so-called non-interference in the affairs of the Danube countries
should be most accurately defined." Simon and Eden exchanged a quick look when I translated these words, and I
suddenly felt as though I were back in Geneva.

That afternoon the English also raised the question of the
League of Nations. "A final settlement of European problems,"
Simon said quietly but emphatically, "is unthinkable unless
Germany again becomes a member of the League of Nations.
Without the return of the Reich to Geneva the necessary confidence cannot be restored amongst the peoples of Europe."
On this matter, too, Hitler was by no means as intransigent as I
had expected. Indeed, he stated that a return of Germany to
the League was well within the bounds of possibility. The
ideals of Geneva were thoroughly praiseworthy, but the manner
in which they had hitherto been put into practice had given
occasion for far too many justified complaints by Germany.
The Reich could return to Geneva only as a completely equal
partner in every respect, and that was impossible so long as the
Treaty of Versailles was linked with the League covenant.
"Moreover, we would have somehow to be given a share in
the system of colonial mandates if we are really to consider
ourselves as a Power having equal rights," he added quickly,

but immediately avoided any further discussion of the colonial question, with the remark that Germany had at that time no colonial demands to bring forward.

This conversation was continued until seven o'clock in the evening, half of the time being naturally taken up with my translation, and Hitler, as was his wont, constantly repeating himself on matters about which he felt strongly. Moreover, in the absence of both chairman and agenda, discussion tended to be diffuse. On the whole, however, it passed off better than I had at first expected, although after the cordial atmosphere of the morning I felt that the English had cooled off a little, no doubt owing to the fact that, despite his marked friendliness and his skilful recourse to Geneva formulas, Hitler had actually said "No" to every point.

Von Neurath gave a dinner in honour of the British visitors attended by about eighty guests, including Hitler, all the Ministers of the Reich, many Secretaries of State, leading figures of the Nazi Party, Sir Eric Phipps, the British Ambassador, and the senior members of his Embassy.

I sat next to Hitler, but had to talk all the time while the most delectable dishes were whisked away untouched, with the result that I left the table hungry. I had not yet devised the technique of eating and working at the same time—while my client stopped eating to give me his text I would eat, and then translate while he ate. This procedure came to be recognised by *chefs de protocole* as an ingenious solution for interpreters at banquets.

The following morning was devoted to a detailed discussion of German armaments. At first there was some tension between Simon and Hitler as Simon again expounded the principles governing the British position, emphasising especially that a discussion of the level of German armaments did not imply that Britain had departed from her original position. She adhered strictly to the view that treaties could be altered only by mutual agreement and not by unilateral denunciation.

Hitler replied with his well-known thesis that it was not Germany but the other Powers that had first broken the disarmament provisions of the Treaty of Versailles, in that they had failed to carry out the clearly expressed undertaking to disarm themselves. He added with a laugh: "Did Wellington, when

Blücher came to his assistance, first ask the legal experts of the British Foreign Office whether the strength of the Prussian forces was consonant with existing treaties?"

Both sides advanced their arguments without any acerbity, the English obviously taking pains to avoid any contretemps on this fundamental question. Such was my impression from the very cautious, almost deprecatory, manner in which Simon expressed the British reservation; Hitler, too, was extremely moderate in his tone, compared with that of his public statements on disarmament, though he was not wanting in clarity. "We shall not let conscription be touched," he stated, "but we are prepared to negotiate regarding the strength of armed forces. Our only condition is parity on land and in the air with our most strongly armed neighbour."

When Simon asked him at what strength he estimated the armaments requirements of Germany under prevailing conditions, Hitler replied: "We could content ourselves with 36 divisions, that is, with an army of 500,000 men." But this, with one SS division and the militarised police, would satisfy all his requirements. This point was somewhat confused by the fact that Hitler, while naming the SS, almost in the same breath denied that the Party organisations in general had any military value, as Heydrich before him had done at Geneva. No doubt remembering the Geneva discussions on this question, in which he had taken part as British delegate, Eden expressed doubt as to whether the Party organisations could be considered as having no military value, and said that they should at least be regarded as reserves.

Wishing to avoid lengthy debate on this very controversial point, Simon immediately steered the discussion to the matter which at that time above all interested the English—the question of the German Air Force. "In your opinion, Herr Reichkanzler," he asked, "what should be the strength of the German Air Force?" Hitler avoided making any precise statement. "We need parity with Great Britain and with France," he said, adding immediately: "Of course, if the Soviet Union were materially to augment their air forces, Germany would have correspondingly to increase her Air Force."

Simon wanted more information: "May I ask how great

Germany's air strength is at the present time?" Hitler hesitated, and then said: "We have already achieved parity with Great Britain." Simon made no comment. For a while nobody said anything. I thought the two Englishmen looked startled and also sceptical about Hitler's statement. This impression was later confirmed by Lord Londonderry, British Air Minister, at whose conversations with Göring I was almost always present as interpreter. The subject of Germany's strength in the air in 1935 constantly cropped up as well as the question of whether Hitler's statement on that occasion had not, after all, been exaggerated.

Hitler and Simon also briefly discussed the conclusion of an Air Pact between the Locarno Powers. Under such an agreement the signatories to the Locarno Treaty would immediately render mutual assistance with their air forces in the event of an attack. "I am prepared to join such a Pact," said Hitler, repeating an assent previously given. "But of course I can only do so if Germany herself has the necessary air force available," he added with a logic to which the English had no reply.

Hitler himself introduced the question of naval strength, making the German demand, later to become famous through the naval agreement, for a ratio of 35 per cent of the British fleet. The Englishmen did not say how they stood with regard to this proposal, but since they raised no objection it could well be assumed that they were inwardly in agreement with it.

At noon there were refreshments at the British Embassy at which Hitler made an appearance; this was the first time that he had been seen at a foreign embassy. Göring and other members of the government were present.

Immediately afterwards discussions were resumed at the Chancellery, but no new points came up on the main subjects. Hitler took up much time with his favourite theme, Soviet Russia. He was particularly vehement about Soviet attempts to push Westwards, and in that connection he called Czecho-Slovakia "Russia's thrust-out arm." Hitler's second obsession at this discussion was German equality of rights. The Reich must of course have all the classes of armaments which other countries possessed, but was prepared to co-operate in agreements whereby armaments defined at Geneva as offensive weapons would be prohibited. Similarly, Germany could agree to supervision of armaments, but of course only on the basis of equality of rights and on the assumption that such supervision were simultaneously exercised over all the other countries concerned.

Simon and Eden listened patiently to all this, with its many repetitions. I often thought of the disarmament negotiations at Geneva. Only two years ago the skies would have fallen if German representatives had put forward such demands as Hitler was doing now as though they were the most natural thing in the world. Nor could I help wondering whether Hitler had not got further with his method of the *fait accompli* than would have been possible with the Foreign Office method of negotiation. I was especially inclined to think this when I observed how placidly Simon and Eden listened. They had naturally made their reservations, and had evidently maintained the line of fidelity to agreements and of security guarantees in the familiar Geneva manner. Indeed, they had been emphatic to Hitler on these matters. Nevertheless, the mere fact of their presence and of this discussion about things which for years had been completely taboo at Geneva greatly impressed me.

These memorable days were concluded by an evening reception given by Hitler to a select company in the old Brüning Chancellery, which had been quietly and tastefully furnished. The host himself was unassuming, sometimes almost shy, although without being awkward. During the day he had worn a brown tunic with a red swastika arm band. Now he was wearing tails in which he never looked at ease. Only on rare occasions have I seen him thus "plutocratically" rigged out, and then he gave the impression of having hired the tails for the occasion. That evening, in spite of his unwonted party suit, Hitler was a charming host, moving about amongst his guests as easily as if he had grown up in the atmosphere of a great house. During the concert items I had ample opportunity of observing the English. Simon's friendly interest in Hitler struck me even more than during the negotiations; his gaze would rest for a while with a friendly expression on Hitler, and he would then look at the pictures, the furniture and the flowers. He seemed to feel happy in the German Chancellor's house.

Eden also took in his surroundings with obvious interest and not without sympathy, but his expression indicated a sober, keen observation of men and things. His scepticism was clearly evident, except with regard to the musical entertainment which he followed with unqualified admiration.

Of the Germans present, von Neurath alone was unconstrained and natural in his demeanour. All the others, especially Ribbentrop, were vague and colourless, like subsidiary figures indicated by an artist in the background of an historical picture.

Towards eleven o'clock that evening Eden left for Warsaw and Moscow. In Hitler's entourage this visit to Stalin was taken much amiss, and an old National Socialist at the Chancellery said to me: "It is sheer tactlessness of Eden to go on to the Soviet chieftain immediately after his visit to the Führer." Somewhat later Simon went back to the Hotel Adlon, and flew next morning to London.

As I left next morning for trade negotiations in Rome, I learnt nothing further of the direct impression which the Englishmen had made on Hitler. Hitler had spoken very appreciatively about Simon in the short intervals during the negotiations, and I heard him say to Ribbentrop: "I have the impression that I would get on well with him if we came to a serious discussion with the English." His opinion of Eden was more reserved, mainly because of the questions which Eden had put during the negotiations in order to elicit Hitler's intentions on particular matters. Hitler disliked definite questions, particularly in negotiations with foreign politicians, as I often had occasion to note when working for him. He preferred general surveys on broad lines, historical perspectives and philosophical speculation, evading any concrete details, which would have revealed his real intentions too clearly.

My portable wireless, an inseparable companion on my travels, informed me that Simon stated in the Commons that substantial differences of opinion had emerged in the Berlin conversations.

* * *

On April 11th a conference met at Stresa on Lake Maggiore. Those taking part were the British and French Prime Ministers,

Ramsay MacDonald and Laval, their Foreign Ministers, Sir John Simon and Flandin, and Mussolini. In the final resolution, Britain, France and Italy stated that they were agreed "to oppose with all suitable means any unilateral denunciation of treaties." That was a clear answer by the three great Powers of Western Europe to Hitler's reassumption of German armed sovereignty. This declaration would indeed have seemed far less menacing to us had we known then what we now know from Churchill's Memoirs that at the very beginning of the negotiations the British Foreign Minister had emphasised that he was not in a position to consider the imposition of sanctions against a treaty breaker. At that time only the optimists among us guessed that the common front against us was so flimsy.

A few days later, on April 17th, a second blow followed Germany's action was condemned by the Council of the League of Nations. Through her "arbitrary action" she had "broken the Treaty of Versailles and threatened the security of Europe."

A third blow was the Alliance concluded by Laval with the Soviet Union on May 2nd. When I got back to Berlin I found people at the Foreign Office very depressed. Germany seemed to be completely isolated. In reply to Hitler's methods of foreign policy an anti-German coalition had been formed of all the Great Powers of Europe, including the Soviet Union. However, I was soon to learn in Poland and in London that this coalition had little cohesion.

To my surprise I received instructions to go with Göring to Warsaw and Cracow for the funeral of Marshal Pilsudski, as there was the possibility that an opportunity for political discussions with Laval might arise. So on the evening of May 16th I left the Friedrichstrasse Station with Göring and a small delegation in his saloon coach. At that time the future Reich Marshal did not travel by special train, but contented himself with having his coach attached to the ordinary train. I had just settled down comfortably in my compartment to hear the evening news on my indispensable portable radio, when the massive Göring suddenly stood at my door. To my extreme astonishment he said: "I must apologise to you for your accommodation in this confined sleeping compartment.

I am usually a better host, but my people have been careless. The culprit will get a telling-off for this."

I answered that I hadn't the slightest complaint to make about my accommodation, and would certainly sleep splendidly. But with a laugh he pointed out that I had been put in the kitchen of his coach. I hadn't noticed this kitchen, skilfully screened behind a sliding panel.

Von Moltke, the German Ambassador, was waiting for us in the early morning at the station, and took us to the Embassy, whence we went straight to the funeral service at Warsaw Cathedral.

The cathedral was most tastefully decorated with Polish flags. There was crêpe over the windows, so that the vast building seemed gloomy and ill lit. A spotlight from the roof illuminated the coffin of the Polish national hero, on which lay the Marshal's sword and his famous legionary's cap. In the dim nave there were many brilliant uniforms; I made out Marshal Pétain in full dress uniform sitting on a front seat next to Laval, who had just returned from Moscow. Just behind was a contingent of British officers, and then followed the German delegation with Göring in the uniform of an Air Force General. I also noticed a Soviet contingent, whose uniforms were the simplest in this brilliant assembly.

The ceremony lasted almost two hours, and my thoughts went back to Geneva, where I had known the Marshal years before, when the dispute between Poland and Lithuania came before the League Council. "I have come here to hear the word peace," he had said. "Anything else is nonsense, which I leave for my Foreign Minister to handle."

After the service Pilsudski's coffin was borne on a gun carriage through the whole of Warsaw to the Mokotow parade ground. The funeral procession was most impressive and took four hours to pass through the streets of the Polish capital. It was May and already very warm, almost oppressive, so that the slow march, followed by the long period of standing at the memorial parade, was an exceptionally severe strain on visitors unaccustomed to such exertions. Göring, with heavy steps, marched panting beside me, but he stuck it to the end, whereas the aged Marshal Pétain after a while got into a carriage for the remainder of the ceremony. Huge crowds stood on either side of the streets through which the procession moved.

Next morning there was another three hour procession in Cracow, followed by the final lowering of the coffin into the prepared grave in Wawel Castle. Foreign Minister Beck gave the foreign delegations a breakfast at the Hotel de France, at which I assisted Göring in some short conversations with Pétain, the English, and Laval. Laval and Göring arranged for a long talk during the afternoon.

It was evident that not only Göring desired this discussion, but that Laval also gladly availed himself of the opportunity to talk to us. He brought only *chef de cabinet* Rochat, and I alone accompanied Göring. The discussion, which lasted over two hours, was a compressed form of the talks between Hitler and Simon. Exactly the same subjects were dealt with, and for that very reason the differences between the English and the French were the more noticeable.

Göring, broad and massive, showed little of the considered tactics of Hitler. He went in for forthright utterance, no beating about the bush or diplomatic niceties. "I trust you got on well at Moscow with the Bolsheviks, Monsieur Laval," he said, launching out into the most delicate subject, the Franco-Russian pact of mutual assistance. "We know the Bolshevists better in Germany than you do in France," he continued. "We know that in no circumstances can one have anything to do with them if one wants to avoid trouble. You will find that out in France. You will see what difficulties your Paris communists will cause you." There followed a tirade against the Russians, in which he used the same words that Hitler had spoken when talking to Simon. This was my first experience of what later always struck me about leading National Socialists in their dealings with foreigners—the almost word for word repetition of Hitler's arguments. As interpreter I naturally had to pay the closest attention to individual phrases, and could therefore ascertain how closely Hitler's henchmen followed their master. Sometimes it seemed as though the same gramophone record were being played, though the voice and temperament were different.

I also observed this in other points touched upon by Göring

—disarmament, or rather German re-armament; bilateral pacts in place of collective security; reservations with regard to the League of Nations, without excluding the possibility of Germany's re-entry; an air pact, and much besides. In the short time available, Göring could naturally not go into details, even to the extent that Hitler had done at Berlin. Neither did he ever do so on later occasions, adhering even more than Hitler to generalities and basic ideas. He liked precision even less than did the Führer. Nevertheless, he was not wanting in diplomatic adroitness. I saw him later in very delicate situations, which he handled with a finesse which the German public would not have believed possible in this swashbuckling heavy-weight.

This skill was shown for the first time at Cracow in the discussion of Franco-German relations, naturally the main theme of the conversation with Laval. With very convincing words Göring succeeded in persuading Laval of Germany's desire to achieve a general settlement with France. Concrete details were never mentioned. He brought his personality and eloquence to bear on Laval. An unprejudiced person could not but be convinced that Göring, who had just let off steam about the Russians and the League of Nations in the language of the man in the street, was speaking sincerely when he said: "You may rest assured, Monsieur Laval, that the German people have no keener desire than finally to bury the century-old hatchet with their French neighbour. We esteem your fellow countrymen as brave soldiers, we are full of admiration for the achievements of the French spirit. The old apple of discord in Alsace-Lorraine no longer exists. What then should still keep us from becoming really good neighbours?"

These words did not fail in their effect upon Laval, who emphasised how strongly he had always advocated a Franco-German *rapprochement*, and invited me to testify to the efforts he had made in 1931 during the Berlin conversations with Brüning in the cause of Franco-German understanding. I could confirm this with a clear conscience, for I had got the impression, both during the six-Power Conference at Paris and also at Berlin in the autumn of the same year, that Laval's intentions were sincere, and that he was striving sincerely for

a good-neighbourly relationship between the two countries. Laval did not go into details about the sort of Franco-German settlement he envisaged—although it seemed to me that this was just what was needed. From innumerable discussions in Geneva and Paris I knew how difficult it was to reach results when one really got down to details.

I was also interested to note that Laval, like Eden in Berlin, sought to reassure us about Russia's intentions. "I have found nothing in Moscow," he said, in language almost identical with that of the Lord Privy Seal, "that could suggest that Russia harbours any warlike intentions against Germany." He described Stalin as a man easy to get on with, a man with whom one could talk. Ribbentrop described Stalin to me in similar terms in August 1939, when I accompanied him to Moscow for the conclusion of the sensational Russo-German Pact shortly before the outbreak of war. Roosevelt, too, after his first meeting with Stalin at Yalta, expressed a similar opinion to his son and later to some of his colleagues. When I reflect on what I have heard foreigners say after talking to Hitler, I am almost tempted to believe that dictators somehow exercise a special magic on their listeners.

Laval also represented the conclusion of the Franco-Russian alliance as a necessity imposed by France's internal politics. "Certain events in Germany," he said, "and much that has been written and said in your country against France—in conjunction with German re-armament—have caused such apprehension amongst my countrymen that anything calculated to mitigate it will indirectly contribute to Franco-German understanding." This line of argument was typical of Laval's method of conducting negotiations. He was always the skilled, polished French lawyer. In Cracow I found my earlier impressions of Laval confirmed. He seemed to me to belong to the category of "hommes de bonne volonté," who advocated peace out of conviction. At that time I would without question have put him on a par with Herriot and Briand.

The main impression which I brought back with me to Berlin from this conversation was that it would be possible at any time for Germany, if she pursued a more or less intelligent foreign policy, to emerge from the isolation into which Hitler's psychological mistakes had landed her. The conversation between Göring and Laval seemed to me a definite move away from that isolation of the Reich which had been expressed in April by the Stresa meeting, and in May by the Franco-Soviet Pact. In the Berlin and Cracow conversations I saw clear indications that England and France wished to avoid a final breach with Germany, and to lead the Reich back from its isolation into the community of nations.

Göring, with whom I had a long conversation about the general position during our journey back to Berlin, shared this impression. In contrast to Hitler, he was amenable to suggestion and argument. He questioned me in detail about my earlier impressions of Laval. He asked about the relations between Briand and Stresemann, and listened carefully when I expressed the view that Stresemann had put up a diplomatic record by liberating the Rhineland from foreign troops without an army of his own. "Looking at it like that," he added thoughtfully, "there's truth in what you say." But he was contemptuous about our Foreign Office and its staff. "They spend the morning sharpening pencils and the afternoon at tea-parties," he said.

* * *

Immediately on my return to Berlin I received my next assignment. Although Germany had been officially condemned by the Council of the League on April 17th, a month later the British sent an invitation to the treaty breaker for naval talks. Ribbentrop was appointed "Ambassador Extraordinary" and entrusted by Hitler with the conduct of these negotiations. I was to go with him as interpreter. We flew to London by special plane at the beginning of June. This was the first of many air trips I was to make to European capitals in that three-engined Junker. In later years I made the trip between London and Berlin so often that I could have navigated a plane to London without a map.

The negotiations opened at the Foreign Office. Simon was present, and Ribbentrop soon laid his cards on the table. Germany demanded the right to 35 per cent of the British naval strength. With a somewhat exaggerated display of forcefulness he declared: "If the British Government does not immediately accept this condition, there is no point at all in continuing these negotiations. We must insist upon an immediate decision." If this principle were conceded all technical details regarding the programme of naval construction and the classes of ships could easily be settled.

I must confess that I did not consider these tactics very intelligent. It was obvious, in view of the fact that the Reich had just been officially condemned for breaking the Treaty of Versailles, that the English could not suddenly reverse their position and give official approval to a breach of the naval provisions of the same Treaty. At that time I did not know Ribbentrop very well, and wondered why he brought up the most difficult question of all so undiplomatically right at the start, thereby risking the collapse of the negotiations before they had properly begun. Was it lack of experience of international conferences? Was it a typical National Socialist attempt to be unconventional at all costs? Or was he blindly following instructions without using his own imagination? Later I realised that his conduct was that of the terrier of the "His Master's Voice" gramophone advertisements. Just as the terrier listens fascinated to the voice coming out of the horn, Ribbentrop absorbed Hitler's words and then repeated them. On this account he gave the impression both at home and abroad of being stupid—an impression which he strengthened by his arrogance, vanity and extreme suspiciousness. I must say that in the innumerable negotiations at which I was to interpret for him he was never at a loss for counter-arguments. He could formulate his ideas with some clarity, and had the relevant facts and details firmly in his head. But it never occurred to me to consider him a statesman or a Foreign Minister. At the Nuremberg International Court he described himself as Hitler's foreign political secretary, which I think fairly well describes his position. His relationship to Hitler was one of extreme dependency. If Hitler was displeased with him, Ribbentrop went sick and took to his bed like a hysterical woman. He was indeed nothing but his master's voice, and thus seemed to many of us a dangerous fool.

During that London visit my opinion that Ribbentrop had

made a mistake by his "bull in a china shop" technique seemed confirmed by Simon's reaction. As I translated Ribbentrop's words, Simon flushed with anger. He replied with some heat: "It is not usual to make such conditions at the very beginning of negotiations," and concluded brusquely by saying: "I can, of course, make no statement on the subject." He then left the session with a frigid bow. I was already wondering what the weather would be like on our return flight to Berlin. I felt sure, from previous experience, that even if negotiations did not completely break down, the conference would at any rate be adjourned for a long time. But I was mistaken.

For one or two days nothing was heard from the English, and then another session was arranged, not at the Foreign Office, but at the Admiralty. The discussion took place in the historic Board Room where, as we were told, many an important decision affecting the British Navy had been taken. It was a large panelled room in the centre of which was a long table with red leather seats on either side. My seat, as interpreter, at the head of the table, was normally occupied by the First Lord of the Admiralty and was particularly comfortable. If it be true that clothes make the man, it may also be said that the position of the seat makes the interpreter. In the forthcoming naval negotiations I had a dominating position between the two parties, and thanks to my point of vantage I never lost the thread even in the most complicated technical questions regarding types of ship, displacement, and the like.

On my left was the German delegation, headed by Ribbentrop and Admiral Schuster; on my right were Sir Robert Craigie, Under-Secretary of State at the Foreign Office, Admiral Little and Captain Danckwerts. On the wall behind the British delegation there was a wind indicator connected with a weather vane on the roof. "When the British Navy still consisted of sailing ships," Admiral Little explained to us, "the direction of the wind was of decisive significance for the operational decisions taken by the admirals in this room." Pointing to a particular spot on the wind indicator he added with a laugh: "When the wind was blowing from this quarter, the French fleet could not leave Brest, and we had the Channel completely at our disposal." The days of sailing ships were long over, but in this venerable room the wind indicator still swung to the changing wind. Another object of interest was a little mark on the wall which, as our kindly instructor the Admiral told us, indicated Nelson's height. We were rather surprised to see that the British naval hero was so short a man.

In spite of the coldness caused by the clash between Ribbentrop and Simon at the start of the negotiations, a very friendly atmosphere now prevailed. To my astonishment Sir Robert Craigie opened with a statement to the effect that the British Government was prepared to agree to Ribbentrop's demand. The only reservation was that this should have effect only if agreement had been reached in all other matters. I scarcely believed my own ears when I heard Craigie make this wholly unexpected statement. I had reluctantly to admit that Ribbentrop's methods, which I had disliked and criticised so much, seemed to have been successful. The British must have been extraordinarily anxious to come to an agreement to give in so completely in a few days. It made me very uncertain in the future in my judgment of Hitler's methods. I often thought of this scene when I was later called on to translate statements by Hitler or Ribbentrop, which were in complete contrast to the methods of the pre-1933 German statesmen.

After this agreement in principle, it was not very long before full agreement was achieved. Ribbentrop had reason to be proud of the success of his negotiations. His rather awkward manner with Englishmen changed almost to that sociable attitude to which I was accustomed in international discussions. The inferiority complex which he tried to overcome by an assumed brusqueness now disappeared, with only occasional lapses. For instance, towards the end of the negotiations, when he was casually asked by the English how long the agreement should last, he drew himself up and with his most solemn expression said only one word: "Ewig" (for ever). My colleague, Kordt, grinned at me, amused at my embarrassment. With Ribbentrop's expression the words "For Ever" in English could only be sung to the accompaniment of a church organ. I wondered how I should interpret without producing a comic effect. I soon found a way out: "It is to be a permanent agreement," I interpreted, with relief, and this was the phrase incorporated in the text.

On my return home I was often asked why Ribbentrop, who spoke quite good English, should have had everything translated. I had prudently raised this question with him just before the negotiations, suggesting that if he wanted to speak English he should first have the text or the main points of his remarks written out in English.

"I could quite well negotiate in English myself," he had answered, "but I want to concentrate my thoughts wholly on the matter in hand, and not to be bothered by English syntax or phrases."

Ribbentrop's monstrously suspicious nature struck me especially during these negotiations. At discussions in his room at the Carlton we German members of the delegation had to huddle round him in the middle of the room, talking in whispers, as the wicked English might have fixed up a microphone in the wall to hear our secrets. It was sometimes difficult not to burst out laughing at the sight of the naval delegation in the middle of the large room like a lot of chickens around Ribbentrop, whispering about battleships, destroyers and tons displacement.

After the exchange of documents between the new British Foreign Minister, Sir Samuel Hoare, and Ribbentrop, defining the naval agreement, we remained in London for a few more days to finish off the technical details. Ribbentrop made a triumphant return to Germany as "a great statesman." Hitler especially regarded him as a skilful diplomat after this sensational success, while the rest of the world rubbed its eyes at what the German "Special Ambassador and Commissioner for Armaments Questions" had achieved in England. The French sent the English an unfriendly note. "A question which affects all the signatories of the Treaty of Versailles has been treated more or less as a private matter between Germany and Great Britain. . . . France reserves her freedom of action in naval matters." Laval wrote angrily to the British Foreign Minister. Even Italy handed in a critical note. Eden was sent to soothe feelings in Paris. Hitler seemed to have won all along the line.

* *
*

During this year of Anglo-German *rapprochement* I had again to work for Hitler on an important occasion. On July 15th he received a delegation of the British Legion at the Chancellery, conversing for nearly two hours with Major Fetherston-Godley and the five Englishmen accompanying him. He asked each of them to tell him in detail on which sector of the front he had fought, and exchanged war memories with the visitors. But for the difference in language it might have been a typical meeting of old comrades. At the end there was a suggestion of politics in Hitler's short speech. After expressing his hearty pleasure at the visit, he emphasised the special value he attached, in the interests of peace, to collaboration between soldiers who had fought in the last war.

At a breakfast to the English visitors just before the reception, Major Fetherston-Godley had said that the English had only once fought against the Germans, and that in the opinion of the British Legion this had been a mistake—a mistake which would not be repeated. He now spoke in similar terms to Hitler.

On leaving the Chancellery these visitors undoubtedly felt much impressed by the manner in which Hitler had received them, but I now noticed something which in the following years was often to strike me. Hitler's effect on his visitors faded out as time went by. During the next few days I accompanied the delegation, showing them round, and I noticed how their attitude to Germany became daily more critical. Things they saw for themselves in National Socialist Germany seemed to confirm what they had heard about Germany in their own country, rather than what Hitler and his colleagues had told them so persuasively.

* *
*

During the last months of 1935 the conflict between Italy and the League of Nations, particularly England and France, gradually came into the foreground. Mussolini, who had expected, in return for his support of the Western Powers against Germany, to be given a free hand in Abyssinia, now suddenly found himself facing unexpected difficulties, largely due to British policy in the League of Nations. He automatically broke away from the "unity" of Stresa, and was drawn over to Hitler's side.

Altogether 1935 had been a year of triumphs for Hitler in the field of foreign politics. There had been the successful outcome of the Anglo-German conversations of March, the May meeting between Göring and Laval, and the Naval Agreement of June. Most important of all, as far as the majority of Germans were concerned, was the achievement of military equality. As a result of those successes many people entirely misjudged Hitler's diplomatic methods. At the time it was not possible to see that he owed his success less to his own statecraft than to the lack of decision and unity amongst his opponents. It was not until events in the following years repeatedly revealed this indecision amongst the Western Powers that those who had a close view of events saw the real explanation of the otherwise inexplicable triumphs of the German dictator.

CHAPTER II

(1936)

WHEN in March, 1946, I gave evidence before the Nuremberg Court, and looked at the long row of accused on my right, my gaze lingered involuntarily on the scarcely recognisable face of Ribbentrop. My mind went back to another tribunal before which, almost precisely ten years earlier, Ribbentrop had stood. The tribunal was the Council of the League of Nations, summoned to a special session in London, and Ribbentrop, as the representative of Germany, was called to account for her breach of the Locarno Agreement of 1925 by Hitler's re-militarisation of the Rhineland.

That was indeed a contrast to the severely businesslike American scene presented by the great court room at Nuremberg, where the blue neon lights diffused an atmosphere of unreality, making judges, the public and accused look like men long dead. Bright daylight shone through the windows of St. James's Palace, where the Council sat. The walls were hung with silken tapestry and impressive old portraits. A huge mirror above the fireplace added to the friendliness of the warm colours of carpets and hangings. On the fireplace stood a magnificent old clock which, together with the room in general, vividly recalled the Hall of Clocks at the Quai d'Orsay, and the more hopeful days when Stresemann had signed the Kellogg Pact there. The only symbols of modern times were the horseshoe Council table from Geneva and its microphone, at which I sat next to Ribbentrop.

All eyes were on the representative of National Socialist Germany, who was the sensation of the day in that old-fashioned diplomatic environment. The Australian delegate, Bruce, presided; he was a tall, dark man with typical Anglo-Saxon features and an equally typical calm. On his right sat Flandin, who had recently become French Foreign Minister, and whom I

39

remembered from Paris and Geneva. Next to him sat the Italian Foreign Minister, Grandi. At the Council table I recognised many other old acquaintances. Next to Ribbentrop sat Titulescu, who constantly tried to engage him in conversation in German in the most friendly way. But Ribbentrop remained aloof, and only responded to the Rumanian Foreign Minister's overtures with the minimum of courtesy. On the other side of Bruce sat Eden, and the bespectacled Litvinov. The Soviet Union at the Council of the League! That indeed was sensational, and the most obvious sign of how, with Hitler's help, things had changed in this supreme international body.

It was only natural that I should recognise many old acquaintances amongst the various delegates. When I greeted them before the session I felt that they were as pleased as I was at our unexpected meeting. Ribbentrop, however, was somewhat disapproving: "Well, you seem to be pretty popular here," he remarked. Perhaps he expected that the reason for our presence there—Hitler's denunciation of the Locarno Treaty and the entry of German troops into the Rhineland—would affect my personal relations with my French and English colleagues and acquaintances.

Following on the introduction of compulsory military service in the preceding year, Germany had once again found herself completely isolated from all other countries, great and small. On March 7th, 1936, shortly after the ratification of the Franco-Soviet Pact of mutual assistance, Hitler had occupied the Rhineland. He justified this action by the statement that the Pact constituted such a grave breach of the Locarno Agreement that the latter no longer existed, and that therefore Germany was no longer bound by its provisions regarding the demilitarised zone of the Rhineland. We were kept so busy translating protest notes and counter-arguments that we felt sure that the paper war would almost certainly lead to a shooting war. "Germany has broken the Locarno Treaty," wrote the French and the Belgians. "France broke it first," replied the Reich, pointing to the Franco-Soviet Pact.

On March 7th a Foreign Office friend had expressed an opinion very widely held in our department: "If France attaches the slightest value to her security," he said, "then she must march into the Rhineland now." More than once, even during the war, I heard Hitler say: "The forty-eight hours after the march into the Rhineland were the most nerve-racking in my life." He always added: "If the French had then marched into the Rhineland, we would have had to withdraw with our tails between our legs, for the military resources at our disposal would have been wholly inadequate for even a moderate resistance."

For reasons which were still unintelligible to us in the Foreign Office, France had contented herself with calling a meeting of the League Council, which I attended as Ribbentrop's interpreter. "I have undertaken this mission with real personal satisfaction," Ribbentrop said, addressing the Council, "convinced as I am that never has a cause so just, in the highest sense of that word, come before this Council of Nations." Then, turning immediately to the new Franco-Soviet military alliance, he said with emphasis: "This Pact constitutes the alliance of two states comprising some 275 million people. The two contracting parties are the two strongest military powers in the world. Soviet Russia, so far distant from Germany that she could not possibly be attacked by that country, has indirectly advanced to the German frontier by means of a similar military alliance with Czecho-Slovakia." Litvinov was busily making notes. "France and Russia," Ribbentrop continued, "can, by virtue of their agreement, proceed to war against Germany at their own discretion." Litvinov shook his head vehemently, and Flandin derisively turned down the corners of his mouth. "This alliance is directed exclusively against Germany," I continued with my translation, while all present—delegates, secretaries, legal advisers and interpreters—followed my words with the closest attention.

After arguing the purely legal aspect, Ribbentrop passed to Hitler's earlier offers regarding disarmament. "The offer of absolute disarmament was refused. The offer of an army of 200,000, applying equally to all, was refused. The offer of an army of 300,000 was refused. The offer of an air pact was refused. . . . The offer of a general European settlement made in May 1935 was simply passed over, except for the proposal which afterwards provided the basis of the Anglo-German naval agreement." Thus he described Hitler's peace efforts in a summary which, so far as I could see, did not fail to have an effect upon some delegates and upon several Press representatives. "The Government of the German Reich must therefore reject as unjust and unwarranted the charge of having unilaterally contravened the Treaty of Locarno," Ribbentrop concluded, without referring to the real question before the Council—the contravention of the Treaty.

At one of the Council sessions preceding our arrival in London, Flandin had said: "If the German Government was not convinced (by the French counter-arguments in the matter of the Russian Pact), then it was her duty, by virtue of the Treaty of Arbitration, concluded simultaneously with the Locarno Agreement, to submit the matter to arbitration. This she never attempted to do. Although I myself stated in the Chamber that we would accept the finding of the Hague Court in this matter, the German Government ignored this suggestion. Neither did it attempt to discuss the matter through a meeting of the Locarno Powers; it simply declared as null and void a treaty whose contracting parties expressly forwent the right to terminate it, and which could he terminated only by the Council of the League of Nations on their application."

Hitler had obviously instructed Ribbentrop to follow his own favourite tactics of evading precise questions by giving vague and generalised assurances. "The German people," he declaimed, "who now, after seventeen years, at last see themselves reinstated in freedom and honour . . . . sincerely desire to live in peace and friendship with their neighbours and henceforward to cooperate to the utmost in the construction of true European solidarity. . . . They wish to end the long period of Franco-German tension, crises and wars, and to help to inaugurate a better understanding and friendship between these two great nations. This the German people long for from the bottom of their hearts. In this spirit the German Chancellor has made an historical and indeed a unique and unparalleled offer to the world to unite Europe and ensure peace for the next twenty-five years . . ." This speech may not have made much of an impression at the Council table, but it had an unmistakable effect on the Press, and set the tone for the diplomatic activity of the next few weeks, which can best be described as the period of bigger and better peace plans.

After my French colleague, Mathieu, had translated my English rendering of Ribbentrop's speech into French, the session adjourned for lunch. The German Ambassador in London, von Hoesch, had had to plead hard with Bruce to get this adjournment, for the Council had originally intended to pronounce its verdict of guilty immediately after hearing Ribbentrop, without further discussion of the matter. This would have been the closure by silence, which I had often seen at Geneva, and the effectiveness of which had first been brought home to me at the preparatory Disarmament Commission. At that time the most telling arguments of our representative, Count Bernstorff, former German Ambassador at Washington, had been met with complete silence. In fact his case was unanswerable. The efforts of our London Ambassador, and the understanding shown by Bruce and the English, prevented such high-handed action, at any rate in its crudest form. Judgment was not pronounced until the afternoon. But it was unanimously agreed that no member of the Council should reply to Ribbentrop's arguments, which, as Press reaction was to show, were not wholly beside the point.

Litvinov alone did not agree to this. While I was giving the speech in English, I had noticed him busily making notes, and shaking his head in emphatic disagreement at many of the points—causing Eden, who sat next to him, to look at him uneasily. During the French translation, however, I noticed the tall figure of Flandin talking emphatically to the short, dumpy Litvinov. It was not difficult to guess what this excited conversation was about. It was obvious that Litvinov, as the Soviet representative, wished to enjoy this opportunity of really going for National Socialist Germany in public, in much the same way, as Vyshinski, after 1945, never missed an opportunity of attacking America at the meetings of the Security Council. As I watched Flandin and Litvinov in heated discussion I looked forward to the Litvinov-Ribbentrop duel that seemed inevitable. Rows are easy to translate, and I would have been glad if the Council's plan of action had failed and I could once again have interpreted a real hammer-and-tongs debate. But things worked out otherwise. On the opening of the afternoon session no one offered to speak. Flandin had evidently won his argument with Litvinov.

"The Council of the League of Nations declares that the German Government has committed a breach of Article 43 of the Treaty of Versailles, in that, on March 7th, 1936, it caused military forces to march into the demilitarised zone as specified in Article 42 and the following Articles of that Treaty and in the Treaty of Locarno." This was the Franco-Belgian resolution which the Council passed unanimously, thus branding Germany as a treaty-breaker.

But there was one big surprise. Shortly before the vote was taken, the President of the Council, Bruce, speaking as the Australian representative, said: "The work of the Council is not completed with the acceptance of this resolution. . . . The Powers principally concerned must proceed to find a solution amongst themselves." I naturally thought that he had in mind the Locarno Powers, excluding the treaty-breaker Germany. To my utter astonishment, however, Bruce continued: "The moderation of the statement by France and Belgium has aroused the greatest admiration in the world. On the other hand, Reich Chancellor Hitler has frequently expressed his will to co-operate; this morning the German representative has again done so."

It reminded me of what had happened the year before when the English, after protesting against the German breach of Versailles by the restoration of conscription, went on to ask whether the visit of Simon and Eden to Berlin would be convenient.

The last thing I expected, after the tremendous excitement caused by the German march into the Rhineland, now occurred. "In these circumstances," I heard Bruce continue, "I definitely expect that a solution will be possible."

I was too intent upon the reaction of France and Belgium fully to appreciate the grotesque contradiction in this last sentence. Nobody objected to the President of the Council's suggestion that negotiations with us should now be resumed. Ribbentrop again briefly protested against the "resolution which the Council had recently passed, which will stand condemned by the verdict of history." Then Flandin again suggested that the legal question should be decided by the Permanent Court of

International Justice. This closed one of the most remarkable sessions of the Council.

Negotiations between Eden and Ribbentrop now began as though nothing had happened. Whereas, in the German view, the Locarno Agreement no longer existed, the other Locarno Powers stated that for them the obligations under that Treaty were still valid. They had promised France and Belgium to come to their assistance in the event of a German attack. It was under these circumstances that the English, during the following days, proceeded to negotiate with Ribbentrop how Hitler's offer of twenty-five years peace, made simultaneously with his march into the Rhineland, could somehow be incorporated into the Locarno Treaty! Hitler certainly seemed to have achieved the desired effect upon the English by his peace offer—namely, the softening of their reaction to his unilateral denunciation of the Locarno Treaty.

Eden tried to get from Ribbentrop at least an undertaking that no fortifications should be set up in the Rhineland, at any rate for a period. Ribbentrop countered by objecting to the proposed Anglo-French staff talks which were to decide what action should be taken if France and Belgium were actually attacked. The phrase "staff talks" to Ribbentrop at that time was like a red rag to a bull. He felt instinctively that concrete military agreements between England and France would be a very high price to pay for the militarisation of the Rhineland. He protested against them to Eden and other Englishmen in much the same way as Stalin now protests against the military agreements within the framework of the Atlantic Pact.

The astonishing change from condemnation to negotiation made me doubt more and more my own ability to judge the international situation. I felt rather foolish, along with my Foreign Office friends, when our confident predictions about the consequences of Hitler's action failed to come about. Hitler seemed once more to have been proved right.

We know now that we were nearer to war then than we thought. The French Ambassador, François-Poncet, writes in his Memoirs: "The possibility of military intervention was very seriously considered. It was proposed that a force of one army corps should march into the Saar territory. . . . The

civilian Ministers, however, were against this.   General Gamelin
expressed the view that even a restricted military operation
would be a risk and could not therefore be undertaken without
general mobilisation. . . .   The Government recoiled from
such a possibility . . .   The peace current is still very strong.
The idea of war encounters strong opposition."

We know from Flandin, then French Foreign Minister, what
efforts he made to secure British support.   Churchill, in his
war history, says that Flandin told him of his intention to propose
to the British Government a simultaneous mobilisation of the
land, sea and air forces of both countries, saying that France
already had promises of support from all the nations of the Little
Entente.   The following diary entry in the biography of Neville
Chamberlain throws a striking light on the British position:
"12th March.   Talked to Flandin, emphasising that public
opinion here would not support us in sanctions of any kind.   His
view is that, if a firm front is maintained by France and England,
Germany will yield without war.   We cannot accept this as a
reliable estimate of a mad dictator's reactions."

"The whole world, especially the small nations, today looks
to England," Flandin once said in Churchill's presence at a
gathering of leading Englishmen.   "If England acts now, she
can lead Europe . . . it is her last chance; if you do not now
hold Germany in check, all is lost."

Churchill, in his war history, has expressed the opinion that
if France had been equal to her task she would have immediately
ordered general mobilisation, and thereby have compelled all
the others to join her.   For France it was a question of to be or
not to be.   Any French government worthy of the name should
have acted on its own responsibility and relied on treaty
obligations.

Then, I knew nothing of all this.   I only remembered the
voice of the French Premier Sarraut as I had heard it on my
portable wireless just after the German march into the Rhineland, saying with great emotion: "France will never negotiate
as long as Strasbourg is within range of German guns."   I had
heard the Council of the League pronounce the verdict "Guilty,"
and yet I was meeting Eden with Ribbentrop almost daily.
The haggling at these negotiations had reached the point where

a compromise was being unsuccessfully sought, on the basis of "no fortifications, no staff talks." But the "guilty party" declined even to postpone the fortification of the Rhineland.

**

Throughout March and April we made frequent flights between London and Berlin in Ribbentrop's special plane, the familiar Ju 52 with the registration letters AMYY—often regarded as a very hopeful symbol for a diplomatic mission by well disposed English people. Hitler had seen, from the reaction of British statesmen and above all from public opinion, that his tactic of screening the Rhineland adventure with peace proposals had succeeded, and he pursued this method with renewed zeal.

One afternoon at the end of April we took off from the Templehof in AMYY with a large-scale peace plan of Hitler's. It was, if possible, to be handed to the English that evening, so that I had to translate it in the air. I arranged for our Languages Section to make a rough translation, the last sheets of which were handed to me by special messenger just before the plane took off. I set to work feverishly. Normally the flight from Berlin to London took about four hours—not by any means too long for the study of such a highly important diplomatic document. Moreover, during the flight a fair copy had to be made for transmission to the British Government by Ribbentrop's secretary. "I hope we have a head wind," she said. "That'll give us a little more time."

As we were flying over the Wannsee I read the first sentence of the document, which was cleverly attuned to the mood in London as I had found it—to my astonishment—a few days before. "The German Government sincerely concurs in what it has learnt from its Ambassador Ribbentrop to be the desire of the British Government and the British people—namely, as soon as possible to start with the practical work of a true pacification of Europe." It was clear that Hitler thought that he had now regained the initiative, and his language sometimes became overbearing. "Germany," he wrote, "concluded the Armistice in 1918 on the basis of Wilson's Fourteen Points. The demilitarised zone itself arose only in consequence of the previous contravention of an undertaking that was also binding upon the Allies. The German Government rejects all proposals which unilaterally impose obligations on Germany, and are thus discriminatory." As I revised the English draft, it was passed forward sheet by sheet, and the typewriter, a fixture in the nose of this flying office, was kept busy. We had too much head wind to be comfortable. The papers often slipped off my improvised desk, and it was a good thing that the typewriter was firmly fixed. But it is well known that if one is busy one does not feel air-sick, and our miniature Languages Service worked without stomach-trouble until we reached relative calm over the North Sea.

Meanwhile I had come to the revision of the second part of our document, the actual German peace proposals. These consisted of 19 Points: "Equality of rights," "No increase in the strength of the forces in the Rhineland," "Troops not to be brought nearer to the Belgian and French frontiers for the time being," "Supervision by British and Italian military attachés," "25 year non-aggression or security pact between France, Belgium and Germany," "Inclusion of the Netherlands," "Instruction of youth in Germany and France," "Germany prepared to rejoin the League of Nations," . . . "Equality of status in colonial matters," . . . "Separation of the League from all connection with the Treaty of Versailles," . . . "Practical measures to be taken against armaments race."

I had not finished the translation by the time we landed, but to my relief Eden could not see us until the following morning. This gave me time for revision and to translate Hitler's proposals in the disarmament portion of his peace plan. These were—"Prohibition of gas, poison and incendiary bombs," "Prohibition of the bombing of open localities," "Prohibition of the bombardment of open localities with long-range guns," "Abolition of tanks," "Abolition of heavy artillery"

The document I had translated between Berlin and London was undoubtedly impressive and contained some interesting proposals It also seemed to me more concrete and precise than I was accustomed to from Hitler It contained, however, no word about the question which the Locarno Powers, England,

France, Italy and Belgium, had raised at the beginning of their own proposals Eden had spoken to Ribbentrop about it immediately after our condemnation: "(The four Powers) request the German Government to submit to the Permanent International Court of Justice at the Hague the question of whether the Pact of Mutual Assistance between France and Russia can be reconciled with the Locarno Treaty, and to undertake to recognise as final the decision of that Court. " Neither was anything said about the Rhineland fortifications— a matter constantly raised by Eden in previous discussions.

The conversations which took place between Eden and Ribbentrop brought no result. Ribbentrop was particularly enraged at his inability to prevent the hated staff talks between England, France and Belgium. "Contact between the General Staffs of our two countries," Eden wrote in an official note of April 1st to the French Ambassador, "shall be established and maintained." It was on the morning of that day that Ribbentrop had handed in the peace plan.

A few days later we flew back to Germany, having failed in our mission. General distrust of Hitler's surprise tactics in foreign affairs had blocked our peace offensive from the start.

On April 7th the French submitted a counter-proposal, which once more set out all the stock in trade of the Disarmament Conference, such as collective security, etc. On May 7th Sir Eric Phipps, British Ambassador in Berlin, handed in the famous questionnaire which so enraged Hitler, always averse to any precise statement, that he left it unanswered. Thus Germany's diplomatic initiative came finally to a halt.

The British questionnaire, after expressing regret that the German Government had been unable to make any tangible contribution to the restoration of confidence, so essential for the comprehensive negotiations which both Governments had in view, asked "whether Germany regards herself as now in a position to conclude genuine treaties . . . It is of course clear that negotiations for a treaty would be useless if one of the parties hereafter felt free to deny its obligations on the ground that that party was not at the time in a condition to conclude a binding treaty." The Note continued: "The question is really whether Germany now considers that a point has been reached at which she can signify that she recognises and intends to respect the existing territorial and political status of Europe." As I read this questionnaire I realised that we had worked so feverishly in the AMYY in vain. Hitler's attempt, by making grandiose general proposals, to divert attention from his highly unusual method of treating urgent specific questions, had finally failed—at least so far as the Foreign Offices of the other Powers were concerned.

**

Nevertheless, Hitler's diversionary manœuvres had been temporarily successful in misleading world opinion. I particularly noticed this during the August, 1936, Olympiad, which was held in Berlin. It would require a whole book to record the hundreds of conversations at which I interpreted for Hitler, Göring, Gœbbels and other leaders as they conversed with foreign notabilities—kings, heirs apparent, politicians, men of learning and men of the people from almost every country in the world.

I had at the beginning of that year worked in the same capacity, and made similar observations, in the more intimate framework of the winter Olympiad at Garmisch. Now, in August, the anxiety aroused in all minds by the German march into the Rhineland had subsided, the threat of war, which had seemed imminent in March, had receded, and many eloquent pleas for peace had been uttered by the Germans. Not one of the foreign visitors whose words I translated refrained from expressing his joy at the fortunate turn events seemed to have taken. Many emphatically expressed their admiration for Hitler and his endeavours for peace, and for the achievements of National Socialist Germany. Those days seemed to me a virtual apotheosis of Hitler and the Third Reich. During the conversations, which were usually rather brief, I noted that almost without exception Hitler was looked upon by the foreign visitors with the greatest interest, and often with real admiration. Only rarely was a certain scepticism apparent, as in Hitler's conversation with Lord Vansittart. On this occasion he made a remark to me which I often thought about during the war, and which now seems to me especially relevant. "The next war," Vansittart said, "will not be confined within national boundaries. The fronts will go through individual peoples, for it will be a war not of nations but of ideologies."

Much has been written about the grandiose setting in which Germany staged that Olympiad. The production of this fantastic show was first class, and those who witnessed it, whether they were afterwards friends or foes, will always remember it.

As I have already said, I had to perform an interpreting Marathon. At the very start Göring's adjutant said to Hitler's adjutant: "Göring declines to welcome the Olympic Committee in the Old Museum on behalf of the Government unless he has the services of the chief interpreter of the Foreign Office." "The Führer needs Schmidt himself, so he cannot work for Göring," was the reply. "I'll get you a police car which can get through all barriers," said Meissner, who always found a way out. "Then you will be back in the Chancellery in time."

At eleven o'clock I spoke the closing words of the address to the Olympic Committee into the microphone at the Old Museum. As soon as I was out of sight of that solemn gathering I broke into an undignified trot to the police car, and reached the Chancellery just as the last of the foreign delegations whom Hitler was receiving entered his office. Meissner had been right, and I was on the spot in time.

One of the many festivities was a dinner given by Ribbentrop at his Dahlem villa. But the host was in a very ill humour. He had that day been appointed Ambassador to London, instead of Foreign Minister, which was his great ambition. Now the hated Neurath would continue in charge of the Ministry in Berlin; while he himself would be in London, far away from his Führer, a rival might be stealing his place in Hitler's favour. This angered him beyond all measure, and it was actually for this reason that, contrary to all rules of international courtesy, he so long delayed taking up his London appointment, and then offended the British by frequent long absences from London. In normal times an ambassador who thus neglected his duty because, like an offended prima donna, he wanted another rôle, would have promptly been retired. But for some inexplicable reason, on this as on subsequent occasions, Hitler passed over Ribbentrop's gross breach of discipline.

Next day I drove from a picturesque evening entertainment at the Charlottenburg Schloss to an "Italian Night" on the Pfaueninsel. Gœbbels had invited about a hundred people, of whom more than half were foreigners, to an open air dinner. Over the large meadow in the middle of the island glowed innumerable Chinese lanterns. Dining, dancing . . . and interpreting. After-dinner speeches, toasts, and individual conversations—"Oh Herr Schmidt, do help me, I would like to speak to Lord Londonderry," "Monsieur Schmidt, deux mots seulement avec le docteur Gœbbels," "Do you know where Göring is?" One after another. I didn't get hoarse, for there was no shortage of "the right stuff" with which to lubricate my throat, but I slept for two days after the Olympic fires were extinguished.

I had the impression of having taken part in a great event uniting the peoples, and to an interpreter that is always a very pleasant feeling. I had seen the masterly talent of the National Socialist leaders for stage production, and how powerful had been the effect of this truly superb spectacle on the international public, both in the boxes and in the gallery. Only later did I realise, together with those enthralled spectators, that stragecraft and statecraft are wholly different.

It was not only on these festive occasions that I had noticed the keen interest in Hitler and Göring shown by the foreign visitors for whom I interpreted. It was exactly the same in personal man-to-man discussions. Lord Londonderry, the former British Air Minister, was a fairly frequent guest of Göring's who often invited him to go hunting. He usually came to Berlin with his wife and daughter in his private plane, and spent a few days in the capital. I first interpreted for him in February, 1936, and it was thus that I first visited the famous Karinhall, Göring's country estate in the middle of the Schorfheide, forty miles north of Berlin.

In those days Karinhall was just a long log house after the
Scandinavian style, containing only a few rooms. It was
nothing more than a very comfortable hunting lodge, built of
crude logs, but provided with all the most modern devices for
lighting, heating and water supply—a comfortable home away
from the noisy capital, in the huge Schorfheide forest on the
banks of a lake. In the middle of it was a long room with a
rough wooden table and massive wooden seats for several
people. Seated at this table, Londonderry and Göring discussed
the political situation. It was of course not the kind of diplomatic or political discussion with which I usually dealt, but
more in the nature of a pleasant chat. General questions and
personal views were talked about rather than concrete problems.
Much of the conversation was actually about hunting, for which I
had to learn a new vocabulary, so as to be able to translate the
talk about aurochs, elk and deer. The second great theme was
naturally the Air Force, on which they talked technical "shop,"
so that my experience on the Air Committee of the Disarmament
Conference (the square-root of the horse power multiplied by
the wing surface) as well as my experience as an enthusiastic
passenger stood me in good stead. Göring was often surprisingly
frank when proudly recounting the latest achievements of the
Luftwaffe. Lord Londonderry often referred to the talks
between Hitler and Simon, asking whether Germany had really
achieved air parity with England at that time. According to
the Air Ministry's very careful investigations, he said this could
not possibly have been the case. From Lord Londonderry's
insistence on this point it was evident that, as Air Minister at
that time, the parity claimed by Hitler must have caused him
much embarrassment.

When Anglo-German relations were discussed Göring con-
veyed with remarkable skill the impression that Germany
desired nothing more ardently than to be on friendly terms with
England. "If Germany and England stand together," Göring
emphasised more than once, "there is no combination of Powers
in the whole world that can oppose us." Londonderry spoke
with more reserve. "We must, above all, build up world
confidence," he was apt to reply somewhat evasively to Göring's
power politics. But he, too, was a devotee of Anglo-German

friendship. More than once he emphasised the close kinship between the two peoples, the many characteristics they had in common, and the favourable conditions thereby provided for common political action. Listening to the tall, spare Englishman, who faintly resembled the King of Sweden, as he somewhat hesitatingly sought for the right words, one knew at once that this man sincerely desired an understanding with Germany. Göring must also have had this impression, for I have seldom heard him speak with less reserve than in his conversations with Lord Londonderry. There grew up finally between the two men a kind of mutual confidence which the country atmosphere of Karinhall, the family meals, and their long walks together naturally fostered.

The German Air Minister, Prime Minister of Prussia, would stride across the heath, wearing a huge hunter's hat, wielding a sort of old Germanic spear, clad in a white-sleeved leather jerkin, accompanied by the English Lord and his Lady, and sometimes their daughter. At the bison enclosure he would blow his horn. At the sound all the huge beasts came up, giving the impression that they knew Göring personally. But their little eyes gleamed angrily as they approached and butted their horns against the fence, almost breaking it. The lord of the Schorfheide would laugh noisily, as he turned proudly to his English guests, who watched this curious spectacle with smiling interest. They had obviously not seen anything of the kind in England, and were clearly amused at their host's behaviour and the way he was rigged out. But there was no condescension or contempt in their laughter. They obviously liked the man in the jerkin with his strange spear and almost childish delight, which he made no attempt to conceal. They regarded him with the sympathetic understanding which Englishmen usually feel for anyone who is original or eccentric.

No doubt the Londonderrys realised that there was also another Göring besides their cheery Karinhall host—a man who could act with ruthless energy and brutality. This was apparent from various remarks dropped by mother and daughter during meals. "To live in the upper levels of National Socialist Germany may be quite pleasant," Lady Londonderry once said to me, "but woe to the poor folk who do not belong to the upper orders." Nor did she hesitate to make such critical remarks to Göring, who did not take them amiss, as Hitler would certainly have done, but usually answered with some humorous observation. On the whole he seemed to understand such criticism quite well.

Emmy Göring played her part as hostess well. Quiet and modest, she created an atmosphere of hospitality in the best sense of the word, occasionally smiling deprecatingly when her Hermann got carried away and used coarse language. She herself said very little, just unobtrusively contributing to the pleasant family atmosphere of those Anglo-German conversations at the Schorfheide.

During this February visit, the first of a whole series of meetings between Göring and Londonderry, the latter was received by Hitler at the Chancellery. Hitler spoke about the political situation and Anglo-German relations exactly as Göring had done—except that Göring had been more emphatic and forthright and therefore more convincing. No doubt Göring had been carefully instructed by Hitler. At that time the policy was to concentrate on an understanding with Great Britain. It was almost as if Hitler was wooing the coy Britannia. This was most noticeable during the talk with Londonderry. "How often, during the war," Hitler said, "when I was opposite British troops, did I say to myself that it was absolute madness to be fighting against these men who might well have belonged to our own people! That must never happen again."

Londonderry listened with friendly and sympathetic interest, and sought for the right phrases to express similar hopes as convincingly as possible. Hitler's eloquent words about Anglo-German relations had visibly impressed him. Once again I noticed how strongly foreign visitors were influenced by Hitler at such interviews.

* * *

I interpreted for a whole series of foreigners who came to see Hitler during that year of 1936. They included Frenchmen, such as Labeyrie, Governor of the Bank of France, and Bastide, Minister of Commerce. These were not very important conversations, but they confirmed my impression that foreign countries, at any rate so far as their visitors to Germany were representative of them, regarded Hitler at that time with an extraordinary close and by no means unfriendly interest. "Hitler has impressed Europe as an exceptional personality. He arouses not only fear and aversion, he inspires curiosity and also wins sympathy. His reputation grows. The power of the attraction which he exercises extends beyond the frontiers of his country. Kings, princes, and celebrities of all kinds come to the capital to meet this man of destiny, who seems to hold the fate of the continent in his hands, and also to see this Germany which with irresistible compulsion he has changed and invigorated." In these very apt words François-Poncet has described what I experienced at all these meetings.

One of the most noteworthy of these meetings was that between Lloyd George and Hitler at the Obersalzberg near Berchtesgaden at the beginning of September. "I am exceptionally pleased," said Hitler, as he went to meet the former British Prime Minister with outstretched hand, "to be able to welcome to my house the man whom we in Germany have always regarded as the actual victor of the World War." Lloyd George smilingly disclaimed this with a wave of the hand, but I thought I detected a certain satisfaction at this compliment from the German ex-corporal. "And I deem myself lucky," Lloyd George readily answered, "to meet the man who, after defeat, has united the whole German people behind him and led them to recovery." Looking out of the big window over the sunny Berchtesgaden landscape, he said: "What a splendid place you have found up here."

We sat at a table near the window, Hitler, Lloyd George, Ribbentrop and myself. Ribbentrop was like a shadow; during the whole talk he scarcely uttered a word.

Lloyd George's flowing white hair contrasted vividly with his youthful, expressive face and merry, penetrating eyes. His movements too showed an almost youthful elasticity as he enlivened his talk with vivacious gestures of his small shapely hands. The victor of the first world war! And facing him was the man who, as it then seemed, was in a fair way to bring Lloyd George's work to naught.

It was one of Hitler's best days. Refreshed by his stay in the mountains, slightly bronzed by the sun, obviously delighted by the recognition implied in this visit from the world-famous statesman, he began to speak with excitement of his experiences as a humble soldier at the front. "I often faced the English," he said, enumerating many well known places on the western front. He praised the English soldiers, and went into details about their equipment and tactics. Lloyd George was astonishingly well informed about all these matters. He was able to tell Hitler exactly why any particular offensive had been launched on any particular day.

After more of this they began to discuss politics. "Alliances are always dangerous," said Lloyd George. "In the last war they extended the hostilities like a prairie fire. But for them the conflict might have been localised." Consciously or unconsciously, he had exactly expressed Hitler's opinion on collective security. One of Hitler's favourite mottoes was: "No multilateral undertakings, but only mutual non-aggression pacts between neighbours." Hitler elaborated this theme as though he had only been waiting for a cue, expounding the peace plan which I had translated in the plane to London in March, and which had since somewhat sunk into oblivion. Lloyd George took this opportunity of expressing himself very definitely, if in quite general terms, about the German peace efforts, "which," he said, "have unfortunately been frustrated by the staff talks." Intentionally or not, he had again touched upon a favourite theme of Hitler's.

Somewhat abruptly Lloyd George then turned the conversation from politics to the social measures "by which Germany has always distinguished herself." National Socialism had embarked on experiments in this field which were especially interesting to England. "They are not experiments, but well worked out plans," interposed Hitler, who thought the word experiment implied some criticism. But Lloyd George was far from implying any such thing. With eloquent enthusiasm he spoke of the German measures for abolishing unemployment, of health insurance, social welfare and holidays. He had already investigated much of what was being done on the labour front, and seemed to be deeply impressed by what he had seen.

Hitler was quite enchanted by his visitor. Afterwards, he constantly referred to his conversation "with the great English statesman, Lloyd George." He pressed him to visit the forthcoming rally at Nuremberg, but Lloyd George declined very definitely. "I did not come to Germany for politics," he said. "I only wanted to study your social measures, and above all your solution of the unemployment problem, which is such a menace in England too." If he went to Nuremberg, he said it would be taken very amiss in England. It was some time before the conversation recovered from the chill caused by this remark.

The sun was low on the horizon when, after nearly three hours, this memorable conversation ended. The old victor of the first war took a warm leave of the young dictator. They arranged that Lloyd George should come to tea next day, bringing his daughter Megan and his son. Gwilym, who were with him on his visit. "The whole Liberal Party has gone to Germany with him," the newspapers in England maliciously reported.

Ribbentrop remained with Hitler whilst I went back with Lloyd George. He was at his most genial, asking exactly where I had been in the war. I was able to tell him of my experiences as a machine gunner near Rheims, and of the first great turn in events when Foch started the counter-offensive in July 1918. He asked in great detail from what positions we had then retired and what had been the moral effect of the allied counter-attack, cross-examining me minutely.

I was encouraged, in due course, to put some questions to him, and I asked him to confirm the following story. Briand had once told Stresemann in my presence that Lloyd George had congratulated him on the particularly brave conduct of a Breton regiment from his home province. "Well, you know, Monsieur Lloyd George," Briand had replied, "we Bretons do not so easily adjust ourselves to new relationships. These troops were therefore told before the action that they would be attacking the English, and that is why they fought so bravely." Lloyd George laughed heartily, saying: "I remember that very well. Old Briand was always an incorrigible jester."

I also asked him to confirm a second story, and he said: "By all means—if it is as amusing." In Clemenceau's Memoirs I had read that at a dinner on Armistice Day he and Lloyd George had discussed Germany's future, Lloyd George's opinions being materially different from Clemenceau's. "What's come over you?" Clemenceau had asked rather bluntly. "You seem to have changed completely." To which Lloyd George replied: "Yes—hadn't you heard that I have become pro-German?" Lloyd George confirmed this story too. As our car stopped at his hotel door, his daughter laughingly greeted him with the Nazi salute, saying "Heil Hitler!" Thereupon the aged Lloyd George became quite serious and answered with quiet decision: "Certainly, Heil Hitler! I say it too, for he is really a great man."

In his war history Churchill says: "No one was more completely misled than Mr. Lloyd George, whose rapturous accounts of his conversations make odd reading today."

CHAPTER III

(1937)

"The period of surprises is over. Peace is now our highest aim" our Languages Service translated from a speech Hitler made on January 30th, 1937. I hoped, rather than believed, that he meant this statement seriously.

In his conversations with foreigners, which were still frequent during 1937, I noted that Hitler was becoming stiffer in his attitude towards the rest of the world. This may have been partly because he had achieved such wide recognition, but he undoubtedly also became more uncompromising as the anti-Nazi coalition weakened. Whereas at Stresa Mussolini had stood on the opposite side together with France and Britain, he had now, as a result of the Abyssinian conflict, been pushed into Germany's arms.

I had followed from a distance with lively interest the conflict over Abyssinia as it was enacted at Geneva. From my experience of Geneva I would not have thought it possible that the whole League of Nations would unite in a common front against Italy, and seek by means of economic sanctions to hinder her from carrying out her plan of aggression. I profoundly hoped that the League would succeed, for I believed that nothing would have a more salutary effect upon Hitler than Mussolini's failure. In 1938, on the eve of the Munich Conference, Mussolini admitted that the League of Nations had very nearly succeeded in countering aggression by means of collective security. "If the League of Nations had followed Eden's advice in the Abyssinian dispute," he said to Hitler, "and had extended economic sanctions to oil, I would have had to withdraw from Abyssinia within a week. That would have been an incalculable disaster for me."

It was owing to the opposition of the French Government,

the protagonist of collective security, oddly enough, that oil sanctions were not applied. Laval did not want an open breach with Italy. When, during the war, he repeatedly complained to me about the difficulties caused to France by Italy, I was able on one occasion to retort with some justification: "How ungrateful of Mussolini, Prime Minister, for you saved his life in the Abyssinian dispute. He admitted as much at Munich in my presence." Quick though he was, Laval had no answer. How different history might have been had the League been successful in bringing Mussolini to heel!

As Hitler had announced in his speech in January, 1937, there were no more surprises——that year. Looking back on it now, one could almost call it a year of calm before the storm. I was nevertheless kept busy with a great variety of assignments. The coronation celebrations in London, the International Exhibition in Paris, the Party Rally in Nuremberg, and Mussolini's state visit to Germany—these were the highlights. But my varied programme included also the following: the meeting between Hitler and the former leader of the British Labour Party, the aged Lansbury, in March; Göring's conversations with Mussolini in Rome in April; the Duke of Windsor's visit to the Obersalzberg; the negotiations between Hitler and Lord Halifax at Berchtesgaden, and between Göring and Halifax in Berlin; the visits of the Aga Khan, of the British Fascist leader, Sir Oswald Mosley, and of a descendant of Confucius, Chiang Kai-Shek's brother-in-law, the Finance Minister Kung.

It was shortly before Hitler's birthday that I interpreted the conversation he had with Lansbury. The world-famous pacifist, "the patriarch of decent feelings," as a German paper called him, was laying a plan before Hitler for a peace conference which should be called by the President of the United States. This was a purely private undertaking of Lansbury's and well-meaning pacifist circles in England, and the plan was discussed only in broad outline and very superficially. One could tell from his eloquent exposition how enthusiastic Lansbury was. I noticed, however, that most of the time Hitler's thoughts were elsewhere. This was the first time that I saw that other Hitler— a man pale from sleeplessness, his complexion almost grey, with somewhat puffy features, whose absent-minded expression clearly showed that he was brooding on other things. Only occasionally did he attend to what Lansbury was saying through me, and make some vague, noncommittal remark about Germany's participation in a peace conference, or about the peace policy that he himself wanted to pursue. I almost felt sorry for the old gentleman from England. Again and again he advanced his pacific plans with great enthusiasm and persistence. He seemed wholly unaware of Hitler's lack of interest, being obviously delighted with his replies, vague though they might be. He plainly regarded the man who sat there lost in dreams as one of the pacifist idealists whom he had so often met at international gatherings. The longer the conversation lasted, and the more monosyllabic Hitler became, the more did Lansbury warm to his theme. After all, Hitler had not once contradicted him; he had agreed that Germany would attend the peace conference; he had pronounced the word freedom with appropriate emphasis!

Hitler terminated the conversation somewhat abruptly. It had begun to bore him. It was hardly to be expected that a practising pacifist would have any effect on him. What seemed to me extraordinary was that Lansbury left the Chancellery highly satisfied, and that his statements to the Press and on the wireless were very confident. "I return to England," he said, "with the conviction that the catastrophe of war will be avoided."

I was surprised, a few days later, to receive instructions to go to Rome for talks between Göring and Mussolini. The morning after our arrival I went with Göring to the Palazzo Chigi, the Italian Foreign Office, for a short call on Count Ciano. Our main topic was the Spanish Civil War, then in full swing, in which Italy and Germany were giving Franco military assistance.

In the afternoon, together with Göring, I entered the famous Palazzo Venezia for the first time. A small lift with accommodation for only two people took Göring and the Italian *chef de protocole* to the first floor, so that I had to rush up the historical staircase two steps at a time, meeting my chief, breathless, at the lift door. This was a performance I was later often to repeat. We were taken along passages decorated with mediæval armour and other trophies to the hall of the

Fascist High Council, a medium-sized, sombre room. The long tables and Mussolini's raised daïs, and also the seats, were all covered with dark blue velvet. We went on to Mussolini's anteroom, where Ciano greeted us. Then the door opened on to the Italian' dictator's much described study. My impression was of a vast, sober, bare room. In the far distance, on the side facing us, there were a few solitary pieces of furniture and a globe. With its cold marble floor and grey walls, the room struck me as forbidding, unfriendly and un-Italian.

As we entered a figure rose up at the far end, where, looking closely, I saw a long smooth table and some simple chairs in Venetian style. It was Mussolini, who came walking down the whole length of the room to meet us. He raised his arm in the Fascist salute, shook hands with Göring and gave me a friendly nod. Bareness was the outstanding feature of this office. There were a few books, but no papers anywhere.

We sat down—Mussolini at his desk, with myself and Göring opposite him on visitors' chairs. Ciano, to whom his father-in-law did not pay much attention, found himself a seat next to us. The situation in Spain was the first subject to be discussed. Various technical details about the military were somewhat guardedly exchanged, both parties keeping up the pretence, even to one another, that the Germans and Italians fighting for Franco were volunteers having no official connection with their Governments. In the course of the conversation Göring became franker, giving with obvious satisfaction all the details of how, at the beginning of the Spanish Civil War, Franco's Moroccan troops were flown to Spain with the help of German Ju 52 transport planes. "Franco has much to thank us for," Göring said—adding, somewhat thoughtfully: "I hope he'll remember it later."

Both violently criticised the Spanish strategy and tactics, though the bravery of the Spaniards, including Franco's opponents, the so-called Reds, was fully recognised by both Mussolini and Göring. Both spoke disparagingly of the war material supplied to the Republicans by Russia, especially the aircraft, and both were completely confident of their own superiority over the Red Army.

They passed on to discuss the general political situation in

Europe, and Mussolini used strong language in condemning
the League of Nations and the sanctions policy of England
and France. Listening to him one would never have thought
that but two years ago at Stresa he, together with England and
France, had condemned the introduction of conscription in
Germany, or that only a year earlier he had sent Italian divisions
to the Brenner frontier when Dollfuss was murdered during a
National Socialist putsch in Austria. Times had changed,
and the discussion of the Austrian question itself showed how
fundamentally Mussolini's attitude had altered. Göring was
very outspoken on this matter, frankly telling Mussolini that
the *Anschluss* would and must come and that the event could
not be delayed.

Mussolini, who spoke good German, listened to Göring
attentively, but he evidently could not have understood this
passage, for it was only in the course of my translating it into
French that he shook his head vehemently. It was the only
sign of opposition he gave on that day—just a year before
Austria's *Anschluss* with Germany became a fact. His silence
was a clear indication that, although he continued to regard
the *Anschluss* with somewhat mixed feelings, he realised that it
"would and must come," as Göring had put it. I naturally did
not know what instructions Hitler had given Göring for Rome,
but from the talk with Mussolini I formed the impression that
the main purpose of the visit was to sound out the Italians on
the *Anschluss* question.

I was more interested than surprised to see how far Mussolini
had already parted company with the Western Powers, and how
he now shared Germany's views on fundamental questions
of European policy. Sitting there, with his short, squat body,
very upright, with expressive looks and few gestures, he gave
his opinions with concise Latin clarity. As he looked penetratingly with his big brown eyes at Göring or myself, I felt
that here was a man with little of the vague visionary about
him—a clear-sighted, matter-of-fact Roman with both feet on
the ground, who knew exactly what he wanted. In conversations that afterwards took place between him and Hitler I was
constantly struck by this clear, concise and realistic phrasing
of Mussolini's, in contrast to Hitler's vague generalities. This

was the great difference between the two dictators—so long, at any rate, as Italy and Mussolini were able to make more or less independent decisions. As the Italian gradually declined to the status of a vassal of Hitler's, he became more and more silent. When I now look back at the gradual change in his demeanour during their many conversations, I am inclined to think that Mussolini realised before many others did whither the journey was taking them, and that he certainly foresaw the catastrophe looming ahead long before his German partner did. But by that time he had already lost his freedom to act independently.

Another sudden change of scene for me. From the Italian dictator's bare office in the Palazzo Venezia I flew home a few days later on the Rome-Berlin air axis, to start off again immediately on the much more familiar and shorter air route to London, for the coronation of King George VI. I was to be available in London to interpret at political discussions for the War Minister, von Blomberg, the leader of the German delegation. The Third Reich still hoped for a Berlin-London agreement, although all the time the gap between the two capitals was widening in proportion as that between Rome and Berlin narrowed.

The morning after my arrival in London I was awakened at seven o'clock by a military band which passed the German Embassy. I had a room overlooking the Mall, along which the coronation procession was to pass. From eight o'clock onwards this room, with the terrace in front of it, was no longer my own. The Ambassador, von Ribbentrop, had provided accommodation for the entire German colony in the rooms of the Embassy, and I had a large share of the guests. Even so, I had an excellent view of the procession.

First came the Lord Mayor of London in a glass coach. This traditional vehicle seemed to come straight out of Grimm's fairy tales—I felt like rubbing my eyes to make sure that I was not dreaming. The members of the royal family, each with their splendidly uniformed escorts, brought up the rear of

the procession.   Already in the distance one could see slowly
approaching the golden state-coach drawn by eight greys, in
which were seated the royal pair.   Surrounded by the pageantry
of this centuries-old tradition, the King and Queen, symbols of
the greatest Empire in the world, made an unforgettable
impression on me.   I could not but envy the way in which the
ordinary Englishman took this manifestation of the might of the
British Commonwealth for granted.   There was nothing
extravagant or overdone about it.   The applause was not
hysterical, but came naturally and spontaneously from the heart
of the common man.   Here the ceremonial uniforms did not
seem out of place.   They clearly derived from an unbroken line
of ancient tradition.

Ribbentrop had invited some leading party members to
come to London for the coronation, and I was interested in their
reaction.   It did not win their approval, mostly because it was
too "historical."   "We National Socialists do this kind of thing
much better," said one of the party men to me.   "We dispense
with all this traditional mumbo jumbo.   You don't see so many
old greyheads with us.   We give youth and the modern uniform
of the brown shirt precedence over age and historical tradition."

On this memorable occasion Britain seemed to me like a
weathered oak—gnarled but still vital.   Compared with this
our National Socialist displays in Germany seemed like brilliant
hothouse plants, prize blooms forced by every conceivable device
of modern horticulture, about whose staying power one might
well feel sceptical.

The day after the coronation I accompanied our War
Minister, von Blomberg, to see the Prime Minister, Mr. Baldwin,
at No.10 Downing Street, which I had first entered with Stresemann in 1924.   Nothing seemed to have changed here, and
Baldwin himself gave the impression of having been part of the
house for a long time.   The short, heavily-built man sat
smoking his pipe at his desk, looking like an English bulldog.
From all that he said I got the impression that he was expressing
carefully considered opinions which he had held for a long time.
His every movement expressed unshakable calm and self-
confidence.

We already knew that he was soon to be succeeded by the

Chancellor of the Exchequer, Neville Chamberlain, and we also knew that Baldwin had never been much interested in questions of foreign policy. In these circumstances hardly anything was said of the relations between Germany and England. Both parties confined themselves to expressing the wish that existing difficulties might be eliminated. Blomberg pointed out that the attitude of the British Press caused great displeasure to National Socialist circles in Germany, without however specifying any particular wishes in this matter. Baldwin contented himself with the answer, often enough made later to Hitler and other Germans when they complained about the British Press: "England is the land of a free Press, and the British Government cannot possibly influence newspapers."

On the afternoon of the same day I went to see Neville Chamberlain—who the following year was to play such an important part in the Munich crisis. The difference between him and Baldwin was striking. Compared with the almost phlegmatic Baldwin, Chamberlain seemed—for London— almost lively. He was not a man of fixed, immutable opinions. He was obviously interested in the most recent developments in Germany, and enquired about various details of the administrative organisation of the Third Reich. Although he expressed them with a certain reserve his wishes for friendly relations between Germany and England were far more convincing. No doubt he was naturally reserved, but the fact that he was officially still only Chancellor of the Exchequer understandably made him more so on this occasion. This was little more than a courtesy visit.

I also went with Blomberg to pay a brief call on Eden at the Foreign Office. Eden was extraordinarily reticent, which I attributed to the fact that the English would have liked the Foreign Minister, von Neurath, to represent Germany at the coronation. I was told that a hint to this effect had been given, but that Ribbentrop was determined not to have his rôle as Germany's political representative questioned, and had therefore successfully intrigued to prevent the Foreign Minister being sent over for the occasion.

After my return I was kept extremely busy in Germany. Von Neurath, just like Stresemann and Curtius in earlier days, made me available as interpreter to other notabilities, including members of the Cabinet and leading figures in the Third Reich.

I also did much interpreting for Gœbbels at official Press functions and at private conversations. On these occasions he was the wolf in exceptionally well-tailored sheep's clothing. Before his suicide in 1945, an eye-witness told me, when the National Socialist Reich lay in ruins all around him, he tore off the mask and said to his most faithful colleagues: "Now you see what you get for having worked for us. Now your number's up too and the whole German people are getting what they deserved." But in those earlier days, when I interpreted for Gœbbels and his foreign visitors, he was invariables the cultivated intellectual—affable, well groomed and smiling—the very antithesis of the raging demagogue which he often showed himself to be in his radio speeches and election meetings. Perhaps the contrast was too great for the impression on his foreign visitors to be lasting. One who was not taken in by him was the future French Premier, Paul Reynaud. I once interpreted for them in Berlin, and it was clear that Gœbbels, for all his skill, had met his match in the shrewd Frenchman.

One of the many assignments that followed in quick succession was that of attending the Nuremberg Party Congress to interpret for the many distinguished foreign visitors. It was not the first time that I had done this job, and it was exacting work. My hotel was full of English and French guests who could hardly contain themselves in their enthusiasm for Hitler.

It was one of my duties to drive in an open car a few yards behind Hitler with the most prominent English and French guests, on the day of Hitler's triumphal procession through Nuremberg. A triumphal procession it undoubtedly was. A mighty crowd of people ecstatically applauding Hitler created an overwhelming impression. It was as though at the sight of him mass intoxication had seized the untold thousands all along the way. They greeted him deliriously with outstretched arms, and shouts of:

"Heil!" To drive through the midst of this frenzied applause was physically exhausting. One felt one had to keep a grip on oneself in order not to be carried away by the jubilation. Fortunately my attention was constantly diverted by having to interpret, but I have seen Englishmen and Frenchmen moved almost to tears by such scenes, and even some hardboiled international journalists were shaken to the core.

When the procession was over, Hitler, with a few party leaders, would give a banquet to the foreigners. After the gruelling experience of the morning scarcely any of the visitors were capable of sensible conversation.

The diplomatic corps was fully represented at the Nuremberg Party Rally held for the first time in 1937. This year the ambassadors of France and Britain, and the U.S.A. chargé d'affaires (not the ambassador) were present. The ambassadors of the Argentine, Brazil, Chile, China, France, Great Britain, Italy, Japan, Poland, Spain and Turkey had been brought to Nuremberg in two long trains composed of sleeping-cars, and in another train there followed the Ministers of the smaller countries, as well as the chargés d'affaires of the U.S.A., the Union of South Africa, Czecho-Slovakia, Lithuania, Afghanistan and Iran.

On one of the days during the Nuremberg week Hitler was in the habit of holding a reception at the Deutscher Hof, at which I used to translate his speech into French. François-Poncet, who spoke excellent German, would reply as senior ambassador, and seldom failed to introduce one of the witty remarks for which he was famous in diplomatic circles in Berlin. "You speak so well," Hitler once said to him, "that I would very much like to have you as Reich spokesman." "I would gladly accept the office, but only as speaker extraordinary (*zur besonderen Verwendung*)," François-Poncet readily replied, with a dig at the prevalent mania in the Third Reich for "z.b.V." appointments of ambassadors-extraordinary, commissioners-extraordinary, etc. On these occasions François-Poncet could also introduce a serious note. "The finest laurel wreath," he said with slow emphasis a year later, when the Sudeten crisis was threatening war, "will always be the one that can be made without a single mother having to shed her tears."

* *
*

My next big political assignment was Mussolini's state visit to Germany—an elaborately staged demonstration of the increasing solidarity between the two countries. I waited with the German Escort of Honour at the small German frontier station of Kiefersfelden to receive Mussolini and Ciano as they arrived by special train on the morning of September 25th. This was the first time that I boarded one of the famous special trains which Mussolini and Hitler used on their political journeys. The Italian train had ten large saloon, dining, and sleeping cars, and two Mitropa sleeping cars were attached to it for our use. Mussolini and Ciano greeted me heartily, for I was one of the few in the German party whom they already knew. I was conspicuous as the only person in the whole train wearing mufti. Both the Germans and the Italians were all wearing gorgeous gold and silver braided uniforms. Conversations between the Italian guests and the German reception committee, which included two Reich Ministers, Hess and Frank, was not exactly hearty. In Mussolini's swaying saloon the Germans and the Italians contented themselves with sickly smiles at each other, while the members of the Escort of Honour were at pains, like tourist guides, to point out even the smallest and least significant features of the landscape in order to make some show of conversation. In Munich the ordeal came to an end.

At the Central Station, completely transformed by all its banners and decorations, Hitler was surrounded by a vast entourage, all in uniform. He held out both hands to Mussolini who was standing at the carriage window. The music of bands, the roll of drums and the yells of "Heil!" and "Duce!" echoed back from the station roof, and the tumult continued as we made our way to the exit along a red carpet which stretched right through the main hall. I had no interpreting to do not only because Mussolini spoke German very well, but also because nobody could possibly have made himself heard above the din.

In our drive through the cordoned-off streets I at once noticed a marked difference from the drive through Nuremberg a few days before. The public applause was very cool—no one would have been moved to tears here. "It's all the fault of the Chief of Police," I heard Hitler shout a little later to his adjutants.

The talks that followed in Hitler's five-roomed apartment were the first between the two dictators since they had met some years before in Venice. As they spoke in German, I had ample opportunity of observing and of comparing them. There was little about Hitler that fitted in with the popular conception of the typical German. When he got excited the much-caricatured lock of his long black hair fell over his receding forehead, giving him an untidy Bohemian appearance. I noticed his coarse nose and undistinguished mouth with its little moustache. His voice was rough and often hoarse as he flung out sentences full of rolling *r*'s either at me or at Mussolini. Sometimes his eyes blazed suddenly, and then equally suddenly became dull as if in a fit of absent-mindedness.

Mussolini sitting opposite him was of a wholly different type. Firmly erect, swaying from the hips as he talked, his Caesarian head might have been modelled from the old Romans, with its powerful forehead and broad, square chin thrust forward under a wide mouth. He had a much more vivacious expression than Hitler when his turn came to thunder against the Bolshevists or the League of Nations. Indignation, contempt, determination and cunning alternately lit up his highly mobile face, and he had the histrionic sense native to Latins. At particularly eloquent passages his gleaming dark brown eyes seemed ready to start from his head. He never said a word too much, and everything he uttered could have been sent straight to the printers. The differences in their laughs were also interesting. Hitler's always had a flavour of derision and sarcasm. It showed traces of past disappointments and suppressed ambitions, whereas Mussolini's laugh was free and whole-hearted, a liberating laugh that showed he had a sense of humour. The conversation began with what was, for me, an amusing ceremony —Hitler being appointed by Mussolini an honorary corporal in the Fascist Militia.

The discussion itself lasted only about an hour, and was general rather than particular as indeed were all the subsequent conversations. Hitler discoursed vaguely and at great length, while Mussolini spoke briefly and clearly, yet without giving anything away.

All that emerged from this conversation was that both countries were pretty well agreed on a friendly attitude to Japan, the greatest possible support to Franco, and contempt for the western democracies, Britain and France. This was actually the only political talk between Hitler and Mussolini during the whole visit. The "Festival Programme" left scarcely a quiet moment for really serious discussion. Parades in Munich, manœuvres in Mecklenburg, inspection of the Krupp works in Essen, and other activities of this kind, followed one another without respite.

I travelled all over Germany with Mussolini in his special train. Hitler always accompanied him to the station, and then followed in his own brand-new special train, passing us on the way so as to be able to receive his guest again at our destination, like the fable of the race between the hare and the tortoise.

Undoubtedly the most splendid ceremony of Mussolini's German visit was his triumphal entry into Berlin. Hitler's train unexpectedly drew alongside Mussolini's at Spandau-West station, on the adjacent track, and from there kept exactly level with us—a masterpiece of train driving. The two heavy trains each had two locomotives, and I later learned that the engine drivers had rehearsed the operation for days beforehand. Thus, for a quarter of an hour the trains ran along side by side, and we could comfortably carry on a conversation with the occupants of the other train. Just before Heerstrasse Station the German train began to gain almost imperceptibly, so that it reached the terminus platform a few seconds before our Italian train. This had also been carefully timed by the Reichsbahn, so that Hitler could walk the few paces along the platform, and hold out his hand to Mussolini the moment the latter's train stopped.

Later, as we drove through Berlin, my car got a special ovation, because I was the only one among the Germans and Italians who was in mufti, and my top hat attracted special attention. Berliners like a joke—they had come there to shout, and were glad of the opportunity I had unwittingly given them.

On the following day there were parades, banquets, a visit

to Karinhall, and, in the evening, a great public meeting at the Olympia Stadium. "Italy, and particularly Fascist Italy, has no part in the humiliations of our people," said Hitler to the masses. The speech was broadcast, to the "115 million citizens of our two countries who are sharing with deep emotion in this historic event." He spoke of "community, not only of opinion, but also of action. Germany is once again a World Power. The strength of our two nations constitutes . . . the strongest guarantee for the preservation of a civilised Europe, true to her cultural mission, and armed against disruptive forces."

A sudden cloudburst drenched the "one million people" who were in and around the Stadium as Mussolini's turn came at the microphone. "The Berlin-Rome Axis was formed in the autumn of 1935, and during the last two years it has worked splendidly for the ever closer association of our two peoples and for European peace," he said. "My visit must not be judged by the same standards as ordinary diplomatic or political visits are judged. . . . Tomorrow I am not going on somewhere else" (an obvious allusion to Eden's journey from Hitler to Stalin). "The greatest and most genuine democracies that the world knows today are Germany and Italy." Despite the pouring rain, the return journey was made with the cars still open—special orders were given to this effect.

When it was all over, a storm of another kind broke over my innocent head at the Chancellery. With my "plutocratic" top hat and morning coat I had attracted Hitler's very unfavourable attention as the only civilian among the uniformed Axis officials. The fact was brought to his notice again when he saw the Press photographs from Munich that evening. I was not at all displeased with my suit, and had long since become inured to taunts by Party men, such as: "You look like the President of the Republic," or the sarcastic observations of staff officers at manoeuvres, such as: "If you look straight past the gentleman in mufti you will see the advancing tanks;" or: "You look like the owner of the battlefield assessing the damage to his land." But now I was finally told that my suit was "impossible," and that I must henceforward appear in uniform when interpreting for Hitler in public. Hitler provided me with an SS uniform, and Göring with an Air Force uniform.

Some time afterwards the bewildered director of personnel at the Air Ministry asked me: "What on earth was the Field Marshal thinking of when he gave you an Air Force uniform? Officially that is not allowed." In the next great show, however, which was Hitler's return visit to Italy, I wore neither of these uniforms, but appeared looking rather like an admiral in the new dark blue uniform of the Foreign Office, especially created for that occasion. In fact the Italians when they saw us coming actually greeted us with cries of: "Here come the Amiranti!"

As I had expected, the programme of Mussolini's visit to Germany allowed no time for serious political discussion. Not even was a final communiqué issued; and it was only in the toasts exchanged between Hitler and Mussolini at a Chancellery banquet that serious matters were touched upon. Hitler spoke of Italy and Germany having been drawn together in sincere friendship by a common political purpose, saying that they would "strive to secure peace and a general international understanding." Mussolini replied: "German-Italian solidarity is a living and active solidarity. . . . Italy and Germany are ready to work together with all other peoples. . . . They are immune against any attempt to separate them."

On the afternoon of September 29th I left the Lehrter Station in Mussolini's train. Hitler saw the Duce off. The strenuous days of this first "Axis Conversation" were ended.

* * *

I had only just got back to Berlin when, at the beginning of October, I was called upon to interpret for the Duke and Duchess of Windsor on the occasion of their visit to Göring at Karinhall. They were at that time studying our social system.

Karinhall had been greatly enlarged since Lord Londonderry's visit. Göring, with childish pride, showed the Duke and Duchess over the whole house, including his gymnasium in the basement, with its elaborate massage apparatus. With all his Orders tinkling on his uniform he forced his generously proportioned body between one of the pairs of rollers to show the smiling Duchess how they worked. The spacious attic was entirely taken up with an elaborate model railway for the benefit of one of Göring's nephews. Göring switched the current on and the two men were soon quite absorbed with the fascinating toy. Finally Göring sent a toy aeroplane, attached to an overhead wire, flying across the room. As it flew over the railway it actually dropped some small wooden bombs.

At tea afterwards I did not have to translate for the Duke, who speaks German fairly well, but I kept up a running commentary for the Duchess.

Two days later the Windsors were received by Hitler at the Obersalzberg. The Duke expressed his admiration for the industrial welfare arrangements he had seen, especially at the Krupp works in Essen. Social progress in Germany was the principal subject of conversation between Hitler and the Windsors during the afternoon. Hitler was evidently making an effort to be as amiable as possible towards the Duke, whom he regarded as Germany's friend, having especially in mind a speech the Duke had made several years before, extending the hand of friendship to German ex-servicemen associations. In these conversations there was, so far as I could see, nothing whatever to indicate whether the Duke of Windsor really sympathised with the ideology and practices of the Third Reich, as Hitler seemed to assume he did. Apart from some appreciative words for the measures taken in Germany in the field of social welfare the Duke did not discuss political questions. He was frank and friendly with Hitler, and displayed the social charm for which he is known throughout the world. The Duchess joined only occasionally in the conversation, and then with great reserve, when any social question of special interest to women arose. She was simply and appropriately dressed, and made a lasting impression on Hitler. "She would have made a good Queen," he said when they had gone.

My next assignment was as interpreter for the visit of Lord Halifax, which received so much publicity. The pretence was made that the visit was purely private, and that Lord Halifax had come to see the international hunting exhibition elaborately staged by Göring. The Berliners at once nicknamed him "Lord Halalifax" (*Halali* is the German equivalent of Tally Ho!) Actually, Halifax's journey formed part of the effort then being made by Chamberlain to establish good, or at least tolerable, relations with Germany. Halifax was briefed to sound Göring and Hitler on this subject. After staying a few days in Berlin he left for Berchtesgaden with Neurath and myself, on the evening of November 18th, and the following afternoon had a fairly long conversation with Hitler.

Hitler met him on the steps with a friendly smile, and showed him over the house, after which we settled down at the inconveniently low table in his study. "I have brought no new proposals from London," was Halifax's opening remark. "I have chiefly come to ascertain the German Government's views on the existing political situation, and to see what possibilities of a solution there may be."

This was dangerously reminiscent of Eden's questionnaire which had so provoked Hitler, and he reacted accordingly. As I translated Halifax's words he frowned angrily, and I thought he would sulk and refuse to speak. But Hitler found it hard to remain silent for long. So, in spite of his annoyance, he embarked on a lengthy dissertation, and presented Germany's wishes in the form of highly categorical demands. This angry Hitler was very different from the quiet, friendly Chancellor who had spoken with Simon and Eden two years before. He was no longer cautiously feeling his way, as in 1935, but obviously confident of his own strength and of the others' weakness.

He began by complaining bitterly about the British Press, which, he said, had tried to torpedo Halifax's visit by publishing alleged German demands. Halifax, to Hitler's further annoyance, produced in reply the stereotyped justification about the freedom of the British Press. The Führer went on to speak about Germany's relations with South-East Europe. A close union between Austria and the Reich was absolutely imperative, and had been urgently desired by the Austrian people ever since 1919. Nor could the Czechs any longer be allowed to oppress the Sudeten Germans. Finally, Germany must be able freely to extend her economic relations with South-Eastern and

Eastern Europe, for those areas provided the natural comple-
ment to the German economy. Germany was the principal
European importer of the products of all those countries.
"Obstacles are repeatedly being put in my way in South-East
Europe by the Western Powers," Hitler shouted, "and political
ambitions which I have never entertained are attributed to me."

Halifax observed that England was ready to consider any
solution, provided that it was not based on force. "That also
applies to Austria," he added with emphasis.

Hitler again became excited. The question of applying
force in the case of Austria could not arise; the wishes of the
people were clearly evident. Then he turned to Danzig and
the Polish Corridor. Here again Halifax said that he was
prepared to discuss any solution not brought about by force.
Hitler at great length stressed Germany's desire for peace, and I
felt that Halifax was impressed by the way he based this on
Germany's need of peace for her internal development programme. But, on the whole, the meeting was not auspicious.
One could scarcely have conceived a greater contrast between
two men. Halifax, the deeply religious Yorkshire nobleman,
the enthusiastic protagonist of peace, and Hitler, wilful and
uncompromising by nature, and now rendered even more so by
his recent successes and the now manifest weakness of his
opponents.

When the conversation turned to fundamental ideas the two
were completely at cross purposes. Hitler's racial theories were
just as foreign to Halifax as the latter's religious conception of
neighbourly love was to Hitler. Later on he sometimes slight-
ingly spoke of him as the "English Parson." When the conversation ended, about noon, I felt that a battle for peace had
been lost. Neurath also looked pensive.

The conversation over dinner brought nothing new, although
Hitler had got over his bad temper and was once more the
amiable and attentive host I knew so well. Halifax gave no
sign of emotion or disappointment. He remained the whole
time the typical, quiet, phlegmatic Englishman, and said
goodbye to Hitler apparently without annoyance.

We returned to Berlin by the night train, and next morning I
drove to Karinhall, on instructions from Hitler, to give Göring

an account of the Berchtesgaden conversation before Halifax's arrival. I did not conceal how badly things had gone, and expressed the fear that Halifax would return to England with a very poor opinion of the chances of reaching an agreement with Germany. Göring listened very attentively but made no comment.

I realised from his conversation with Halifax that afternoon that he must have received precise instructions from Hitler. He dealt with exactly the same questions as Hitler had done, only with infinitely more diplomacy. He remained quite calm, even about Austria, and treated matters as though the solutions sought by Germany were inevitable and unquestionable. "Under no circumstances shall we use force," he said reassuringly. On this matter, too, he seemed to have been given a hint either by Hitler or Neurath, as he added: "This would be completely unnecessary."

Everything could be settled quite well by negotiation. Later conversations showed me that this was in fact Göring's innermost conviction and it came out constantly in his conversation with Halifax. We know from Chamberlain's diary that Halifax went back with a favourable report—and I am convinced that this was mainly due to his talk with Göring at Karinhall.

Hitler had kept his word in 1937—there were no surprises. But he had prepared both militarily and politically for coming events. That year of peace was followed by a year in which Germany came within a hair's breadth of world war.

CHAPTER IV
(1938)

Right from the beginning of 1938 it was clear, despite what Hitler had said in 1937, that the period of surprises was by no means over. First came the internal crisis of February, in the course of which Neurath was sacked and succeeded by Ribbentrop at the Foreign Office. Then the entry of German troops into Austria, and finally the Czech crisis of September, when for many days Europe hovered on the brink of war.

Hitler's state visit to Mussolini in the first half of May, amidst all these storms, was like an Indian summer interlude, reminding me of the festivals of 1936 and 1937. Mussolini had suggested this visit in my presence under the influence of the magnificently organised reception accorded to him in Germany. Whether the invitation would have been so hearty if the *Anschluss* had already been an accomplished fact seems to me somewhat doubtful in view of the emphatic way Mussolini shook his head when Göring sounded him on the matter in April, 1937. Since then the subject had not been mentioned to Mussolini again in my presence.

It was only just before the march into Austria that Hitler sent Prince Philip of Hesse, son-in-law of the King of Italy, with a letter to the Italian dictator, setting out the reasons for his action. " Pale but resolute, the Prince of Hesse left by plane early this morning to see Mussolini," became an almost routine Foreign Office joke later on whenever Hitler sent a messenger to inform Mussolini at the last moment of some startling new move he had decided on. Once I was recalled from leave because the Languages Section could not finish a translation into Italian for Mussolini's benefit quickly enough. Eventually for such emergencies I had to find an airworthy Italian translator, who would be able to translate Hitler's letters during the flight, in the same way as I had translated his peace plan between Berlin and London.

Despite Göring's hint Mussolini was somewhat surprised, but he swallowed the *fait accompli* of the *Anschluss* with a good grace and assured Hitler that he understood the necessity for this action. "Duce, I shall never forget this," Hitler telegraphed in reply. And he kept his word until 1945. If any one of his entourage so much as hinted anything against Mussolini personally, Hitler always mentioned his conduct over the *Anschluss*. I concluded from this that Hitler regarded "Austria's return home" to the Reich as a considerable risk in his foreign policy. Only his relief that it had brought no change in Italy's attitude to Germany can, in my opinion, explain his abiding gratitude. The closer relations between Italy and England after the *Anschluss* showed that Hitler was justified in his fears that Italy might turn away from Germany towards the European anti-Nazi front. This rapprochement was fostered by Chamberlain to such an extent that Eden resigned in protest, and was succeeded by Halifax. On April 16th it led to a whole series of agreements between the two countries, the most important of which was Britain's recognition of the annexation of Abyssinia. We now know that very soon after Hitler's stormy meeting with the Austrian Chancellor Schuschnigg, Ciano told Lord Perth (British Ambassador in Rome) that he had instructed Grandi (Italian Ambassador in London) to press for an early start of conversations in view of "possible future happenings."

Such was the background, completely concealed from the general public, to the German state visit to Italy.

All the Foreign Office members of the delegation spent much time at the tailor's fitting their "Admiral's" uniform, the design of which had been approved by Frau von Ribbentrop. Actually this uniform was no more ornate than the traditional uniform worn by French or British diplomats on formal occasions. But in republican Germany we, Foreign Office officials, like the Americans, had been accustomed to wearing tails.

I set off on May 2nd in this uniform for Italy with Hitler and Ribbentrop. Our delegation, consisting of about five hundred persons, travelled in three special trains. Half the members of the Government, most of the Party leaders, prominent journalists, wives of Ministers, including Frau von Ribbentrop, took part in this "invasion of Italy" as some of us called it. Each of us had a sleeping compartment in which our whole array of uniforms was hung up ready for immediate use. Besides my "Admiral's" outfit I had taken with me a complete Air Force uniform, in case I should have to work for Göring alone.

The *chef de protocole* had prescribed our dress for each hour of the day. During the journey from one Italian city to another we constantly had to change from uniform to mufti, then into tails, then into another uniform, with sword or dagger as the case might be, so that our compartments looked like actors' dressing rooms. Putting on and pulling off heavy riding boots was most exhausting. "I never expected to travel to Italy in a wardrobe," observed a colleague of mine. "You've got your belt on the wrong way round," said one of Hitler's adjutants, whom I ran into on the platform. The only touch of reality on the journey was provided by the familiar faces of friends grinning from their strange costumes.

Until nightfall at Leipzig we saw every station decorated, and were greeted with crowds shouting "Heil!"

Flowers and banners greeted us at the Brenner Station, while the platform was covered with carpet, along the edge of which formations of the Italian Army and of the Fascist Party were lined up. As our train drew in, the national anthems were played, and the Duke of Pistoia, representing the King of Italy, stepped up to the train with a large delegation in splendid uniforms to welcome us. As we travelled through South Tyrol the inhabitants came to look at us at the stations, but they remained noticeably quiet. There were no Fascist salutes, and scarcely a single handkerchief was waved, nor any other greeting accorded. These splendid Germans of the South Tyrol looked thoughtful and serious. I seemed to read on their faces the anxious question: "Are you going to betray us in Rome?" When we reached Bolzano the atmosphere of resigned melancholy suddenly changed, and all the rest of the way to Rome we were greeted with unrestrained enthusiasm.

We reached Rome in the evening. King Victor Emanuel and Mussolini, with the heads of the State and the Party and their entourage, met us at a railway station specially constructed for the occasion. We drove into the city in carriages drawn by four horses, and I reflected as we passed the Cestius Pyramid, and were met by Prince Colonna, the Governor of Rome, at the city's ancient gateway: "Now I am myself sitting in a fairy-tale coach such as I admired last year at the coronation in London." Passing huge illuminated fountains we drove along the old triumphal way of the Romans. This had been widened by Mussolini to form a real Via Triumphalis along the foot of the Palatine. Innumerable lights made it as bright as day up to the Arch of Constantine, through which we went, and on past the Colosseum, whose red flood-lighting made it look as though it were on fire. On either side of the street there were flames flickering up from special metal containers, flood-lit pylons, banners and cheering crowds. Hitler was to stay in the Royal Palace. We juniors were fortunately able to step down from the stage and stay at the Grand Hotel, where Italian hospitality had gone to the lengths of putting magnificent baskets of fruit and bottles of grappa in every room.

We were not disappointed in our programme, which was a rare combination of good taste and magnificence. At Naples there was a naval parade in which, from the battleship *Julio Cesare*, I saw a hundred submarines simultaneously submerge, surface after a few minutes with the precision of clockwork, and fire a shot. I was free to enjoy myself, as Hitler, Mussolini, the King, and the leading personalities were all on the battleship *Cavour*.

The gala performance of *Aida* at the San Carlo Theatre that evening seemed almost dull and commonplace, and Verdi's music grey and subdued, in comparison with the fantastic scenes and exuberant sounds and colours of the preceding days.

One man who did not enjoy that evening was the hapless *chef de protocole*, von Bulow-Schwante. The unfortunate man had allowed Hitler to go bare-headed in evening dress to inspect the guard of honour after leaving the theatre, while the King of Italy was resplendent in full uniform. Hitler was beside himself, and Bulow-Schwante lost his job.

This week of Palace receptions, State banquets and other ceremonial occasions in uninterrupted succession left me with relatively little interpreting to do. Quite apart from the fact that we had brought along two Italian specialists, the festival programme left practically no time for real discussions or negotiations. I had already noted this during Mussolini's visit to Germany, and I got the impression later that it was characteristic of all the meetings between dictators. The chief strain, both for myself and all the others, was the constant change of uniform. By the end of the journey, any one of us could have got a job at any average music hall as a quick change artist. But it was also very exhausting to have to maintain, for anything up to ten or twelve hours a day, an appropriately solemn, dignified or delighted expression. As the great processions passed through the populous Italian cities we were under the eyes of a watchful public, and indoors the élite looked critically at the barbarians from the north.

The main reason why I had an easy time as interpreter was that Mussolini and Ciano were obviously trying to evade any serious political discussion—though Hitler, and more especially Ribbentrop, were constantly seeking it. The programme had been deliberately planned so that there was no time for serious tàlk, but even during the various social meetings, at which Hitler and Ribbentrop were always ready for discussions, Mussolini and Ciano showed quite clearly that they were not. This impression was confirmed beyond all doubt when we handed Ciano a draft treaty for an Italo-German alliance— for despite all the beautiful speeches we were still not formally allies. Hitler no doubt regarded it as vital to his future plans to take this opportunity to bind Italy to him irrevocably. A few days later Ciano handed us an "amended draft" of the treaty. It proved to be a completely meaningless paper, whose emptiness amounted to a plain refusal. In a brief interview Ribbentrop had a very violent argument about it with Ciano—a grotesque contrast to what was being presented to the world on the public stage. Ribbentrop's chief characteristic was the persistence and obstinacy with which he would try to get his own way. I was later often to see him keep at it so long, without the least regard for tact or politeness, that the other side gave in through sheer exhaustion. He tried these tactics on Ciano, but without success. "The solidarity existing between our two Governments," Ciano said with what seemed to me a sarcastic smile, "has been so clearly evinced during these days that a formal treaty of alliance is superfluous." I inferred at the time from these words that the Italians had by no means got over their shock at the Austrian *Anschluss*, and especially at Hitler's methods in carrying it out, and that their eyes were still turned westwards. Outwardly, however, nothing of this could be seen at the time.

"It is my unshakable will and testament to the German people that the frontier of the Alps, erected by nature, providence and history, between us and Italy, shall be regarded as eternally inviolate," said Hitler, turning to Mussolini, as he drank a toast at a state banquet. He also had no doubt noticed that the Austrian affair still caused uneasiness, and wished with this frontier guarantee to allay the anxiety of the Italians—who since March had had a powerful Germany as their immediate neighbour. This was the only political result that emerged from the whirl of festivities. As I listened to Hitler's words that evening my thoughts went back to our people south of the Brenner, now finally a part of Italy.

* * *

On May 21st I interpreted at a stormy meeting between Ribbentrop and Sir Nevile Henderson, at which Czecho-Slovakia was discussed. "You have gone behind my back, Ambassador, and asked General Keitel about alleged German troop movements on the Czecho-Slovakian frontier," Ribbentrop said furiously to Henderson, who was sitting opposite him in Bismarck's historic office in the Wilhelmstrasse. "I shall see to it that in future you are given no information on military matters." "I shall have to report that to my Government," replied Henderson, with unusual warmth. "I can only conclude from your remarks that Keitel's statement to me was incorrect."

The cause for this excitement lay in the growing tension in Sudetenland, for whose inhabitants the Germans were claiming autonomy within the Czech state. Conditions within the Sudeten territory were worsening from day to day, incidents increased and were duly exploited and exaggerated by the German Press. There were many rumours abroad that German troops were massing on the Czech border ready to march into the Sudeten territory just as they had done into Austria in March. These rumours actually were either pure invention, or were circulated by the Czechs for political reasons. Henderson had asked Keitel about this and had received a categorical denial.

There had long been a strong personal antagonism between Keitel and Ribbentrop, and this had naturally contributed to Ribbentrop's annoyance with Henderson. In addition, Ribbentrop had disliked Englishmen in general since his time as Ambassador in London, where his arrogant behaviour had brought him many rebuffs. He now let loose his resentment on Henderson, who was a distinguished Englishman of the old school and was sometimes at a loss to deal with the rudeness of our Foreign Minister.

Ribbentrop raged away about the Czechs. When, with regard to the death of two Sudetens, Henderson said soothingly that this was not as bad as if hundreds of thousands of men had been killed in a war, Ribbentrop replied theatrically that every German was ready to die for his country. These remarks by both sides in the conversation show more clearly than any long description the atmosphere of tension and irritation that prevailed.

Henderson even went so far as to utter a fairly plain warning. He reminded Ribbentrop that France had definite undertakings to Czecho-Slovakia. "The British Government," he said, "cannot guarantee that it may not be inevitably drawn into any conflict that might break out."

"If a general war should result," Ribbentrop replied emphatically, "it would be a war of aggression provoked by France, and Germany would fight, just as she did in 1914."

Henderson saw Ribbentrop twice on that May 21st, and on each occasion he spoke with equal emphasis—indeed, almost threateningly. On the following Sunday he communicated a special personal warning from Halifax which drew attention to the danger of any rash action which might easily lead to a general war that would bring about the destruction of European civilisation.

As will be seen, the English were bringing up very heavy artillery. And at that time it was quite out of place. I knew from a reliable source that there was in fact no truth in the accusations then made against Germany. When I heard the British Ambassador addressing Ribbentrop so heatedly I believed that he was convinced that Hitler was preparing a blow against Czecho-Slovakia, and that that accounted for Ribbentrop's excitement. We now know from Henderson's Memoirs that the British military attaché and his assistant, after an intensive tour of investigation through Saxony and Silesia, had reported that there were no signs of any unusual troop movements, and that other military attachés had also arrived at the same conclusion. I still do not quite understand why, in these circumstances, he took such a strong line. From countless other instances I know that he was not an agitator, and, indeed, always endeavoured to do his best to clear up differences and to preserve peace. I can only assume therefore that it was Ribbentrop's attack at the beginning of the conversation which disconcerted him. Moreover, I noted both before and later that Henderson's way of communicating the ideas of his Government, in the typical manner of Western diplomats, and his general bearing, which was that of the perfect English gentleman, always somehow irritated both Ribbentrop and Hitler, who could not endure "fine people." As far as I can recollect, Hitler was only once open and friendly to Henderson. That was at the 1937 Party Rally, when Hitler assumed that the presence of the diplomatic corps in full strength, and especially the representatives of the Great Powers, was due to the influence of the British Ambassador. On every other occasion the sight of Henderson seemed to arouse Hitler's antagonism.

This antagonism had struck me particularly in a conversation at the Chancellery early in March, 1938, in the course of which Henderson made a very remarkable proposal on his Government's behalf regarding the colonial question. If it had been put into effect Germany would have received colonial territory in Central Africa. This proposal was to pool European possessions in Central Africa and then to distribute them anew, with Germany receiving a share. Here again, it was the manner in which the Ambassador put forward the project that irritated Hitler intensely.

Instead of launching out with a sensational announcement

that he was offering Germany territory in Africa as colonies, Henderson began his statement with a series of reservations. He said that the British Government had not yet discussed its proposal in any detail with any of the other Governments concerned, or arrived at any definite agreements on the plan, so this was an entirely unofficial step. He, as British Ambassador, wanted to ascertain the reaction of the German Government. He made it worse by implying that there would be conditions affecting the transfer of these colonial territories. For instance, he asked whether the German Government would abide by the provisions of the Congo Act regarding the prohibition of military training of the natives, and of the building of fortifications, in addition to the observance of certain humanitarian principles in the treatment of natives.

When Henderson concluded his rather lengthy exposition Hitler showed not the slightest interest, saying there was no hurry at all about the colonial question. But his annoyance was evident from his excited answer to other observations which Henderson made. The Austrian question was acute at that time—only a few days later German troops marched into Austria—and the Sudeten question was being zealously canvassed in the German Press. Henderson had expressed the British Government's attitude, as Halifax did later, saying that with regard to both questions it considered changes to be possible, but only if they were undertaken in a peaceful way.

Hitler, in his answer, gave free rein to his anger, without however raging at Henderson personally as Ribbentrop had done in the May 21st discussion already described. He stated excitedly that only a small percentage of the Austrians supported Schuschnigg. If England opposed a just settlement, and interfered in "German family matters" which were no concern of hers, then Germany would fight. Hitler enlarged at length, and with great indignation, on this theme of "England's intervention in matters that are no concern of hers." He had especially hard words to say against the Press and against religious circles in England for interfering in the German Church dispute. As he spoke, he became more and more agitated, as though his long-restrained resentment against England had suddenly burst the flood-gates. With reference to the Sudeten question, he was particularly violent about the Czecho-Soviet Treaty, saying that it was a crime for European countries to let Russia into Central Europe.

With all this in mind, I could well imagine with what rage Hitler would receive Ribbentrop's report on his conversation with the British Ambassador on May 21st and the British warning expressed therein. After that meeting Ribbentrop flew at once to Munich. On the following day, Sunday, May 22nd, Halifax's personal warning was received. The barometer clearly pointed to stormy.

Moreover, on account of the alleged German troop concentrations the Czechs had carried out a partial mobilisation on May 20th, and when Germany did nothing the world Press announced jubilantly that the German dictator had yielded. One had only to stand up to him, as the Czechs had done, they said, to make him see reason. Anyone deliberately planning to madden Hitler could have thought of no better method. Openly to accuse a dictator of weakness is the thing least likely to make him see reason—all the more so when, as in this case, the whole matter was pure invention. The consequences were not long delayed.

* * *

During the summer my interpreting activity slowed down ominously. The tone of the German Press on Czecho-Slovakia became more and more violent. I twice worked for Göring— wearing the Air Force uniform because purely air force matters were being dealt with. The first occasion was the visit of the Italian Air Minister, Balbo, the second was that of General Vuillemin, head of the French Air Force, who had come to Germany with a group of French airmen on Göring's invitation. Because of my uniform the Italians always addressed me as "Colonello." The French officers made a very good impression on all the Germans they met, and I realised too the profound effect made on them by the state of German air armament. The French visited Göring at Karinhall. "What will France do," Göring asked Vuillemin, "if war breaks out between Germany and Czecho-Slovakia?" Vuillemin promptly replied: "France will keep her word."

On the drive back from Karinhall, according to François-Poncet's Memoirs, the General said to the French Ambassador: "If war does break out at the end of September, as you believe, there won't be a French plane left in a fortnight."

* *

At the beginning of September I was again on duty at the Party Rally. Foreign countries were even more strongly represented than in the previous year. The British Ambassador, who, at the last Rally, had spent only two days at Nuremberg, remained almost until the end, and among the British guests were Lords Stamp, Clive, Hollenden, Brocket and McGowan, as well as Norman Hulbert, M.P. France and other countries were no less strongly represented. From the conversations I translated I sensed the daily increasing tension that prevailed throughout Europe in September, 1938. Rarely had I translated so much about war and the danger of war as during those days. It was noteworthy that one of those who considered the situation with the greatest anxiety was the Spanish Ambassador, who openly expressed his fear that, in the event of war, the French Government, supported by the Spanish Left, would bring about the fall of the Franco regime.

The news that reached Nuremberg from abroad was also alarming. I can still see the anxious faces of some of my colleagues when they handed to me, to translate for Hitler, a statement by the British Government that German aggression against Czecho-Slovakia would be ground for intervention by the Western Powers. At almost the same time I had to translate for Hitler a report from London stating that Britain might be prepared to give military support to Czecho-Slovakia. That was on September 11th.

"I can only tell the representatives of these democracies that, if these tormented creatures (the Sudeten Germans) cannot themselves obtain justice and help, they will receive both from us," Hitler shouted in a speech full of threats against the Czechs on September 12th, the last day of the Party Rally. "The Germans in Czecho-Slovakia are neither defence-

less nor deserted!" I heard it on the loud speaker at the air
port as I left Nuremberg.

With Hitler's threats still ringing in my ears, I got back to
Berlin, where I found not only in the Foreign Office but also
amongst friends and acquaintances generally, profound de-
pression at what was generally felt to be the imminence of war.
I heard many hard words against Hitler, and also learnt of the
opposition's plan to have him summarily arrested by the army
as soon as he ordered general mobilisation. On September
13th the tension had become almost intolerable.

On the morning of September 14th events took a dramatic
and sensational turn. I had to translate for Hitler a seven-line
message: "Having regard to the increasingly critical situation, I
propose to visit you immediately in order to make an attempt
to find a peaceful solution. I could come to you by air and am
ready to leave tomorrow. Please inform me of the earliest time
you can receive me, and tell me the place of meeting. I
should be grateful for a very early reply. Neville Chamberlain."

That same evening I left for Munich in a special train, without uniforms, feeling that this time I was not going to act as an
extra in an international show, but to play a modest, if not
unimportant, part in a real historical drama. "Keep your
mind quite clear," von Weizsäcker, the Foreign Office head,
said to me in the train. "Tomorrow at Berchtesgaden it will
be a matter of war or peace."

Next day at noon I met Chamberlain at the Munich airport
with Ribbentrop, whom Hitler had sent for the purpose. As he
got out of the plane, Chamberlain said to Ribbentrop: "I stood
the passage very well, although we had bad weather part of the
way, and I had never been in an aeroplane before."

With Chamberlain were Sir Horace Wilson, the Prime
Minister's most intimate adviser on all political questions, and
Sir William Strang, head of the Central European section of the
Foreign Office. As we drove in open cars through Munich to
the station, the people greeted Chamberlain very warmly—
considerably more so, as it seemed to me, than they had
Mussolini the year before.

We lunched in Hitler's dining car on the way to Berchtesgaden. The scene is still very clear in my memory. During almost the whole of the three hour journey troop transports rolled past, making a dramatic background, with soldiers in new uniforms and gun barrels pointing skywards. "Peace Envoy Chamberlain," as he was then called in Germany, formed a curious contrast to this warlike picture.

Shortly before we reached Berchtesgaden it began to rain, and as we drove up with Chamberlain to the Berghof the sky darkened and clouds hid the mountains. Hitler received his guests at the foot of the steps leading up to the house. After greetings, hand shakings, introductions, we all sat down round the tea table in the large room with the view towards the Untersberg in which Hitler had received Lloyd George and the Duke of Windsor. Not only was the weather threatening— indoors the tension was noticeable. The protagonists, it was clear, were taking each other's measure for the ensuing conversation, at which the issue would be war or peace.

After conventional remarks about the weather, the size of the room, the possibility of Hitler visiting England, and Chamberlain's journey, Chamberlain asked rather abruptly whether Hitler would speak to him alone or whether he wanted the support of his advisers. "Of course Herr Schmidt must be there as interpreter," said Hitler, "but as an interpreter he is neutral, and forms part of neither group." I already knew that Chamberlain would express the wish to speak to Hitler alone. With Hitler's knowledge this had been settled between the English and the Germans beforehand, behind Ribbentrop's back. Both sides felt that our Foreign Minister would prove a disturbing element in any endeavour to achieve a friendly settlement between England and Germany. Hitler too had noticed the wounded vanity aroused by the English in his former London Ambassador. He had therefore agreed to the plan to exclude him which had the approval of Henderson and Weizsäcker and the warm support of Göring.

Ribbentrop therefore remained angrily in the background, while I went with Hitler and Chamberlain to the office on the first floor. It was the same simple, almost bare, room in which Hitler and Halifax had got on so badly a year before. This conversation also, on which hung the issue of peace or war, was not conducted in an exactly serene atmosphere, and sometimes became quite stormy. It lasted nearly three hours. Hitler, the Party Rally just over, was apparently still attuned to long speeches, and from time to time he was so carried away by his rage against Benes and Czecho-Slovakia that his harangues went on interminably.

Hitler began fairly quietly by presenting in full the list of complaints against Germany's neighbours which he always brought forward. The Versailles Treaty, the League of Nations, and disarmament were discussed in detail, as well as economic difficulties, unemployment and National Socialist reconstruction. Chamberlain was reproached in rising tone with the attitude of the British Press, with Britain's "interference" in German affairs, and in the Reich's relations with South-East Europe, including Austria.

Chamberlain listened attentively, looking frankly at Hitler. Nothing in his clear-cut, typically English features, with their bushy eyebrows, pointed nose and strong mouth, betrayed what went on behind his high forehead. His brother, Sir Austen, sitting opposite Stresemann at Locarno had always looked like that; but Neville Chamberlain had nothing of his brother's aloof frigidity. On the contrary, he dealt in lively manner with individual points brought up by Hitler, giving the stock answer about the freedom of the Press with a friendly, almost conciliatory smile. Then, looking Hitler full in the face, he emphasised that he was prepared to discuss every possibility of righting German grievances, but that in all circumstances the use of force must be excluded.

"Force!" Hitler exclaimed. "Who speaks of force? Herr Benes applies force against my countrymen in the Sudetenland, Herr Benes mobilised in May, not I." Outside it was pouring with rain, and the wind was howling. "I shall not put up with this any longer. I shall settle this question in one way or another. I shall take matters into my own hands." This was the first time, in a discussion with a foreign statesman, that the phrase "in one way or another" had been used—a phrase which I observed then and later to be an extreme danger signal. I rightly translated it "one way or another," but its meaning now and on later occasions amounted to: "Either the other side gives in, or a solution will be found by means of the application of force, invasion, or war."

Now Chamberlain, who had hitherto listened to everything that was said with serious calm, also became excited. "If I have understood you aright," he said, "you are determined to proceed against Czecho-Slovakia in any case." After pausing for a second, he added: "If that is so, why did you let me come to Berchtesgaden? Under the circumstances it is best for me to return at once. Anything else now seems pointless."

Hitler hesitated. If he really wants it to come to war, I thought, now is the moment; and I looked at him in agonised suspense. At that moment the question of peace or war was really poised on a razor's edge. But the astonishing happened: Hitler recoiled.

"If, in considering the Sudeten question, you are prepared to recognise the principle of the right of peoples to self-determination," he said in one of those sudden changes from raging to complete calm and collectedness, "then we can continue the discussion in order to see how that principle can be applied in practice."

I thought that Chamberlain would immediately assent. The principle of self-determination had always played an important part in English political thought, and its relevance to the Sudeten question had been generally admitted by the British Press and by prominent British visitors to Germany. But Chamberlain at once raised an objection—though whether this was because he had been angered by Hitler's aggressive manner, or because, as a practical administrator, he recognised the complications in applying this principle to Czecho-Slovakia, it is difficult to say.

"If, in the application of the right of self-determination in Czecho-Slovakia, a plebiscite were held among the Sudeten Germans, the practical difficulties would be enormous," he replied. Even so Hitler did not get indignant. Had Chamberlain's threat to return home frightened him? Was he really recoiling from the prospect of a war?

"If I am to give you an answer on the question of self-determination," said Chamberlain, "I must first consult my colleagues. I therefore suggest that we break off our conversation at this point, and that I return to England immediately for consultation, and then meet you again." When I translated these words about breaking off the discussion, Hitler looked up uneasily; but when he understood that Chamberlain would meet him again, he agreed with obvious relief. The atmosphere had suddenly become friendly again, and Chamberlain at once availed himself of this change to secure a promise from Hitler that in the interval no aggressive action would be taken against Czecho-Slovakia. Hitler unhesitatingly gave this assurance, but added that it would not apply if any particularly atrocious incident occurred.

Thus the discussion ended. After Hitler's change of direction, the prospects for the maintenance of peace seemed to me more hopeful. I drove with the English to the Berchtesgaden hotel, where we dined and spent the night.

As always after such discussions, I dictated a report the same evening. Henderson kept coming into my room and asking impatiently how I was getting on, as Chamberlain wanted my note that night if possible, in order to be able to give a detailed report to his Cabinet the next day. On similar occasions I had always handed the other party to a discussion a copy of the report as a matter of course if he wanted it. The first time I did so was at the Hague Conference of 1929, when I gave Arthur Henderson an English version of my report on the discussions between the Foreign Ministers of Germany, France, Britain and Belgium. I was always interested in the emendations foreigners wished to make. These always referred to minor matters— sometimes to purely stylistic questions. No one had ever raised an objection on matters of substance. Hitler's and Ribbentrop's corrections usually consisted of the elimination of certain passages in their statements, but their alterations also never made any essential change.

But that evening Ribbentrop suddenly stood angrily beside Henderson in my room. "You think you're still in Geneva," he said when Henderson had left the room, "where all secret papers were freely handed about to everybody. We don't have that sort of thing in National Socialist Germany. This report is intended for the Führer alone. Please note."

I now had the highly unpleasant task of informing Henderson

and Chamberlain that I could not give them my report. I recalled that Hitler had already, at other conversations, suggested to those taking part that a written record would militate against its character as a man-to-man talk. In itself this was a plausible explanation; but as nothing of the kind had been said before the conversation, it was in this case quite unconvincing to Chamberlain. Indeed, he complained emphatically, stating that in these circumstances he must have his own interpreter at the next conversation, or at any rate bring someone with him who could make him a report. I appreciated for the first time what a mark of confidence it had been that none of the foreigners for whom I had interpreted, from Herriot and Briand to Henderson, MacDonald and Laval, had ever in all these years brought their own interpreter, but had always relied on my services. I regretted this contretemps the more because I realised that it was a pure act of spite by Ribbentrop, who wanted to have his revenge for being excluded from the conversation with Chamberlain.

I later had constant difficulties with Ribbentrop about handing my reports of such conversations to foreigners. Even Mussolini had to ask for my report on each occasion. The Duce never had any fault to find with my work—as a matter of fact he often congratulated me on the accuracy with which I reported his words.

Next morning we drove with Chamberlain to Munich, where he took the plane for London exactly twenty-four hours after his arrival. The same evening I returned to Berlin.

The more I reflected on the vital discussions at Berchtesgaden, and recalled how Hitler had shrunk from taking the fatal step, the more hopeful I felt. Profound pessimism still prevailed, however, in Berlin as a result of the Press stories of clashes between Germans and Czechs in the Sudeten territory. Gœbbels stepped up the tone of the German Press day by day. He had almost reached the limit of indignant abuse when, five days later, I left for Cologne by the night train. Chamberlain arrived at noon on September 22nd. We escorted him to his hotel beside the Rhine, opposite Godesberg, and the same afternoon he held his first conversation with Hitler at the Hotel Dreesen, Godesberg.

Hitler met Chamberlain at the hotel entrance with very friendly enquiries about his journey and his accommodation at the Hotel Petersberg. The conference room had a glorious view over the Rhine and the Siebengebirge. But the statesmen had no eyes for natural scenery and without a glance out of the window they sat down at the end of the long conference table. Owing to the incident about my report, Chamberlain had brought with him Sir Ivone Kirkpatrick, now British High Commissioner in Germany, who speaks excellent German.

Chamberlain opened the session with an account of his talks in London, recalling that he had agreed to get the Cabinet's views on the recognition of the Sudetenland's right to self-determination. The Cabinet had agreed to this, and so had the French Ministers, who had come to London at his invitation. Even the Czecho-Slovak Government had expressed its agreement. Together with the French, he had drawn up a plan in London whereby the territories inhabited by Sudeten Germans were to be transferred to Germany. Even the details of a new frontier were provided for in the plan. Chamberlain then outlined a comprehensive and complicated system of agreements providing for relatively protracted handing over periods. He concluded by announcing the guarantee which France and Britain were prepared to give to the new German-Czecho-Slovak frontier. Germany, on her side, was to conclude a non-aggression pact with Czecho-Slovakia.

Chamberlain leant back after this exposition with an expression of satisfaction, as much as to say: "Haven't I worked splendidly during these five days?" That was what I felt, too, for the agreement of the French, and still more of the Czecho-Slovaks, to a definite cession of territory seemed to me an extraordinary concession. I was the more surprised to hear Hitler say quietly, almost regretfully, but quite definitely: "I am exceedingly sorry, Mr. Chamberlain, but I can no longer discuss these matters. This solution, after the developments of the last few days, is no longer practicable."

Chamberlain sat up with a start. He flushed with anger at Hitler's attitude, at the ingratitude for his pains. I noticed that his kindly eyes could gleam very angrily under their bushy brows. Chamberlain was extremely surprised and indignant: he said he could not understand why Hitler should now suddenly say that the solution was no longer practicable, when the demands he had made at Berchtesgaden had been met.

Hitler at first evaded a direct reply, saying that he could not conclude a non-aggression pact with Czecho-Slovakia while the claims of Poland and Hungary on that country remained unsatisfied. Then, speaking relatively very calmly, he criticised the individual points of the plan elaborated by Chamberlain. Above all, the period of transfer contemplated was far too long. "The occupation of the Sudeten territories to be ceded must take place forthwith," he stated.

Chamberlain justly pointed out that this constituted a completely new demand, going far beyond the request put forward at Berchtesgaden; but Hitler continued to demand the immediate occupation of the Sudeten territories. As the conversation proceeded, he became more and more excited, more and more violent in his abuse of Benes and Czecho-Slovakia: Chamberlain became more reserved and withdrawn.

"The oppression of the Sudeten Germans and the terror exercised by Benes admit of no delay," Hitler declared hoarsely, and propounded the settlement he himself envisaged. This amounted to almost unconditional capitulation by Czecho-Slovakia.

Thus that first meeting in the ill-starred Godesberg conference room ended with complete discord. Chamberlain returned angrily to his hotel. The only ray of hope was that another meeting had been agreed upon for the following morning, and Hitler, at Chamberlain's express request, had renewed his Berchtesgaden promise not to take any action against Czecho-Slovakia during the course of the negotiations.

We received a letter from Chamberlain next morning, however, which amounted more or less to a rejection of Hitler's ideas. "I do not think," he wrote, "you have realised the impossibility of my agreeing to put forward any plan unless I have reason to suppose that it will be considered by public opinion in my country, in France, and indeed in the world generally, as carrying out the principles already agreed in an orderly fashion, and free from the threat of force. . . . In the event of German troops moving into the areas as you propose, there is no doubt that the Czech Government would have no option but to order their forces to resist."

Although the letter was couched in quite a friendly form, beginning "My dear Reich Chancellor," its impact was explosive. The negotiations seemed to have reached a deadlock on the first day. There were feverish discussions between Hitler, Ribbentrop and their advisers. Finally, Hitler dictated a reply, which amounted to a long, far from friendly, repetition of what he had said the preceding day. "When Your Excellency informs me that the cession to the Reich of the Sudeten territories has been recognised in principle, I must regretfully point out that theoretical recognition of principles with regard to Germany has been accorded before." He reminded Chamberlain of Wilson's fourteen points, whose promises had been "most shamefully broken." "I am interested, Excellency," he wrote, "not in the recognition of the principle, but solely in its realisation, and in such a way that in the shortest possible time the sufferings of the unhappy victims of Czech tyranny will be ended, and, at the same time, the dignity of a Great Power will receive its due." He continued thus for four or five sheets, and, there being no time for a written translation, Hitler instructed me to hand the letter personally to Chamberlain, and to translate it verbally.

The eyes of the world were on Godesberg. Tension over the hitch in the negotiations was increasing hourly. The representatives of the world Press were receiving continually more pressing enquiries from their editors in Europe and America. Were negotiations broken off? Would there be war over Czecho-Slovakia? These were the newspaper headlines, and the anxious speculations of broadcasters. The Press representatives at the Petersberg, and probably also the British delegation with Chamberlain at its head, gazed with hourly growing disquiet across the Rhine at the Hotel Dreesen. There, however, nothing stirred. The ferry boat which was exclusively reserved for carrying delegation cars over the Rhine remained at the bank.

I was well aware of all this as I left Hotel Dreesen at about three o'clock that afternoon with a large brown envelope under my arm. I realised that all the field-glasses at the Petersberg would be trained on my car, to drop again in disappointment when it was seen that I was alone with the driver. As I approached the hotel I knew they would have spotted the brown envelope; from afar I saw the journalists thronging round the hotel entrance. I pressed through the lounge with a non-committal expression, saying in reply to all questions that I must get to Chamberlain.

"Do you bring peace or war?" an American whom I knew very well from the Café Bavaria in Geneva shouted to me. I did not even venture to shrug my shoulders, as even the smallest gesture might have been misinterpreted. I was thankful when a member of the British delegation met me on the stairs and at once took me to Chamberlain. He was standing on his balcony. No doubt he, too, had been looking anxiously across the Rhine.

But he did not seem to me in the least excited, greeting me as he might any casually encountered acquaintance. He took me into his office, where I translated the letter in the presence of Sir Horace Wilson, Henderson and Kirkpatrick. It took some time, and I had to add some elucidations verbally, so that it was an hour before I left Chamberlain's room. In order to escape the questions of journalists, who were besieging the lounge, I called on our *chef de protocole*, Freiherr von Dörnberg, and fortified myself with several drops of "the right stuff" to strengthen me for the "break-through battle" below. Then I set off on what soon turned into a flight. I had so many friends amongst the journalists that I could only escape their questions by taking to my heels.

"What did he say? How did he take my letter?" Hitler asked me eagerly on my return. I reported my impressions, and he seemed to feel somewhat easier when I told him that Chamberlain had showed no excitement but had merely stated that he would reply in writing the same day. An hour after my return the reply was handed to Ribbentrop by Henderson and Wilson, and a somewhat confused discussion ensued as to what was to be done next.

In his letter Chamberlain again proved conciliatory, saying that he was ready "as a mediator" to transmit the proposals "on which Your Excellency absolutely insists as you did yesterday evening," to the Czecho-Slovak Government. He therefore asked Hitler to let him have these proposals in the form of a Memorandum, and he announced that he proposed to return to London to make the necessary preparations for passing them on.

During the discussion with Ribbentrop it was agreed that Chamberlain should be asked to come again that evening to receive the Memorandum and hear Hitler's explanatory remarks on it.

This discussion with Chamberlain, which began just before eleven that night of September 23rd, was one of the most dramatic in the whole of the Sudeten crisis. As there were to be a larger number of people present it took place in a small dining room of the hotel. "All the best people are invited," said a colleague, on hearing that Ribbentrop had this time managed to avoid exclusion. Also present were Wilson, Henderson, Weizsäcker, and the head of the Legal Department of the Foreign Office. They sat informally in a semi-circle round Hitler and Chamberlain. I opened the session by translating the Memorandum.

"The news of hourly increasing incidents in the Sudetenland proves that the condition of the Sudeten Germans is quite intolerable, and has therefore become a danger to European peace," I read. The main demand was: Withdrawal of all Czech armed forces from an area shown on an accompanying map, "evacuation of which will start on September 26th, and which will be ceded to Germany on September 28th." "The evacuated territory to be handed over in its present condition," "the Czech Government to release all prisoners of German origin arrested for political offences," "voting (in certain areas) under the supervision of an International Commission"—these were some of the other points in the brief document.

The effect on Chamberlain and the other Englishmen was devastating. "But that's an ultimatum!" exclaimed Chamberlain, lifting his hands in protest. "Ein Diktat," interjected Henderson, who always liked to introduce German words into a discussion. Speaking forcibly, Chamberlain declared that it was quite out of the question for him to transmit such an ultimatum to the Czecho-Slovak Government. Not only the content, but also the tone of the document, on its becoming known, would arouse violent indignation in neutral countries. "With the most profound regret and disappointment, Chancellor, I have to state that you have made no effort to assist my attempts to secure peace."

Hitler seemed surprised by the violence of the reaction. He was put on the defensive. He clumsily tried to counter the reproach that he had handed in an ultimatum by saying that it was headed "Memorandum," not "ultimatum." Chamberlain, Wilson and Henderson returned to the attack, pointing out that his proposals would certainly fail, if only because of his suggested time-table. It would allow the Czecho-Slovak Government scarcely forty-eight hours to give the necessary orders, and the whole territory was to be evacuated in four days. The danger that these circumstances would lead to violence was enormously increased. The consequences of hostilities between Germany and Czecho-Slovakia were unpredictable. A European war would certainly result.

Negotiations had thus come to an absolute deadlock. At that moment, the door opened and an adjutant handed a note to Hitler. After reading it he gave it to me, saying: "Read this to Mr. Chamberlain."

I translated: "Benes has just announced over the wireless general mobilisation of the Czecho-Slovak forces."

The room was dead still. "Now war is unavoidable," I thought; and all present probably thought the same. Although Hitler had promised Chamberlain he would make no move against Czecho-Slovakia, he had always added the proviso: "Unless any exceptional action by the Czechs forces me to act." Had such an eventuality now arisen?

Afterwards, when telling friends of this dramatic scene, I often used the analogy of the kettle-drum beat in a symphony. After the drum beat of "Czech mobilisation" there was silence for a few bars; then the violins lightly took up the melody again. In a scarcely audible voice, Hitler said to the frozen Chamberlain: "Despite this unheard-of provocation, I shall of course keep my promise not to proceed against Czecho-Slovakia during the course of negotiations—at any rate, Mr. Chamberlain, so long as you remain on German soil."

Tension began to relax. Discussion was resumed, in a more

subdued quieter tone. All seemed somehow to be relieved at the postponement of the catastrophe. Negotiations were continuing. That was the great thing.

Hitler was suddenly prepared to discuss the question of evacuation dates, which Chamberlain had cited as the chief difficulty. "To please you, Mr. Chamberlain," he said, "I will make a concession over the matter of the time-table. You are one of the few men for whom I have ever done such a thing. I will agree to October 1st as the date for evacuation." He wrote the relevant correction in his memorandum, adding a few other minor alterations which, so far as I recollect, affected the form rather than the content of the document, which was then sent out for a fair copy to be made.

In the course of further conversation Hitler pointed out that he had supported Chamberlain's endeavours for peace inasmuch as the boundaries of the areas to be ceded were quite different in his proposal from those which he would seize if he had used force against Czecho-Slovakia. Finally Chamberlain said that he was prepared to transmit the German Memorandum to the Czech Government. The crisis had cleared the air like a thunderstorm, and at two o'clock in the morning Chamberlain and Hitler parted in a thoroughly amiable atmosphere, after talking alone, with my assistance, for a short time. In the course of their conversation, Hitler thanked Chamberlain, in words which seemed sincere, for his work on behalf of peace, and said that the Sudeten question was the last great problem which, as far as he was concerned, required solution. He also spoke about closer relations between Germany and England, and about their cooperation. It was evident how much store he set on good relations with the English. He returned to his old theme. "There need be no differences between us," he said. "We shall not get in the way of the exercise of your extra-European interests, while you can leave us a free hand in Central and South-Eastern Europe without harm." Some time the colonial question would have to be settled, too, but there was no hurry about that, and they certainly need not go to war about it. Chamberlain returned to London later that morning.

Two days later, on September 26th, Sir Horace Wilson arrived in Berlin with a personal letter from Chamberlain to Hitler.

Accompanied by Henderson and Kirkpatrick, he was received by Hitler at the Chancellery. At this session Hitler, for the first and only time in my presence, completely lost his nerve.

I do not recollect whether the Englishmen brought a German translation of Chamberlain's letter with them, or whether I had to translate it. In any case, the letter produced one of the most stormy meetings that I have ever experienced.

"The Government of Czecho-Slovakia has just informed me," Chamberlain wrote, "that it regards the proposals contained in your Memorandum as wholly unacceptable." In the course of the letter Chamberlain more or less said "I told you so," and he appeared to support the Czech position. Hitler, who had been listening with growing restlessness, suddenly leapt up, shouting: "There's no point at all in going on with negotiations," and rushed to the door. It was an exceptionally painful scene, especially as Hitler seemed to realise when he reached the door how impossible his behaviour was, and returned to his seat like a defiant boy. He had himself now sufficiently under control, and I was able to continue reading out the letter. When I had ended, however, he let himself go more violently than I ever saw him do during a diplomatic interview. Nevertheless it in no way resembled the legendary fits of rage so frequently described. In the course of my duties I never saw anything which suggested them.

A very confused discussion followed, at which everybody talked at once, except Kirkpatrick and myself. It was one of the rare occasions when I failed to assert myself as an interpreter against Hitler. At other stormy meetings, especially during the conference of the Big Four held at Munich a few days later, I succeeded in restoring order by calling the attention of Hitler, or of some other speaker who had interrupted heatedly, to the fact that I had not finished my translation. Sir Horace Wilson's quiet efforts to persuade Hitler to be reasonable only increased his fury; Henderson combated Ribbentrop's excited talk of Benes as a terrorist and the Czechs as war mongers.

It was in this mood that Hitler made his famous speech at the Sports Palace a few hours later. "The question which has stirred us most deeply these last few weeks is known to you all," he said. "It is called not so much Czecho-Slovakia as Herr

Benes. In this name is summed up all the emotion of millions of people today, that makes them despair or fills them with fanatical determination! . . . He is now driving the Germans out! But that's where his little game must stop. . . . The decision now rests with him. Peace or war! Either he accepts this offer, and at last gives freedom to the Germans, or we will come and fetch that freedom for ourselves!"

But there were other tones in the speech. Hitler spoke in a friendly way about Chamberlain, and added the much quoted, significant sentence: "I have assured Mr. Chamberlain that as soon as the Czechs have settled with their minorities . . . I shall have no further interest in the Czech state. I will guarantee him that. We want no Czechs."

The next day I was again summoned to the Chancellery. There I met Wilson, who had received a new message from Chamberlain during the night for transmission to Hitler. In this the Prime Minister offered a British guarantee to see that Czech evacuation was carried out if Germany, on her side, would abstain from using force.

Hitler refused to discuss this proposal, even when Wilson asked what he was to report back to Chamberlain. Hitler kept saying that there were now only two possibilities open to the Czech Government—acceptance or refusal of the German proposal. "And if they choose to refuse I shall smash Czecho-Slovakia!" he shouted angrily. "If the Czechs have not accepted my demands by 2 p.m. on Wednesday September 28th I shall march into the Sudeten territory on October 1st with the German army." That morning it was quite impossible to talk to Hitler reasonably. Abuse of the Czechs and dark threats were all he would utter. Wilson and his associates sat there helpless: they were not equal to such violence.

Suddenly Wilson rose to his feet. In a firm voice, slowly weighing each word, he said: "In these circumstances, there is a further commission from the Prime Minister that I must carry out. I must request you, Chancellor, to take note of the following communication." Then he read out a short but pregnant message, which I translated to Hitler as slowly and emphatically as possible, so that he could appreciate its significance. "If France, in fulfilment of her treaty obligations, should become actively involved in hostilities against Germany the United Kingdom would deem itself obliged to support France."

Hitler replied furiously that he took note of the communication. "It means," he added, "that if France chooses to attack Germany, England feels it her duty to attack Germany also." Raising his voice he went on: "If France and England want to unleash war, they can do so. It's a matter of complete indifference to me. I am prepared for all eventualities. I can only take note of the position. So—next week we'll all find ourselves at war with each other." That was his last word to Wilson, and his answer to Chamberlain.

The same evening I had to translate a letter to Chamberlain, which Hitler phrased in a rather more conciliatory manner. This was the second time in these critical days that I had the impression that Hitler shrank from the extreme step. Had Wilson's final statement caused him to change his course? In this letter, I still particularly remember, the German dictator said that he was prepared to participate in an international guarantee for the remaining part of Czecho-Slovakia, as soon as the minorities question had been settled.

Hitler's change of tone between exclaiming "war next week" and the writing of the conciliatory letter was perhaps due to a significant sight he had seen late that afternoon. In dull autumn weather a motorised division passed along the Wilhelmstrasse. The completely apathetic and melancholy behaviour of the Berlin populace, which Hitler observed from a window of the Chancellery, made a deep impression on him. I was told at the time by his adjutants that he found the scene most disillusioning.

Next day, September 28th, there was an almost uninterrupted coming and going of ambassadors. François-Poncet, Henderson and the Italian Ambassador, Attolico, passed each other at the door of Hitler's office, and in the neighbouring rooms and passages there was the high-pressure activity of a time of crisis. Ministers and Generals, with their train of Party members, A.D.C.'s, officers and Heads of Departments, who had hurried round to consult Hitler, were sitting or standing everywhere. None of these discussions were held as part of formal meetings.

Hitler strolled the rooms, speaking now to one, now another. Whoever happened to be near could get at him, but nobody could actually get a word in. To anyone who wanted, or did not want, to listen, Hitler made long harangues about his view of the situation. It was just a series of shorter Sports Palace speeches. Only now and then Hitler withdrew to his office for a longer discussion with Ribbentrop, Göring, or one of the Generals —Keitel in particular.

The first Ambassador to appear that morning was François-Poncet. He spoke excellent German, but I was called in "just in case." As it was, having nothing to do, I could listen quietly to a conversation which I often recalled in later years for the statesmanlike wisdom and the extraordinary diplomatic ability with which François-Poncet conducted it. The French Ambassador wrestled for peace. "You deceive yourself, Chancellor," he said, "if you believe that you can confine the conflict to Czecho-Slovakia. If you attack that country you will set all Europe ablaze." He chose his words well, with characteristic thoughtfulness, and spoke a grammatically perfect German, whose faintly French accent somehow contributed to the impressiveness of what he said. "You are naturally confident of winning the war," he continued, "just as we believe that we can defeat you. But why should you take this risk when your essential demands can be met without war?"

Hitler gave no sign of agreement as he abused Benes once again, stressed his endeavours for peace, and stated emphatically that he could wait no longer. François-Poncet was not to be side-tracked; he continued, with great diplomatic skill, to demonstrate the senselessness of the action Hitler proposed to take.

From my corner of the room I closely watched the actors in this tense battle for peace. I observed from Hitler's reactions how, very gradually, the balance tilted in favour of peace. He no longer flared up, and it was only with the greatest difficulty that he could find anything to say to the arguments which François-Poncet advanced with devastating French logic. He became visibly pensive. Ribbentrop tried to intervene once or twice—and not on the side of peace. François-Poncet, who fully realised the danger of even one false word in such a situation, called him sharply to order, with suppressed irritation. Obviously this did not displease Hitler; he was always impressed when someone stood up to anyone other than himself.

Another successful stroke of diplomacy on the part of the French Ambassador was the production of a clearly drawn map showing the separate phases of the evacuation. Hitler often said later, when speaking of the Sudeten crisis: "François-Poncet was the only one who made a sensible proposal. One could see at once from his map that it was the work of military men who understood their job."

Again a door opened and an adjutant came in. I wondered whether this was to be another startling announcement. Had the Czechs perhaps started striking out on their own? I only caught the name Attolico mentioned, and was at once relieved, for I knew that the Italian Ambassador was one of the friends of peace. He belonged to the group, which at that time included Göring, Neurath and Weizsäcker, of those who were doing all they could to divert Hitler from his war plans. Attolico wanted to speak to Hitler at once "on an urgent matter." I left the room with Hitler, as Attolico spoke little German.

The slightly stooping Attolico was breathless, his face flushed with excitement. "I have an urgent message to you from the Duce, Führer!", he shouted unceremoniously from some way off. I then translated his message—"The British Government has just let it be known through its Ambassador in Rome that it will accept the Duce's mediation in the Sudeten question. It regards the area of disagreement as relatively narrow." He made an interesting addition. " The Duce informs you that, whatever you decide, Führer, Fascist Italy stands behind you." But he quickly went on: "The Duce is, however, of the opinion that it would be wise to accept the British proposal, and begs you to refrain from mobilisation." Hitler, already reflective after his talk with François-Poncet, was clearly impressed by Mussolini's message. Attolico watched him intently.

It was at this moment that the decision in favour of peace was made. It was just before noon on September 28th, two hours before the expiry of Hitler's ultimatum. Hitler replied: "Tell the Duce that I accept his proposal."

At that time Mussolini's advice still carried great weight with

Hitler; in addition, I had myself seen him on two occasions shrink back from the extreme brink. After that, his acceptance of Mussolini's proposal convinced me that he had turned away from war.

We went back to his office, where François-Poncet was still waiting with Ribbentrop. "Mussolini has just asked whether I will accept his mediation," Hitler said briefly. He continued his conversation with François-Poncet, but his mind was no longer on it. He was more concerned about Mussolini's message than with anything François-Poncet still had to say, and so the interview was terminated somewhat abruptly shortly afterwards.

François-Poncet had scarcely left when Henderson appeared. He had another message from Chamberlain, which I translated. "After reading your letter," he wrote, "I feel certain that you can get all that is essential without war and without delay. I am ready to come to Berlin myself at once to discuss arrangements for the transfer of territory with you and representatives of the Czech Government, together with representatives of France and Italy if you so desire. . . . I cannot believe that you will take the responsibility of starting a world war which may end civilisation for the sake of a few day's delay in settling this long-standing problem." Hitler replied that he must contact Mussolini about this proposal. "I have postponed German mobilisation for twenty-four hours to meet the wishes of my great Italian ally," Hitler told Henderson. The latter took his leave after a perfectly friendly interview.

The same afternoon Hitler telephoned to Mussolini, and the conversation resulted in the greatest sensation of the interwar period—the decision that Hitler should invite Chamberlain, Daladier and Mussolini to a conference at Munich. That night I went south by special train.

The Munich Conference was regarded at the time as the decisive turning point in the Sudeten crisis. Actually this had occurred the day before, in Hitler's talk with Attolico, after the vital preparatory work carried out by François-Poncet. Indeed, it had been foreshadowed at Berchtesgaden, when Hitler first gave ground to Chamberlain, and at Godesberg where he did so for the second time after the startling news of Czech mobilisation.

The course of the Munich Conference, held in the new Führer building in the Konigsplatz, was described in such detail at the time that it would be redundant for me to write at length about it. It was not in any case the actual peak of the crisis.

Soon after my arrival at Munich I drove with Hitler to Kufstein. There he boarded the Italian special train and talked to Mussolini during the journey—a conversation which confirmed my assumption that peace was assured. Mussolini, in words similar to those used by François-Poncet, emphatically advocated a peaceful solution.

Shortly before two o'clock I took my seat at a round table in the Führer building at Munich (now the Amerikahaus), with the Big Four, Hitler, Chamberlain, Mussolini and Daladier. Ribbentrop, Ciano, Wilson and Alexis Léger, head of the French Foreign Office, were also there. The historic Munich Conference had begun. Its course was far less sensational than was then universally assumed, for, as I have said, the actual decision had already been taken.

The four principals first briefly expounded the attitude of their respective countries. They all spoke against a solution by force, even Hitler emphasising that he was all for a peaceful settlement of the matter. An atmosphere of general goodwill prevailed, broken only once or twice when Hitler violently attacked Benes and Czecho-Slovakia and Daladier took up the challenge.

Daladier was still an unknown figure in that circle. A short man, he sat silent most of the time. He was clearly perturbed by the fact that decisions were being taken about the cession of territory by an ally of France, Czecho-Slovakia, without that country being represented at the conference. I noticed that Alexis Léger several times spoke to him, apparently urging him to oppose some point or other. But Daladier did not react, except on the occasions already mentioned, when he took up a fairly stiff attitude towards Hitler. Hitler, surprisingly enough, was not put out by this. He seemed to like Daladier, and they exchanged war experiences in the breaks. I heard Hitler tell Mussolini: "I can get on very well with Daladier; he's been at the front like we have, and so one can talk sense with him."

There was also a slight clash with Chamberlain at Munich.

He persistently raised a question which, by and large, was of very minor significance. It concerned the transfer of Czecho-Slovak public property to Germany in the ceded territory. Chamberlain kept on asking who would compensate the Czecho-Slovak Government for the buildings and installations which would pass to Germany with the Sudeten territory? It was obvious that here not the Prime Minister and politician, but the former Chancellor of the Exchequer and business man was speaking. Hitler became more and more restive. "These installations and buildings are the result of taxes paid by the Sudeten Germans," he kept saying with growing impatience, "and so there can be no question of indemnification." But this failed to satisfy Chamberlain's sense of tidiness in matters affecting property. Hitler finally exploded. "Our time is too valuable to be wasted on such trivialities", he shouted at Chamberlain. This was when Chamberlain, for full measure, also raised the question of whether cattle were to remain in Sudeten territory or whether some of the livestock might not be driven into what remained of Czecho-Slovakia.

During these arguments between Hitler, Chamberlain and Daladier I was often interrupted by the person addressed as I translated the statement made to him into one of the three conference languages—German, English and French. "I must say something about that at once," one of them would interrupt —but on each occasion I asked to be allowed to translate to the end, so that the other participants were kept in the picture. From my long experience of conferences I knew that it produces great confusion if, as the result of interrupted translations, some of the delegates can no longer follow the argument. Friends who were watching the Big Four session through some glass doors told me that when I demanded that my translations should be heard I looked like a schoolmaster trying to keep an unruly class in order. After that we always used to give Big Four conferences the code-name "classroom", especially during the crisis year, 1939. Even my "clientèle," Göring, for example, took it up.

After Mussolini had submitted a written proposal for the solution of the Sudeten question, the Conference adjourned for a short lunch interval at about three o'clock. Mussolini's proposal was in Italian, but its translation was easy as I had translated it once already from German into French in Berlin. On that critical morning of September 28th, the day before, State Secretary Weizsäcker had handed it to me asking me to translate into French as quickly as possible so that it could be given to the Italian Ambassador for transmission to Mussolini without Ribbentrop having an opportunity to alter it. I was delighted to renew its acquaintance again here in Munich. Although it was presented to the Conference as Mussolini's proposal, it had in fact originated with Göring, Neurath and Weizsäcker.

Negotiations continued somewhat disjointedly after lunch. The meeting was no longer confined to the Big Four with their Foreign Ministers or diplomatic advisers; gradually Göring, François-Poncet, Henderson, Attolico, von Weizsäcker, legal advisers, secretaries and adjutants came into the room and formed a tense audience round the heads of Governments who sat in the middle. Mussolini's draft Agreement had in the meantime been translated into the three Conference languages and from it eventually emerged, with a few minor alterations, the famous Munich Agreement, which was finally signed between 2 and 3 a.m. on September 30th.

In the course of the afternoon and evening the talks tended more and more to break up into a number of individual conversations while the legal experts, in their wearisome manner, argued at length about the final phrasing. In these pauses Hitler had several lively conversations with Daladier. He spoke to Chamberlain, too, but perceptibly more coolly than to Daladier. When, however, Chamberlain suggested that he should call on him next day for a tête-à-tête, Hitler assented with pleasure. I also saw Mussolini and Chamberlain having a lengthy conversation, and remembered the Anglo-Italian agreements and Chamberlain's efforts to come to terms with Italy.

Hitler about nine o'clock had invited everyone to dine with him in the banquet room at the Führer building. Chamberlain and Daladier excused themselves, saying they had to telephone to their Governments; they were obviously not in the mood to attend a banquet. They had secured peace, but at the price of a serious loss of prestige. Under pressure from Hitler they had arranged for an ally of France to cede part of its territory to Germany. As we now know, considerable pressure had to be brought to bear on Czecho-Slovakia both by France and England; it was therefore understandable that Chamberlain and Daladier seemed decidedly depressed that evening.

An exclusively Italo-German company, therefore, sat down with Hitler at a banqueting table that was much too long. It was on this occasion that Mussolini made his statement about the catastrophic consequences that would have ensued for Italy at the time of the Abyssinian war, if the League of Nations had extended its sanctions to oil, even if only for a week.

As far as I was concerned, the Munich Conference lasted without respite for nearly thirteen hours, for I also had to interpret during lunch and dinner. I had to translate everything that was said continuously into three languages, and so spoke literally twice as many words as the Big Four put together.

There was only a brief rest after the signing of the Agreement, for the next morning I was at Hitler's house to interpret the conversation with Chamberlain. Hitler looked quite different as he sat beside me, pale and moody. He listened absent-mindedly to Chamberlain's remarks about Anglo-German relations, disarmament and economic questions, contributing comparatively little to the conversation. Towards the end of the conversation Chamberlain drew the famous Anglo-German Declaration from his pocket: "We regard the Agreement signed last night, and the Anglo-German Naval Agreement, as symbolic of the desire of our two peoples never to go to war with each other again.

"We are resolved that the method of consultation shall be the method adopted to deal with any other questions that may concern our two countries, and we are determined to continue our efforts to remove possible sources of differences, and thus to contribute to assuring the peace of Europe."

Slowly, emphasising each word, I translated this statement to Hitler.

I did not share Chamberlain's impression, expressed in a private letter of his now published, that Hitler eagerly assented to this declaration. My own feeling was that he agreed to the wording with a certain reluctance, and I believe he appended his signature only to please Chamberlain, without promising himself any too much from the effects of the declaration.

I then drove with Chamberlain through Munich in an open car, and experienced at close quarters the enthusiasm with which the people greeted the British Prime Minister. As we drove slowly through the streets he was everywhere immediately recognised. The people shouted their greetings and pressed round our car, many trying to shake his hand. I looked closely at their faces, just as I always did on Hitler's triumphal progress through Nuremberg. In moments of excitement men's expressions speak very plainly. Here in Munich the sight of the elderly Englishman sitting next to me did not excite the ecstatic enthusiasm of Nuremberg, but every face beamed happily. "Thank you, dear old Chamberlain, for having preserved peace for us," was what these thousands of joyous faces were clearly saying.

At the same time for me these obviously spontaneous and unorganised ovations for Chamberlain implied a certain criticism of Hitler. When a crowd in an Authoritarian State so demonstratively applauds, not its own godlike dictator, but a foreign statesman from the democratic West with an unheroic umbrella, this constitutes a very definite expression of public opinion—more significant perhaps than any number of hostile articles in the free Press of a democratic country.

That I was not alone in these thoughts was confirmed to me that afternoon by several prominent National Socialists of Hitler's entourage whom I knew always, almost unconsciously, echoed their master's voice as they heard it in the course of their constant association with Hitler. The German dictator was profoundly disappointed that the German people, in the face of war, reacted so differently from the manner prescribed in the National Socialist hero's handbook. Instead of showing delight at the prospect of taking up arms against the enemy, the populace of Berlin and Munich had demonstrated in no uncertain manner its aversion from war and its joy at the maintenance of peace. A certain tribute of routine applause had indeed been paid to Hitler, the man of war, but, in Munich at least, it lagged far behind the spontaneous manifestations of sympathy which I had myself seen accorded to Chamberlain, and such as he and Daladier received outside their hotels. I also heard that when the conclusion of the Munich Agreement became known in the town that night many joyful gatherings had taken place at which plentiful libations of what was then an excellent brew led to the appearance of innumerable merry, swaying figures in the streets and squares.

Part of Hitler's world must have fallen about his ears when he learned about all this on the following day, and I suddenly realised why he had been so completely changed and self-aborbed when Chamberlain visited him.

Scarcely a fortnight later Hitler said, in his famous Saarbrucken speech: "There were weaklings among us, too, who possibly did not realise that a stern decision had to be taken." This was public confirmation of my impression. This Saarbrucken speech was for many Germans a rude awakening from the dream that the Munich Agreement had settled everything, and that peace had been permanently secured. "I know, what apparently the rest of the world, and some individuals in Germany also, do not, that the people of 1938 are not the people of 1918." Once again, here is clear indication of his disappointment at the bearing of the Germans. "It only needs Mr. Duff Cooper, or Mr. Eden, or Mr. Churchill to come to power in England instead of Chamberlain; we well know that the first aim of these men would be to start a new world war. . . . This makes it our duty to be on guard and to take heed for the safety of the Reich."

I too had cheerfully hoped that, with the settlement of "the last territorial problem," peace would reign for many a day. I saw with infinite regret that the spirit of suspicion and resentment once again had the upper hand in Hitler.

At that time I heard much in the Chancellery of Hitler's indignation at the severe criticism in England and France of the Munich Agreement, and at England's drive to increase her armaments. Hitler did not seem to understand what a severe reverse England and France had suffered at his hand.

"I am now going to a dying man to give him supreme unction," François-Poncet had very aptly said as, in the small hours of September 30th, he went to tell the Czechs, France's allies, of the verdict passed on them in their absence. "But

I have not even got oil with me," he added, "to pour on his wounds."

The British Prime Minister had flown three times to Germany; step by step he had allowed Hitler to push him into a solution which contributed very little to the prestige of the Western Powers.

Hitler was astonished and indignant that the two great countries, after their transitory relief at the maintenance of peace, were not exactly congratulating themselves on the price they had had to pay for it, and that they were naturally determined to do everything possible to see that they were never again in such a helpless position.

It once again became startlingly clear to me during those days how little Hitler understood the mentality of Western Europe.

Despite these unpleasant impressions I, and my colleagues at the Foreign Office, retained up to the end of that eventful year the feeling of relief that the great slaughter had been prevented.

CHAPTER V

(1939)

ALTHOUGH, in 1938, Germany had not plunged into war, I realised in the first months of the fateful year 1939, from the words I had to translate for Hitler and Ribbentrop, that Germany was again approaching the abyss, slowly at first and then at an ever increasing speed.

There can have been no period in my career when I took part in such a plethora of separate talks as between the Munich Conference and September 3rd, 1939. Part of my duties was to make reports on all these conversations, many of which have since been published. I was aware when I wrote them that, together with other documents, they would be the raw material from which historians would form an impartial judgment of the events with which they were concerned. At the same time, I bore in mind the fact that my fellow-countrymen might see for themselves, from these reports, the way in which Hitler conducted his foreign policy. Soon after the Munich Conference my apprehension that catastrophe was inevitable was intensified. But I had as yet no conception of its extent.

I can but indicate the theme running through all these discussions and events. After the fateful German march into Prague, which my friends and I regarded with horror as the prelude to disaster, there followed the shrill discords of August, 1939, which culminated in the final crash when England and France declared war on Germany.

During this period there was a significant absence of the brilliant festivals which had dazzled the world in 1937, and at the beginning of 1938. In retrospect, the main feature of those last months before the outbreak of the second world war seems to me to have been the wide contrast between the continued protestations of peace to the outside world and the busy preparations for war at home.

116

* *
*

An Italo-German tribunal met in October 1938 in the magnificent setting of Schloss Belvedere in Vienna, once the summer residence of Prince Eugene, to settle Hungary's territorial claims on the remnant of Czecho-Slovakia. A map of the disputed territories was spread out on a large table, round which stood Ribbentrop and Ciano with their advisers. Each of the Foreign Ministers held a thick pencil, and as they spoke they corrected the frontier line, which had been drawn up by experts as the basis for arbitration.

"If you go on defending Czech interests like that," Ciano exclaimed to Ribbentrop with a malicious smile, "Hacha will give you a decoration." He altered the line with thick pencil strokes in Hungary's favour. "That's definitely too far," protested Ribbentrop, to whom the Foreign Office expert had whispered; and he re-drew part of the line. The Foreign Ministers went on arguing in this way for quite a while, rubbing out and drawing in new lines, the pencils getting blunter and the frontiers thicker "The boundary commission will find it hard to determine the line," a colleague whispered to me. "These thick pencil marks are each a few kilometres broad."

Seldom have I been made so acutely aware of the contrast between the lighthearted decisions on frontiers taken by statesmen in the splendid apartments of historic castles and the consequences of their decisions in terms of everyday life in the territories affected.

I was aware of a similar conflict between outward form and inner significance in the "friendly visits" on which I accompanied Ribbentrop to Paris and Warsaw in December 1938 and January 1939.

"The German and French Governments share the conviction that peaceful and good-neighbourly relations between Germany and France constitute one of the most essential elements for stabilising conditions in Europe and maintaining peace," ran the statement which was solemnly signed by Ribbentrop and Bonnet on December 6th, 1938, in the Salle de l'Horloge at the Quai d'Orsay. It was in the same room that I had, ten years earlier, seen Stresemann, Briand and Kellogg put their signatures to the Pact outlawing war.

"Both Governments . . . solemnly recognise as final the frontier between their countries as it at present runs," continued the text. I read out the German version while photographers cluttered the room with their apparatus, robbing the occasion of much of its dignity.

"Both Governments are resolved," I read on, "subject to their special relations with third Powers, in all questions affecting their two countries . . . to enter into consultation if the future development of such questions should lead to international difficulties."

This was the deceptive façade behind which, a short time after the statement was signed, a rather disjointed discussion of the general situation took place in another room of the French Foreign Office between Bonnet and Ribbentrop. Ribbentrop sometimes spoke in French, and sometimes I translated what he said for him. Nothing was translated into German, and this perhaps is how the misunderstanding which marked this conversation arose. At one point Bonnet, who had previously expressed France's intention vigorously to develop her colonial empire, had stated that at the Munich Conference France had shown herself disinterested in East Europe. These words were in fact spoken during the discussion, although they were later disputed by the French. Bonnet had probably meant them to refer only to past events in Czecho-Slovakia. Ribbentrop, on the other hand, applied them also, and above all, to France's future attitude to Poland, the more so as Bonnet referred to the desirability of a German-Polish agreement about the Corridor and Danzig. Ribbentrop had some grounds for this interpretation in the tension that had then existed for some time between Paris and Warsaw. This had found expression in severe attacks against Poland in the French and British Press because of the way in which the Polish Government, taking advantage of Czecho-Slovakia's weakness after the Sudeten crisis, had occupied the Olsa area.

Another feature of this conversation was Ribbentrop's violent attack on England. In the harsh words he uttered against the British Government, the British Press, and individual Members of Parliament such as Duff Cooper and Eden, I immediately recognised the angry voice of his master. Hitler at that time was wont to shout: "England is to blame for everything," with the same persistence in foreign affairs as that with which his declaration: "The Jews are to blame for everything," occurred in internal matters. Ribbentrop made such a point in Paris of this "England is to blame for everything" that even the gentle Bonnet rather emphatically replied that in no circumstances would there be any change in Anglo-French co-operation, which must provide the basis for a detente between France and Germany.

I saw at once that Ribbentrop merely echoed Hitler's dislike of England, and was not trying to drive a wedge between England and France when, after Bonnet's emphatic words, he at once changed his tone. He said he approved of close Anglo-French co-operation, which was the counterpart to the Italo-German understanding.

So the atmosphere during this "friendship visit" was anything but one of friendly understanding between France and Germany.

The French could not have taken more pains on the material side, and made such gestures as sending to Berlin for our journey to Paris the coach recently built for the King of England's visit. But during Ribbentrop's talks we kept coming up against French mistrust, particularly from the permanent officials, like Alexis Léger.

We, in our "Admiral's" uniforms, in due course laid a big wreath on the tomb of the Unknown Soldier at the Arc de Triomphe. The swastika ribbon for it actually had to he flown by special courier from Berlin, because our protocol department had forgotten to include it in the hurry of our departure. But we all had the feeling that it was only a theatrical gesture.

Such also was probably the feeling of the people of Paris with regard to the whole visit. In so far as the rigorous police precautions enabled us to get a sight of the Parisians, they showed themselves to be completely apathetic and uninterested. The world's attention was then fixed on Paris in some suspense, with the presumption that much more lay behind the three hours conversation at the Quai d'Orsay than in fact there was in that very superficial exchange of views.

I personally had a most interesting experience during this visit, when I had the good fortune to have a long talk at a German Embassy reception with the famous French writer Jules Romains whom, as the author of the monumental work *Les Hommes de Bonne Volonté*, I highly esteemed. He was clearly agreeably surprised that someone who had come to Paris with Ribbentrop should speak with so much enthusiasm of his work, and even be able to quote from it. I had met enough men *de bonne volonté*, men of good will, in politics to realise that the world's salvation at that time—and now—depends upon these men, and that fanatics, of whatever nationality or race, are the real enemies of mankind.

* *
*

At the end of January, 1939, I accompanied Ribbentrop to Warsaw on another "goodwill" visit. Here the difference between the outward show and the inner reality was greater even than in Paris.

The station of the Polish capital, when we arrived there in the afternoon of January 26th, was decorated with swastika banners, there was a guard of honour, and military bands played the national anthems. Beck, the Foreign Minister, received us; he was accompanied by a numerous entourage, as well as by his wife, who presented Frau von Ribbentrop with a bouquet. Here also we laid a wreath on the tomb of Poland's unknown soldier. Although protestations of friendship were only moderately expressed in the toasts proposed at a banquet, none of the difficulties between the two countries, which had appeared fairly sharply during a visit Beck made to Obersalzberg early in the year, were openly mentioned. They were, however, touched on in the conversations between Ribbentrop and Beck.

During the course of Beck's earlier visit to Hitler I had been able to foresee plainly the impending Polish-German trouble which was to culminate in the British Ambassador handing me on September 3rd, 1939, the ultimatum which plunged the world into war.

At that talk Hitler had again spoken of a proposal which had just emerged after the Munich Agreement. The meeting had, incidentally, been arranged at a time when Polish objections were being made known regarding the declaration of the independence of the Carpathian Ukraine, which had previously belonged to Czecho-Slovakia. Poland stated that, in her view, the Carpathian Ukraine should be annexed by Hungary, and she opposed the undertaking given by Hitler at Munich in connection with his guarantee to the remaining part of Czecho-Slovakia.

German demands were principally concerned with the return of Danzig, although Poland's economic interests in that city were to be safeguarded. Hitler also demanded the construction of an extra-territorial motor road and railway through the Corridor to secure communications between Reich territory and East Prussia, and offered in return a guarantee of the German-Polish frontier and a renewal of the German-Polish non-aggression pact. The conclusion of this pact on January 26th, 1934, had been Hitler's first major act of foreign policy.

The day before Beck saw Hitler at the Obersalzberg, Ribbentrop had hammered away at him for hours with that peculiar insistence which observers and victims have rather aptly called "insistent penetration", in order to induce him to accept the German requirements, as a basis of discussion. Beck had persistently refused, with equal obstinacy, being especially resolute concerning Danzig. If he had had his way, a precisely opposite arrangement would have been made: he offered Germany safeguards for her economic interests in the city, but refused to consider any political re-incorporation. "I cannot ask public opinion in Poland to agree to that," was always his answer.

This argument had been repeated by the large window in Hitler's room at the Berghof, although Beck then expressed his refusal more mildly. He had gone so far as to agree to an examination of the question as a whole, but with the clear implication that the Polish attitude would be negative.

These differences were naturally very fresh in my mind during the meetings at Warsaw. Ribbentrop tried again, with even greater persistence than before, to get Beck to agree to the German proposals. He was again met with a refusal which was no less definite for the polite and tortuous form in which Poland's Foreign Minister knew how to deliver it. This was the last major attempt to reach agreement with Poland by peaceful negotiation.

* *

In the early hours of the fateful March 15th, 1939, which I personally regard as the beginning of the end, Hitler received Dr. Hacha, the Czech President, and his Foreign Minister, Chvalkovsky, at the Chancellery for the mysterious discussion which resulted in the sensational creation of a German Protectorate over Bohemia and Moravia. The detailed circumstances of this move caused much speculation both at the time and later. The dark panelling of the room, lighted only by a few bronze lamps, produced a sinister atmosphere—a suitable framework for the tragic scene of that night.

The short, elderly man with dark eyes set in a face flushed with agitation who was shown into this room shortly after 1 a.m. was the successor to Benes—President Hacha. He had done his best to give no occasion for criticism to his giant neighbour Germany, which surrounded the diminished Czecho-Slovakia on three sides. I had often been present at discussions in Berlin when his Foreign Minister, Chvalkovsky, had, as it were, tried to divine Ribbentrop's wishes from his expression, lest by some mischance he should give Ribbentrop the least offence. In the commercial field he had expressed his readiness for a customs union, and for generally granting Germany preferential treatment, and in political matters he had acquiesced in every conceivable way. This short, dark-skinned Foreign Minister expressed his pathetic anxiety to please in a sentence which could not better have summed up the situation: "And in foreign matters we would like to depend on you, Herr Reich-minister, if we may."

But all had been to no avail; the Czechs were like a red rag to Hitler. At the time, I ascribed this to his Austrian past, whereas I now connect his unreasoning rage against the Czechs with the theory that he himself had Czech blood in his veins. I had already heard it said in the Chancellery early in January that Hitler had decided to liquidate the Czech State. I was appalled by this report, for had I not myself, during the Sudeten crisis, several times translated Hitler's assurance to Chamberlain that the Sudeten problem constituted his last territorial demand. The phrase: "We want no Czechs," from his Sports Palace speech still sounded in my ears. Hitler and Chamberlain had assured each other that they were "resolved to deal with other matters, also . . . by the method of consultation."

If Chamberlain, the exponent of a friendly policy towards the Reich, were to be thus blatantly repudiated; if this man, highly esteemed throughout the world (including Germany, as I had seen for myself), were made to look ridiculous by having all promises, written or verbal, torn up and flung defiantly at his feet, the day of reckoning could not be long delayed.

My awareness of Hitler's true intentions showed me the motives behind the Press campaign against the remnant of Czecho-Slovakia, and the declaration of Slovakia's and Carpathian Ukraine's independence. I was not surprised when, a few days before March 13th, I learnt that the march into Czech territory had been fixed for the early hours of March 15th.

Hacha and Chvalkovsky too had seen the approach of disaster, and this was their last-minute, desperate effort to save their country. They sought an interview with Hitler, who agreed to receive them in Berlin. They were met at the station with all the honours due to the head of a State; when they reached the Chancellery they were welcomed in the courtyard by a company of the SS bodyguard, whose band played the regimental march, and who, as a final touch of irony, were inspected by Hacha.

In Hitler's gloomy office the realities of the situation emerged by contrast, even more starkly. Here was no intimate discussion between man and man. There were a number of people present, but Hacha, Chvalkovsky, and the rest, even Göring and Ribbentrop, were the audience, Hitler the speaker.

I had worked for Hitler at longer sessions than this talk, which lasted scarcely three quarters of an hour, and I had seen him much more excited than at this encounter with the Czechs; but I have never reported a more fateful discussion. Indeed, it scarcely could be called a discussion at all; it consisted rather of one long accusation against the Czechs by Hitler, who now repeated the same calender of crimes which he had already exhaustively enumerated to the British and the French. No new point was raised. As compared with the Benes regime, Hitler asserted, nothing had changed—under the surface the Benes spirit lived on in the new Czecho-Slovakia. He did not mean, he said, to imply any distrust of Hacha; in Germany they were convinced of his loyalty. But, for the security of the Reich, it was necessary for Germany to assume a protectorate over the remnant of Czecho-Slovakia.

Hitler said this with considerable fervour—indeed, he never could speak quietly about the Czechs and Benes. There were, however, none of those turbulent scenes that night between him and Hacha which have been described in the foreign Press. As I have said, I had already seen Hitler a good deal more excited on other occasions—for instance, at the discussion with Sir Horace Wilson at the end of September, 1938.

Hacha and Chvalkovsky sat as though turned to stone while Hitler spoke. Only their eyes showed that they were alive. It must have been an extraordinarily heavy blow to learn from Hitler's mouth that the end of their country had come. They had set out from Prague in the hope that they would be able to treat with Hitler, but already, just before Hacha inspected the guard of honour at Berlin station, they had been told by the Czech Minister in Berlin that German troops had crossed their frontier at Ostrau. Then Hacha had had to sit and wait for hours at the Adlon Hotel for a telephone call from the Chancellery. Hitler finally received him at one o'clock in the morning.

It was astonishing how the old gentleman kept his composure with Hitler after all this strain. "The German troops' entry can't he hindered," said Hitler. "If you want to avoid bloodshed, you had better telephone to Prague at once, and instruct your Minister of War to order the Czech forces to offer no resistance." With these words Hitler brought the interview to an end.

But the telephone line to Prague was out of order. A nervy Ribbentrop told me to find out "who's gone and let us down." I moved heaven and earth with the Post Office but could only get the information that the German line was in order, but that Prague did not answer.

"Call the Postmaster-General at once, for me personally," screamed Ribbentrop, scarlet with rage. I redoubled my efforts, with the knowledge that failure to get through might cost many lives.

Meanwhile Göring was talking to Hacha in another room. Prague suddenly came through, and I rushed in in order to take the call in there. They were sitting quietly at the table, talking without any sign of excitement. Hacha immediately went to the telephone, and I stayed a moment to make sure that he really got through. This was just as well, for a moment later the connection was broken off again. I left the room, and Ribbentrop told me to "get the Postmaster-General out of his bed," with an angry allusion to "Ministers who sleep during such a situation while we're hard at work here!"

I had only just started dialling again when I heard Göring shouting for Professor Morell, Hitler's personal physician. "Hacha has fainted!", said Göring with great agitation, "I hope nothing happens to him." He added thoughtfully: "It has been a very strenuous day for such an old man."

"If anything happens to Hacha," I thought, "the whole world will say tomorrow that he was murdered at the Chancellery." I was abruptly recalled from these grim reflections by the Foreign Office central exchange (they had been told by Ribbentrop that they would be sacked at once, with their superintendent, "if they didn't get the connection within an hour") who told me that Prague was now at last on the line.

I went back to the room where were Hacha and Göring, and found them still there, talking in low tones. Outwardly, at any rate, Hacha showed scarcely a sign of his fainting attack. Morell's injection had apparently done the trick.

Hacha and Chvalkovsky spoke to Prague, and Göring and I left the room while they continued their conversation in Czech. The connection did not seem very good, for Chvalkovsky, who spoke first, had to raise his voice and speak very slowly.

I was now busy preparing a fair copy, only a few lines long, of the communiqué: "At the meeting (of Hitler and Hacha) the serious situation arising from the events of recent weeks in what was formerly Czecho-Slovak territory was frankly considered. The conviction was expressed on both sides that all endeavours must be directed to securing tranquillity, order and peace in that part of Central Europe. The President of the State of Czecho-Slovakia has declared that, in order to serve this aim and final pacification, he confidently lays the fate of the Czech people and country in the hands of the Führer of the German Reich. The Führer has accepted this declaration, and has announced his decision to take the Czech people under the protection of the German Reich, and to accord it the autonomous development of its national life in accordance with its special characteristics."

This text, which had been prepared beforehand by Hitler, was signed by him and Hacha as well as by Ribbentrop and Chvalkovsky, on March 15th at 3.55 a.m. It occurred to only a few of those concerned, as they left the great grey building on the Wilhelmsplatz shortly afterwards, that the end of Czecho-Slovakia was at the same time the beginning of the end of Germany.

A few days later, I translated Chamberlain's speech, delivered on March 17th, at Birmingham, two days after this event: "Public opinion in the world has received a sharper shock than has ever yet been administered to it . . . Speaking with great earnestness at Godesberg, Herr Hitler repeated to me what he had already said at Berchtesgaden, namely that this was the last of his territorial ambitions in Europe, and that he had no wish to include in the Reich people of other than German race." I could clearly remember these words of Hitler's, having myself translated them to Chamberlain. Chamberlain continued: "Herr Hitler himself confirmed this account of the conversation in the speech which he made at the Sportpalast in Berlin. 'I have no further interest in the Czech State; this I can guarantee. We do not want any Czechs'." The Prime Minister proceeded in his indictment of Hitler to call attention to the Munich Agreement, signed by Hitler, of which paragraph 6 provided that the final determination of the boundaries of Czecho-Slovakia should be fixed by an International Committee; he put special emphasis on the word "final." In conclusion he pointed out that in the Anglo-German Declaration, signed by himself and Hitler, "We declared that any other question which might concern our two countries should be dealt with by the method of consultation. . . . Does not the question inevitably arise in our minds, if it is so easy to discover good reasons for ignoring assurances so solemnly and so repeatedly given, what reliance can be placed upon any other assurances coming from the same source?" Whether Hitler ever saw my translation of the speech, I do not know; but even without reading Chamberlain's words he must have been aware of the breach of faith he had committed.

"Hitler has gone behind my back, he has made me look ridiculous," Daladier said to the German Ambassador in Paris. But: "The time for words is past," he declared in the Chamber. He was granted extraordinary powers for the strengthening of the armed forces. France and England entered upon immediate negotiations with regard to the protection of Poland and Rumania. Europe was on the move.

* * *

In the course of the following weeks my work mirrored the re-alignment of forces which was taking place. Friend and foe began to be recognisable as such: between them were the hesitant and uncertain, who wavered between Berlin and the Western Democracies.

On the evening of April 14th I met Göring in Rome, and on the following day he explained to a worried-looking Duce the necessity of the German action against Czecho-Slovakia, and the advantages it brought, particularly the acquisition of the Skoda Works.

While I was in Rome an Albanian delegation, in native costume, was evidence of Mussolini's recent coup against that country, of which the Italian Ambassador had given Hitler a hint just before the march into Prague. I had gathered that, after the achievements of his fellow dictator against Austria and Czecho-Slovakia, Mussolini had felt a pressing need to be able to report some success of his own. Hitler had at first thought that Mussolini's plans were directed against France, and had warned him against hasty action. I inferred that he was anxious about the reactions of the Western Powers to his Prague venture and did not want any further complications at that moment.

Another important event occurred at the time of our visit to Rome. Alarmed by the march into Prague, the United States intervened in the European scene. Roosevelt sent a personal message to Hitler and Mussolini, in which he referred to the fact that "three nations in Europe and one in Africa have lost their independence." Although Cordell Hull has since explicitly said so in his Memoirs, even at the time it was quite clear that Roosevelt was referring to Austria, Czecho-Slovakia and Abyssinia. He also stated that a large area of another independent nation in the Far East had been occupied by a neighbouring State, and continued: "Reports, which we trust are not true, indicate further acts of planned aggression against other independent nations." This was a clear reference to Poland, at least so Göring, to whom I translated Roosevelt's appeal, at once assumed. "Are you prepared," Roosevelt asked Hitler and Mussolini, "to give an assurance that your forces will not attack or invade the territory or possessions of the following independent nations?" Then followed a list of thirty named countries, both European and otherwise. Roosevelt proposed that this promise of non-aggression should be valid for ten to twenty-five years, and that it should be mutually agreed with the countries concerned. He also offered American mediation for the settlement of European difficulties at the conference table.

"I have taken the trouble," Hitler replied, in addressing the Reichstag on April 28th, "to ascertain from the States mentioned . . . whether they feel themselves to be threatened, and whether Mr. Roosevelt made this enquiry at their suggestion, or at least with their assent. The reply was in the negative, and, in some cases, an emphatic repudiation." In an angry speech the Führer expressed his rage at the reaction abroad to his Prague adventure: "Since England now, officially and in its Press, voices the opinion that action must be taken against Germany, and applies this by the familiar policy of encirclement, then the conditions for the Naval Agreement are no longer valid. I have decided so to inform the British Government today." Ribbentrop's diplomatic laurels of 1935 thus sank withered in the dust. "I regard the agreement concluded between myself and Marshal Pilsudski as having been unilaterally broken by Poland, and therefore as no longer valid. I have communicated this to the Polish Government"—this was Hitler's angry reply to the Anglo-French guarantee to Poland. This speech was translated, and defiantly sent to the American Embassy with the observation that it was the answer to Roosevelt's appeal.

* * *

Among the waverers, who had not yet declared for either side, was Rumania's Foreign Minister, Gafencu, who visited Berlin on April 19th. He was severely reproached by Ribbentrop for having, in the moment of shock following the march into Prague and the occupation of Albania, accepted a British guarantee. From Berlin he went on to London and Paris.

Another waverer was Paul, Prince Regent of Yugoslavia, who was staying in Berlin at the beginning of June. This highly cultured man, interested in the arts, often said in my presence that he very much regretted that he was called upon to succeed the murdered King Alexander. Hitler tried to impress him with a display of German military power. Preparing for the celebrations of his fiftieth birthday, Hitler had said to Ribbentrop: "As many cowardly civilians and democrats as possible must be invited to see a parade of the most modern of all armies;" and in June he subjected Prince Paul to this treatment, though without any better success than he met with in the case of Gafencu. His conversations with Kiosseivanov, the Bulgarian Prime Minister, whom I had met in Sofia in 1938, had a similar outcome.

There was also a complete misfire with the Secretary-General of the Turkish Foreign Office, Numan Menemencoglu, who in July had a protracted discussion with Ribbentrop at his Sonnenburg country house. With stupefying persistence Ribbentrop kept on pressing him to clear the way for Turkey's accession to the Axis, and to include Germany in the Montreux Convention on the Dardanelles. But with astonishing, almost acrobatic, adroitness Numan always evaded the issue, and after hours of talk even the obstinate Ribbentrop sulkily gave up the struggle.

At the end of May and early in June I also took part in brief

negotiations in Berlin between Ribbentrop and the Foreign
Ministers of Denmark and of the Baltic States of Esthonia and
Latvia, at which non-aggression pacts were concluded between
these countries and Germany. These were an indirect consequence of Roosevelt's appeal.

*
* *

As a result of the Western Democracies' counter-measures,
there was a substantial consolidation of our association with
Italy. On May 4th I went with Ribbentrop to Milan, where
he met Ciano. The two Foreign Ministers, after a long discussion, agreed on a formal alliance, of which Article III provided:
"If one of the contracting parties is involved in war with another
Power, the other contracting party shall immediately come to
its assistance as an ally, and support it with all its military forces
by land, sea and air." By the terms of Article V both countries
undertook: "in the event of a war jointly conducted, to conclude
an armistice and peace only by mutual agreement."

It was not until May 22nd that this so called "Pact of Steel"
was signed with great ceremony by Ribbentrop and Ciano in
Hitler's presence in the new Chancellery in Berlin. It represented Hitler's aggressive reply to the defensive measures taken
by Britain and France—closer Anglo-French co-operation,
Anglo-French guarantees to Poland and Rumania, plenary
powers given to Daladier by the Chamber for the development
of national defence, and the introduction of conscription in
England on April 27th, 1939.

The future alignment of forces was becoming more clearly
marked. Italy had now finally tied herself to Germany; but
just as at Göring's conversations in Rome, so now in Berlin
I noticed a certain reserve in Ciano, as though he were alarmed
by his own boldness. In his conversations with Ribbentrop
and Hitler the Italian Foreign Minister had made a point of
emphasising the common need of both Axis partners for a fair
period of peaceful development. This he estimated should
last for at least three years.

Throughout the summer tension in Europe increased daily.
Preparations for war were put in hand more or less openly in

every country; menaces, warnings, and challenges filled the
ether and the columns of the Press.

After the series of visits which ended in July with the fruitless
conversations between Ribbentrop and Menemencoglu I went
on leave to Norderney with an uneasy presentiment that I should
probably be extremely busy the following month. I had just
managed to settle in when I was called to the telephone. "We
are very sorry," said the voice of a friend in the Foreign Office,
"but you must interrupt your leave. The Foreign Office's
special plane has already left for you. Please be at the aerodrome in two hours time."

The old AMYY arrived punctually. The pilot, a namesake
of mine, did not know where we were to go. "I'll get my
instructions just before taking off," he said mysteriously. We
flew to the other end of the Reich—to Salzburg, where I was
wanted for a surprise visit of Ciano's. He arrived there on
August 11th.

* *

I found the Italian delegation in a great state of excitement.
"You can take my word for it," Attolico told me, "England and
France are resolved to let it come to war if Germany proceeds
against Poland as she did against Czecho-Slovakia." I agreed
without hesitation: "I need no convincing of that. If your
Foreign Minister expresses this opinion in his conversation with
Hitler, you may rely on me to translate what he says with full
conviction and great emphasis."

"You are going to be very busy," Attolico replied. "You
will in fact have to translate just what I have been telling you
to the Chancellor. That is the reason why Mussolini has sent
Ciano to Hitler."

We drove out to Schloss Fuschl, one of Ribbentrop's country
estates, where Ciano, though he spoke like an angel, and under-
lined Italy's weakness, made no impression on Ribbentrop,
who was like a hound at the leash, raging against England,
France and Poland, and boasting grotesquely about the might
of Germany. After the discussion at Fuschl, we made an excur-
ion with Ciano to St. Wolfgang, where a jolly folk festival

was going on, and dined at the Weisse Rossl amongst the unsus-
pecting summer visitors. In the same way, a few weeks before,
on the conclusion of the military alliance at Milan, the Italians
had entertained us as the Villa d'Este, on Lake Como. These
gay and attractive occasions were in striking contrast to the
storm clouds massing over Europe.

At the meeting next day, Hitler was set on war. That Ribbentrop had again been the echo of his master was obvious
from the identity of his arguments with Hitler's. "It's all the
fault of the English," was Hitler's main theme. "The Poles
need a severe lesson. The democracies are not as powerful as
Germany and will not fight," was the refrain; the military and
technical supremacy of the Reich underlay everything.

On this first day Ciano stood up to Hitler very energetically.
He had received detailed instructions from the Duce, as he
revealed in his Diary, to point out to Hitler the "madness"
of embarking on war. With all the eloquence at his command
he more than once pointed out that a war against Poland would
in no way be confined to that country. This time the Western
Democracies would certainly declare war. Obviously acting
on the Duce's instructions, Ciano kept returning to the theme of
Italy's weakness and unpreparedness, bluntly telling Hitler
that Italy could not remain in a war for more than a few months
at most; the position with regard to war materials alone made
it impossible for her to fight any longer. He could not have
been more explicit.

In conclusion he submitted the draft of a communiqué which
suggested international negotiations for the settlement of the
problems threatening the peace of Europe. Ribbentrop had
already turned down this communiqué, and had, instead, put
forward a draft which confined itself to speaking of the "impres-
sively close alliance of the two nations."

During the meeting with Ciano at the Berghof next day Hitler
spoke a sentence which still echoes in my ears: "I am un-
shakably convinced that neither England nor France will embark
upon a general war." On this second day Ciano made no
further effort to impress Mussolini's advice on Hitler. He said
no more of Italy's incapacity for taking part in hostilities.
Quite inexplicably, he folded up like a jack-knife. "You have

been proved right so often before when we others held the opposite view," he said, "that I think it very possible that this time, too, you see things more clearly than we do."

I was profoundly disappointed, and Attolico, when I told him that Ciano had shifted his ground, expressed to the other Italians his deep concern at the results which might flow from the Foreign Minister's new attitude. In these circumstances the question of the Press communiqué was naturally dropped. Ciano did not point out that Italy was entitled, by virtue of her treaty with Germany, to insist upon a common decision on the attitude to be taken regarding Poland.

Ciano left Salzburg the same afternoon. "I return to Rome," he noted in his Diary, "full of disgust with Germany, her Führer and their conduct."

I was naturally not allotted a plane to take me back to the North Sea, and was only too thankful that Ribbentrop let me continue my leave. I arrived once more at Norderney the following afternoon.

* * *

A few days later, I was again rung up by the Foreign Office. "Unfortunately you must interrupt your leave once more," I was told. To my angry question as to what was up now, my friend would give no reply. "You will probably be able to bathe in the North Sea again in a few days," was all that I could get out of him. Flight-Captain Schmidt, too, who appeared over the island two hours later, had no idea where I was to go.

"I am only to take you to Berlin. Beyond that I know nothing," he said as we flew over the Frisian Islands.

When I reached Berlin, a sensation awaited me in the shape of a sealed envelope on my Foreign Office desk. My instructions were to fly to Moscow with Ribbentrop in order to be present at discussions with Stalin. In this case I was not going as an interpreter, since I do not speak Russian. My function was to make a report of the course of the negotiations and to record any agreements there might be. It was the very last thing I had expected. An interpreter, by the nature of his calling, is unlikely to find himself speechless; but on this occasion words would have failed me had I tried to give expression to my surprise. I had, indeed, been given hints by my friends that Hitler had been flirting with the idea of an approach to the Soviet Union for some time. Ribbentrop's liaison man with Hitler, Hewel, had also told me how admiringly, almost enthusiastically, Hitler had spoken about Stalin when a Russian news reel was being shown at the Chancellery in which the Russian dictator was seen nodding in a friendly manner to his soldiers on parade. But I had not attached any particular significance to these things, with the result that the new turn was almost as sensational to me as to Germany and the world. "The sinister news broke upon the world like an explosion," Churchill writes in *The Gathering Storm*.

The impression made by this news on friends and acquaintances in Berlin, who naturally envied me my journey to "the distant planet," was, after the first shock of surprise, by no means a sinister one. On the contrary, the prevailing feeling in Berlin, and no doubt throughout Germany, was a sense of relief—at any rate as far as the general public was concerned. It was felt that a German-Soviet agreement, such as this visit seemed to portend, would obviate war. The opinion was commonly held that the encirclement of Germany would thus be broken, and that in the circumstances France and England would not go to war on Poland's account; in the preceding year, after all, when the groupings were far more favourable, they had not taken up arms for Czecho-Slovakia.

On August 22nd I accordingly set out by air for Moscow with Ribbentrop and a large delegation. We spent a night at Königsberg, but there was no question of rest. Throughout the night Ribbentrop prepared the material for his discussions with Stalin, filling many sheets with notes in handwriting which grew larger and larger as the night wore on, telephoning to Berlin and Berchtesgaden, asking for the most un-get-at-able papers, and keeping the whole delegation on the run.

We younger members availed ourselves of time off from this statesmanlike activity to drink a farewell toast to peace in the bar of the Park Hotel, where we were staying. Unlike the general public in Germany, we were far from soothed by the prospect of an understanding with the Russians. I, especially, by now knew Hitler well enough to realise that, with his rear protected by Stalin, he would become still more rash and irresponsible in his foreign policy.

Next day we proceeded to Moscow, flying over the endless Russian plain, with its vast forests, its widely scattered villages and lonely farmsteads with their dark thatched roofs, which made one realise immediately after crossing the frontier that one was no longer over Germany, where the red tiled roofs had looked bright amongst the cultivated fields. After four hours flying we reached Moscow, whose sea of houses looked just like Berlin or London from the air. The whole delegation, including Ribbentrop, stared fascinated through the windows. The great moment of landing "on the distant planet" had arrived.

What first struck me on leaving the plane was the sight of a shield with the word "Moscou" in French and at its side the swastika flag in friendly contact with the hammer and sickle flag. In front was standing Potemkin, Deputy People's Commissar for Foreign Affairs, whose name seemed to me symbolic of the unreality of the whole scene. He was the head of a delegation of high Russian officials who had come to welcome us. With him were the Italian Ambassador, Rosso, whom I had known at Geneva, and the German Ambassador, Count von der Schulenburg. We drove to Moscow in Russian cars, which were very comfortable and looked like American Buicks. "Dictators seem to delight in the magnificence of wide roads," I reflected, as we drove along the very broad, dead-straight road to Moscow. The surroundings of this road seemed to me as bleak and dreary as are now those of its Berlin counterpart in the Tiergarten—whose present state is a direct, and one hopes final, consequence of the Moscow visit.

The whole delegation were billeted in the German Embassy or at the homes of individual members of it. After a hasty meal Ribbentrop immediately drove to see Molotov in the Kremlin. We were obviously in a great hurry. I ought to have gone with him, but my luggage containing the dark suit, regarded as essential even in Moscow, had gone astray on the way from the aerodrome.

I availed myself of this opportunity to go round Moscow

with my host's wife, who spoke Russian perfectly. With its
large broad streets, squares with churches, overcrowded trams,
crowded thoroughfares and fairly heavy motor and horse-drawn
traffic, it bore at first sight an almost disappointing resemblance
to other great European cities. Only when I looked more
closely was I struck by the essential difference. Cheerfulness,
which I was accustomed to see on the faces of crowds in the
streets of Berlin, Paris or London, seemed to be missing here
in Moscow. The people stared seriously and almost absent-
mindedly straight in front of them. Only very rarely during
my walk of several hours did I see a smiling face.

As laughter was absent from the faces, so colour seemed to
me to be lacking from the clothing of the Muscovites. Occasional
white head-dresses alone brought a little life into the grey of
faces and clothes. Although almost all the people were cleanly
and neatly clad, with hardly anybody in rags, yet a melancholy
grey pall seemed to hang over everyone and everything. In
the case of the houses this effect was due to the fact that they had
not been cleaned or painted for a long time. Many of them
produced an effect similar to that of the district round the
Schlesische Station at Berlin immediately after the first world
war and the 1918 revolution.

Some new skyscrapers, built on the American model to house
Ministries, made an impressive appearance. I felt the same
admiration as is expressed by all Western visitors to Moscow
when I went in the famous Underground. The line did not
run far, but its stations, with their ornamental marble and good
lighting, the comfort and cleanliness of the ultra-modern
carriages, the superb ventilation, put the undergrounds of
Berlin, London, Paris and Madrid to shame. The Muscovites
standing near me stared silently with expressionless faces. As
my companion explained, they at once recognised me as a
foreigner from my clothes, especially my leather shoes. Had I
been wearing my white sand shoes from Norderney I would
have been less noticeable, for grey or white canvas shoes seemed
at that time to be the height of fashion in Moscow.

I had thought of committing a capitalist act in the communist
capital by making some purchases; but I had no luck here. In
shops whose windows displayed a few articles, the daily quota

had long before been sold. Even before the outbreak of war the shortage was as acute as it became in Berlin during the war, and my companion was answered with the Russian equivalent of "We haven't got it and we won't be getting it"—the refrain in all Berlin shops towards the end of the war.

When I got back to the Embassy late in the afternoon Ribbentrop came in from the Kremlin. He was positively bubbling over with enthusiasm about Molotov and Stalin, who, it seemed, had joined the discussion later. "Things are going splendidly with the Russians," Ribbentrop kept exclaiming as he made a hurried dinner. "We shall certainly arrive at an agreement before the evening is out."

The line delimiting the Russian and German spheres of interest in Poland, which was to become so famous, and which involved a new partition of that country, had apparently already been discussed at the afternoon session. Ribbentrop put an enquiry through by telephone from the Embassy asking Hitler whether he agreed to the Baltic ports of Libau and Windau coming within the Russian sphere of interest. Within half an hour Hitler's affirmative answer had arrived.

Immediately after his hasty meal Ribbentrop rushed back to the Kremlin with Schulenburg and Dr. Gaus, the Head of the Legal Division. To my regret, I did not go with them. Hilger, who was acting as Russian interpreter, was also to make the reports of the discussions. "I don't want a new face to crop up suddenly among those taking part in the negotiations," Ribbentrop explained. I was somewhat grieved to realise that the luggage lorry had deprived me of the opportunity of making Stalin's personal acquaintance. Molotov I was to get to know at very close quarters when he came to Berlin in 1940 for discussions with Hitler—on that occasion I resumed my old job of recording the meeting. But I nevertheless learnt the substance of the Kremlin discussions when Ribbentrop and his companions reappeared at the Embassy after the conclusion of the negotiations. They were in the best of spirits. Ribbentrop in elaborating on the individual points of the discussion enthused to anyone who cared to listen about Stalin and the "men with strong faces" who worked with him. He seemed particularly happy about the spheres of interest allotted to Germany and

Russia in Eastern Europe, details of which were kept secret for some time afterwards. That very night I had a look at the secret protocol dealing with this matter signed by Ribbentrop and Molotov. The introductory words, highly ominous in the political situation as it then was, read. "In the event of a territorial and political reorientation. . . . ." It provided that of the Baltic States Finland, Estonia and Latvia should fall into the Russian sphere of interest. For the "Polish State Territory" the demarcation line should follow "approximately the course of the rivers Narev, Vistula and San." The question whether an independent Polish State should continue to exist was to be determined later between the two parties. "With regard to South-East Europe," I read with intense interest: "Soviet Russia emphasises her interest in Bessarabia. Germany for her part expresses complete lack of political interest in these territories."

The intentions of the two contracting parties could scarcely have been more clearly expressed. I realised that we had not been unreasonable when we drank our farewell toast to peace at Königsberg.

Ribbentrop and his companions then enthusiastically described the little celebration which Stalin had improvised after the signature of the agreement. "Like a good paterfamilias," Stalin had personally concerned himself with the welfare of his guests. In accordance with the Russian custom, one toast followed another. Stalin had led off by drinking the health of Hitler, with the words: "I know how much the German people loves its Führer. I would therefore like to drink his health."

I was also interested to hear what the others who had been at the discussions had to say about Stalin's remarks on the questions of the hour. "England is to blame for everything" had naturally been Ribbentrop's refrain. Stalin had agreed, and had added some observations about England's military weakness, though, he said, however weak she was, England would fight hard and obstinately. Stalin seemed to estimate the strength of France higher than did Ribbentrop. With regard to Italy, Stalin put the question, interesting in view of subsequent developments, as to whether the Italians had annexed Albania, with certain ideas about Greece in mind.

Stalin was very uncommunicative with regard to Japan. When Ribbentrop offered German mediation, Stalin did not decline it, but said in his forthright way: "I know the Asiatics better. They want rough handling occasionally."

Having followed the conclusion of the treaty with Russia as intimately as I did, I found it of great interest to read in Churchill's war history the statement which Stalin made to him at the Kremlin in August 1942. The Russians, Stalin said, had the impression that the British and French were not resolved to go to war if Poland were attacked, but rather that they hoped to scare Hitler off by a united front composed of Britain, France and Russia. The Russians, however, were convinced that Hitler would not allow himself to be scared off. Churchill quotes this statement in connection with the week-long negotiations which an Anglo-French Mission was then carrying on at Moscow in an attempt to bring Russia into the "diplomatic front" against Germany. We did not see the members of the Mission during our stay, though they were in Moscow at the same time. They left empty-handed.

"The two contracting parties undertake to refrain from any act of force, any aggressive action, and any attack against one another"—thus ran Article 1 of the "Non-Aggression Pact between Germany and the Union of Socialist Soviet Republics" which Ribbentrop, beaming with delight, displayed at the Embassy in the early hours of the morning, duly signed by Molotov and himself.

We left for Berlin at 1 p.m. on August 24th, having stayed in Moscow only twenty-four hours. Ribbentrop had undoubtedly set up a diplomatic speed record, even by present-day standards. By their surprise move in this round of the diplomatic contest, Hitler and Stalin had checkmated England and France.

Before leaving Moscow I went to see the Red Square and the Lenin Mausoleum. A long queue of Russian peasants was patiently waiting in front of the Mausoleum to see Stalin's waxen predecessor in his glass coffin. In their bearing and expression the Russians looked like devout pilgrims. "Amongst Russian country folk," a member of the Embassy told me, "anyone who has been to Moscow and not seen Lenin doesn't count."

The great wall of the Kremlin was an impressive sight, so too was the Kremlin itself with its many towers, on which I had seen the great red stars gleaming the evening before.

Our delegation was so large that two Condor machines were required for our transport. One was to take Ribbentrop straight to Hitler at Berchtesgaden, while the other flew to Berlin. As I was the only "tourist"—having fulfilled no function and yet been present,—I got a seat in the second machine, which did not take off until an hour after the first. I thought that there would also be this interval of an hour when we stopped at Königsberg, and calmly watched Ribbentrop's plane take off—but the second Condor took the air directly afterwards. In the course of my work among the V.I.P.'s of Europe I have often been photographed, and I have always regretted that there is no record of the moment when I stood foolishly on the ground watching my plane fly away.

In the course of a brief visit to the aerodrome restaurant, I had learnt that both Condors were having fighter cover. In the last few days, such was the tension which had already developed between Germany and Poland, Lufthansa machines had frequently come under Polish anti-aircraft fire. "Railway connection with the Reich was suspended today," a bystander told me when I asked about trains. I hurried to the Air Office. "Run to the other end of the field as quickly as you can. A reserve machine is taking off empty for Berlin at any moment." I trotted off and wildly gesticulated at the machine, the engines of which were already running. I was relieved to see that the pilot slowed them down slightly. The little door at the end of the Ju 52 opened, the wirelers operator helped me in, and I sank panting into the nearest seat. We took off at once.

"May I see your pass?" said the pilot. "As things are, one can't be too careful." He too spoke about Polish anti-aircraft fire. "We are not so grand as those others," he said—meaning Ribbentrop and his delegation. "We get no fighter cover; but we fly far out over the Baltic, where the Poles can't get at us unless they chase us with fighters and then force us to land." As a precaution I prepared my papers for destruction. I had to make sure they did not fall into Polish hands in the event of a forced landing. But nothing happened, and I landed in

Berlin half an hour after Ribbentrop.   He had been re-directed
to Berlin because Hitler himself was on the way there.

This whole episode brought home to me how near war between
Poland and Germany really was.

* *

During my absence in Moscow a colleague had accompanied
the British Ambassador to Berchtesgaden.   Henderson handed
Hitler a personal letter from Chamberlain.   The Prime Minister
said, inter alia: "Apparently the announcement of a German-
Soviet Agreement is taken, in some circles in Berlin, to indicate
that intervention by Great Britain on behalf of Poland is no
longer a contingency that need be reckoned with.   No greater
mistake could be made.   Whatever may prove to be the nature
of the German-Soviet Agreement, it cannot alter Great Britain's
obligation to Poland, which His Majesty's Government has
stated in public repeatedly and plainly, and which it is determined to fulfil."

To this warning Chamberlain added these words: "It has
been alleged that, if His Majesty's Government had made
its position clearer in 1914, the great catastrophe would have
been avoided.   Whether or not there is any force in that
allegation, His Majesty's Government is resolved that on this
occasion there shall be no such tragic misunderstanding."

This was plain enough; but Chamberlain, painfully dis-
illusioned by Hitler's march into Prague, expressed himself
still more clearly and unmistakably in the following words:
"If the need should arise, His Majesty's Government is resolved,
and prepared, to employ without delay all the forces at its
command, and it is impossible to foresee the end of hostilities
once engaged.   It would be a dangerous illusion to think that,
if war once starts, it will come to an early end even if a success
on any one of the several fronts on which it will be fought should
have been secured."

Chamberlain combined this clear and unambiguous warning
with a proposal for friendly negotiations, and for a truce in the
German-Polish propaganda campaign.   He also suggested
that direct negotiations between Germany and Poland should be

entered upon forthwith. "In view of the grave consequence
to humanity which may follow from the action of their rulers, I
trust that Your Excellency will weigh with the utmost delibera-
tion the considerations which I have put before you."

I found the English text of this letter on my desk when I
returned from Moscow.

Hitler in his reply made violent accusations against Poland.
He referred to the German proposals regarding Danzig and the
Corridor, and concluded with sharp criticism of England:
"The unconditional guarantee England has given to Poland,
whereby under all circumstances she would come to that
country's assistance in any conflict, without regard to its causes,
could be interpreted in Poland only as an encouragement to
initiate forthwith a reign of terror against the one and a half
million Germans living there." Cruelties, insupportable to a
Great Power such as the German Reich, breach of obligations
with regard to the Free City of Danzig, economic strangulation
—such were the other main points of Hitler's letter, which
concluded: "I have therefore to inform Your Excellency that,
if the military measures announced (by England) are carried
out, I shall immediately order the mobilisation of the German
Wehrmacht."

The next morning, August 25th, I was summoned to the
Chancellery to translate for Hitler some especially striking
passages from the statements made by Chamberlain and Halifax
in the two Houses of Parliament. "I do not attempt to conceal
from the House," Chamberlain said in the Commons, "that
the announcement (of a Russo-German Non-Aggression Pact)
came to the Government as a surprise, and a surprise of a very unpleasant character." "In Berlin," he went on, "the announcement
has been hailed with extraordinary cynicism as a great
diplomatic victory which removed any danger of war since
France and ourselves would no longer be likely to fulfil our
obligations to Poland. We felt it our first duty to remove any
such dangerous illusion." Halifax's statement in the Lords was
easy to translate, since it was almost identical. These words
made Hitler pensive, but he said nothing.

I noticed that Chamberlain's letter and his statement to the
Commons had made a certain impression on Hitler when, at

about 1 p.m. the British Ambassador was summoned to the Chancellery. Hitler was comparatively calm and told Henderson that he had thought over the latter's words at Berchtesgaden about Anglo-German understanding, and wished to make a final suggestion for an Anglo-German settlement. He made a reference to the statements by Chamberlain and Halifax which I had translated for him that morning, and got rather excited in doing so. After listing a long series of charges against the Poles, including firing at civilian aircraft, he shouted: "The Macedonian conditions on our Eastern frontier must cease!" The Danzig problem and the question of the Corridor, he said, under all circumstances must be settled.

"Your Prime Minister yesterday made a speech in the House of Commons which does not in the least alter the German attitude. The only result of that speech can be a bloody and unpredictable war between Germany and England. But this time Germany will not have to fight on two fronts, for the agreement with Russia is unconditional and represents a long-term alteration in German foreign policy."

He concluded his speech for the prosecution with a sentence of particular interest in the light of ensuing events: "Russia and Germany will never again take up arms against each other." There followed his now famous proposal for a guarantee of the continued existence of the British Empire, and even an offer of help "in any part of the world where such help might be needed." Limitation of armaments, frontier guarantees in the West, and other items rounded off this astonishing offer. Nothing further was said on the Polish question except that Hitler declared: "The German-Polish problem must and will be solved."

The proposals contained in this conversation were extracted from my report, and I had to hand them to Henderson at the British Embassy the same day. At Hitler's suggestion the Ambassador took them on the following morning, August 26th, to England by special German plane.

Soon after the British Ambassador's visit, Attolico appeared. Hitler had already written to Mussolini hinting that he would probably very soon be compelled to proceed against Poland, and that he hoped for "Italy's understanding." He awaited the Duce's reply with unconcealed impatience, and he was extremely disappointed when Attolico told him that though his instructions were on their way from Rome he had not yet received them.   Hitler was so anxious for an early reply that he sent Ribbentrop out to telephone to Ciano.   He was, apparently supremely concerned to make sure of Mussolini's "understanding" before he proceeded seriously against Poland.   Ribbentrop came back a short time later, having failed to contact Ciano. Attolico was dismissed with scant courtesy.

As a visit from the French Ambassador was expected immediately afterwards, I remained in Hitler's office.   I thus witnessed the effect on him of the news of the formal pact of mutual aid between England and Poland which had just been concluded.   I could read the report which had been sent him by the Press Section over his shoulder, and then I watched him sit brooding at his desk until the French Ambassador, Coulondre, was announced.

Coulondre was the successor to François-Poncet, who had been transferred to Rome some time after the Munich Conference.   I had known the new French Ambassador for more than ten years; he had been head of the Foreign Trade Section in the French Foreign Office, and had therefore sat opposite me at innumerable sessions of the long Franco-German trade negotiations.   In the course of these negotiations, the elegant, dark, southern Frenchman had always struck me as an *homme de bonne volonté*, concerned to defend the interests of his country with circumspection and skill, and at the same time to look beyond the frontiers of France.   I was delighted when he came as Ambassador to Germany, not only because I had a high personal regard for him, but also because I knew from experience that he had the diplomatic talent necessary in the critical period from 1938 to 1939 if disaster was to be averted.

Just as a year before, at the time of the Sudeten crisis, I had been struck by the statesmanlike wisdom and great diplomatic skill that François-Poncet had displayed, so now his successor, Coulondre, at this critical conversation on August 25th, 1939, stood up to Hitler.   The Führer made very much the same statement as he had four hours earlier to Henderson.   He raged against the Poles, whose provocation he described as intolerable. Even the danger of a war with England and France would not prevent him, he said, from defending German interests. He would especially regret it if France and Germany were to become involved in war, since, after his formal renunciation of Alsace-Lorraine, there was no point of conflict between the two neighbours. Hitler had confirmed his statement to Henderson in writing; he contented himself with asking Coulondre personally to report his views to Daladier.

In the conversation with Coulondre he got heated only when attacking the Poles, and expressed lively regret when he spoke of the possibility of war between Germany and France. I had the impression at times that he was mechanically repeating what he had said to Henderson, and that his thoughts were elsewhere. It was obvious that he was in a hurry to bring the interview to an end.

When, however, at the end of his own statement, he half rose from his seat to indicate the end of the conversation, Coulondre did not simply let himself be dismissed. He asked with great gravity for permission to reply immediately to some of Hitler's statements. Like François-Poncet, he spoke forcibly. His concluding words I have often subsequently recalled: "In a situation as critical as this, Herr Reichkanzler, misunderstandings are the most dangerous things of all. Therefore, to make the matter quite clear, I give you my word of honour as a French officer that the French army will fight by the side of Poland if that country should be attacked." Then, raising his voice, he went on: "But I can also give you my word of honour that the French Government is prepared to do everything for the maintenance of peace right up to the last, and to work for moderation in Warsaw."

"Why, then, did you give Poland a blank cheque to act as she pleased?" Hitler retorted angrily.

As Coulondre was about to reply, Hitler jumped up and launched into another attack on Poland. "It is painful for me to have to go to war against France; but the decision does not depend on me," he said, and held out his hand to Coulondre, thus terminating the interview. He had talked to the French Ambassador for scarcely half an hour.

The next caller was already waiting outside. It was Attolico,

who now brought Mussolini's urgently awaited answer to
Hitler's intimation that he was about to intervene actively in
Poland.   "In one of the most painful moments of my life," wrote
Mussolini, "I have to inform you that Italy is not ready for war."
    The letter was a bombshell.   Hitler seemed to have forgotten
Ciano's clear indication a few days before at Berchtesgaden
that Italy was militarily unprepared. He was bitterly
disappointed at this sudden, and to him completely unexpected,
defection of his ally. "According to what the responsible
heads of the services tell me," Mussolini continued, "the petrol
supplies of the Italian Air Force are so low that they would
last only for three weeks of fighting.   The position is the same
with regard to supplies for the army, and supplies of raw
materials. Only the head of the navy has been able to
acquit himself of culpable negligence; the Fleet is ready for
action and supplied with sufficient fuel.   Please understand my
situation."
    Hitler icily dismissed Mussolini's envoy, contenting himself
with saying that he would answer the letter immediately.
"The Italians are behaving just as they did in 1914," I heard
him say when Attolico had gone; and for the next hour the
Chancellery resounded with disparaging remarks about the
"disloyal Axis partner."
    I remained at the Chancellery, since new talks might take
place at any moment. During the next few days I was there
almost night and day. Until the outbreak of war there was
an unending succession of conversations between Hitler and
the ambassadors. Thus, as well as attending at the diplomatic
conversations, I was able from behind the scenes to find out
more or less the whole course of events. There was much
coming and going in all the rooms and passages of the
Chancellery, with the military element predominating.
    When I left Hitler's room with Attolico and bade him goodbye,
I saw Keitel passing me swiftly on his way in to see Hitler.
While I was still wondering which of the various groups standing
in the hall I should join, Keitel came rushing out again from
Hitler's room.   I heard him speaking excitedly to his adjutant,
and caught the words: "The order to advance must
be delayed again."

The rumours then had been correct; though in the pressure of work during the last few days I had paid little attention to them. An order to advance had actually gone out to the services. Talking to the officers waiting in the hall, I picked up some more details. They all wanted to know whether my "classroom" would reassemble.

"If you can tell me the order to march is cancelled," I replied, "then I would say a resumption of my class at Munich is not impossible."

"There will be frightful confusion, and a good deal of swearing on the frontier roads," a major was saying, "if the troops who are on the march are to be ordered back in time." He added: "You diplomats are to blame for this; you should have thought things out beforehand, and not sent us off just as everything starts to look different." It was a harsh, but deserved, criticism of the "diplomat" Hitler. In the Third Reich not even a Foreign Minister could take decisions, let alone the despised diplomats of the Foreign Office.

That same evening, August 25th, Hitler replied to Mussolini's letter briefly and coolly. He asked for particulars of the raw materials and weapons which Italy needed in order to make war. The following day we translated Mussolini's answer, brought by Attolico. The demands were so exorbitant that Germany could not possibly have met them. It was quite clear that Mussolini was taking evasive action. Italy again came in for abuse—but not Mussolini.

We had to translate yet another letter from Hitler to Mussolini. He asked his ally to keep his decision to remain neutral a strict secret, and to give every appearance of preparing for war, in order to intimidate the Western Powers. A few hours later Attolico reappeared—Mussolini agreed to do both.

In the next few days verbal or written contact with ambassadors in Berlin and statesmen in London, Paris and Rome continued almost without intermission. It was a sort of long-distance conference by telephone and telegraph, and, as interpreter and translator, I was kept just as busy as I had been the previous year at Munich where the negotiating parties faced each other across a table.

"If Poland is attacked the honour of France insists that

she fulfils her undertakings," Daladier wrote to Hitler.

"Would not France act in just the same way if, for instance, Marseilles had for a time been severed from the mother country and its return to France were refused?" replied Hitler.

"Everything turns upon the nature of the settlement with Poland and the methods by which it is reached," I read, as I translated to Hitler London's reply to his comprehensive offer to Great Britain. "On these points, the importance of which cannot be absent from the Chancellor's mind, his message is silent, and His Majesty's Government feels compelled to point out that an understanding on both is essential if further progress is to be achieved." After again emphasising Britain's determination to carry out her undertaking to Poland, the Note declined to discuss Hitler's grandiose offer to collaborate with the British Empire: "His Majesty's Government could not, for any advantage offered to Great Britain, acquiesce in a settlement which would put in jeopardy the independence of a State to whom they have given a guarantee." It proposed as the next step the resumption of direct negotiations between the German and Polish Governments, regarding which "definite assurances from the Government of Poland" had already been received. The Note concluded with the following unequivocal words: "A just settlement of these questions between Germany and Poland may open the way to world peace. Failure to reach it would ruin the hopes of better understanding between Germany and Great Britain, would bring the two countries into conflict, and might well plunge the whole world into war. Such an outcome would be a calamity without parallel in history."

This Note was handed in by Henderson on the evening of August 28th. Hitler's reaction was surprisingly quiet. He appeared to be interested in some way in the British proposal.

During the hours that followed, until late at night, we translated Hitler's reply. It was not restrained: "Barbarous atrocities which cry to heaven," "persecution of the German population in Poland," "the murder of Germans settled in the country, or their compulsory evacuation in the most cruel circumstances," "a state of affairs that is intolerable to a Great Power"—these are some samples which indicate the general tone.

"These conditions have now compelled Germany, after being a passive spectator for months, to take the necessary active steps for assuring legitimate German interests," our translation continued. "The present demands of the German Government accord with a revision of the Treaty of Versailles, which has always been recognised as necessary—namely, the return of Danzig and the Corridor to Germany, and safeguards for the German population in the remainder of Polish territory." Hitler, too, was not lacking in clarity. "Under these circumstances," he wrote, "the German Government accepts the British Government's offer of mediation under which they will arrange that a Polish negotiator with the necessary powers would be sent to Berlin. It expects the arrival of a Polish envoy on Wednesday, August 30th, 1939, and will at once prepare its proposals."

Henderson read this document carefully at a further interview with Hitler the next day, August 29th. "It sounds like an ultimatum," was his comment, on account of the short time allowed for the arrival of the Polish negotiator. "The Poles," he said, "are given barely twenty-four hours to make their plans."

Hitler disputed this pertinent remark of Henderson's on grounds as threadbare as those he had given at Godesberg. "The time is short," he said, "because there is the danger that fresh provocation may result in the outbreak of fighting." The danger of an explosion because of constant incidents did in fact at that time seem to grow almost hourly.

Shortly afterwards Attolico came again to see Hitler. Mussolini reported that the British Government had expressed to him on various occasions its willingness to negotiate. I had the clear impression from this message that Mussolini wanted to take the initiative in calling a conference. Hitler, too, obviously realised this, but he felt no inclination to accept any mediation from "disloyal" Italy. He replied to Attolico with marked coldness that he was already in direct communication with the British, and had stated that he was ready to receive a Polish negotiator.

On the following day, August 30th, comparative peace reigned. Our time was employed in drafting Hitler's proposals regarding the settlement of the Danzig and Corridor questions. When I saw these proposals I could scarcely believe my eyes. They contemplated a plebiscite in the Polish Corridor under the supervision of an International Commission of British, French, Italian and Russian representatives; they left Gdynia to Poland and awarded only Danzig to Germany; they gave Poland an international road and railway through territory which would become German. They were inspired by a spirit which had little in common with National Socialist methods and with the ideas previously expressed by Hitler. It was a real League of Nations proposal. I felt I was back in Geneva.

Shortly before midnight on August 30th, that is just before the expiry of the German ultimatum regarding a Polish envoy, the British Embassy unexpectedly telephoned our Foreign Office. Henderson wanted to hand Ribbentrop the British Government's reply to Hitler's document of the previous day.

The conversation which ensued was the stormiest that I ever experienced during my twenty-three years as an interpreter. The atmosphere was highly charged, the nerves of the two men worn by the protracted negotiations in which they had lately been involved. Ribbentrop had come straight over from the Chancellery, and was obviously in a state of almost shivering excitement.

"What have they decided over there now?," I wondered, as the German Foreign Minister with a pale face, set lips and shining eyes sat down opposite Henderson at the small table in Bismarck's former office. He had greeted Henderson with an icy expression and stiff formality. The conversation was conducted partly in German, for Henderson liked to speak our language although he was not exactly a master of it. In this critical discussion he would have been able to express himself with more clarity and ease in English. He had often on previous occasions shown a tendency to use German, and I assume, therefore, that he meant this to be a friendly gesture.

Henderson began by recalling the messages which had reached us in writing from the British Embassy that day, beginning with the statement that it was "unreasonable" to expect the British Government to be able to produce a Polish envoy in Berlin within twenty-four hours.

Ribbentrop flared up. "The time is up," he said with affected calm. "Where's the Pole your Government was to provide?"

In addition, Henderson handed over a personal communication from Chamberlain to Hitler which stated that the British had made representations in Warsaw to prevent frontier incidents. He also mentioned the British advice to Poland to practise restraint, and requested that Germany should adopt a similar policy.

"The Poles are the aggressors, not we!" retorted Ribbentrop, getting more excited. "You have come to the wrong address."

When Henderson then put forward his Government's suggestion that in dealing with Poland the Reich should follow the normal procedure and transmit the German proposals through the Polish Ambassador in Berlin, Ribbentrop completely lost his self-control. "That's out of the question after what has happened," he shouted at Henderson. "We demand that a negotiator empowered by his Government with full authority should come here to Berlin."

Henderson, too, was beginning to lose the calm, typically British composure which normally characterised him. His face grew red, and his hands began to tremble as he proceeded to read the official answer to Hitler's memorandum. The British Note passed over fairly quickly the proposals regarding Anglo-German relations, and concentrated on the Polish dispute. To avoid incidents, both parties were urged to refrain from troop movements during the negotiations.

As the individual points were read out, Ribbentrop continually interrupted Henderson. "That's an unheard-of suggestion," he said angrily at the recommendation that troop movements should cease. Then he crossed his arms and looked challengingly at Henderson: "Have you anything more to say?" he shouted, in order to indicate that Henderson might continue.

Henderson then, for full measure, made a verbal addition to the British Note. The British Government, he said, possessed information to the effect that Germans were committing acts of sabotage in Poland.

"That's a damned lie of the Polish Government's!" Ribbentrop shouted in a fury. "I can only tell you, Herr Henderson, that the position is damned serious!"

Now the British Ambassador also lost his temper. Lifting a forefinger in admonition, he shouted: "You have just said 'damned.' That's no word for a statesman to use in so grave a situation."

Ribbentrop's breath was taken away. One of the "cowardly" diplomats, an ambassador, and an arrogant Englishman at that, had dared to reprimand him as he might a schoolboy. Ribbentrop jumped up from his chair. "What did you say?" he roared. Henderson, too, had risen to his feet. Both men glared at each other.

According to diplomatic convention I too should have risen; but to be frank I did not quite know how an interpreter should behave when speakers passed from words to deeds—and I really feared they might do so now. I therefore remained quietly seated and pretended to be writing in my notebook. Above me, I heard the two fighting cocks, breathing heavily. The least that can now happen, I thought, is that the Foreign Minister of the Reich will throw His Britannic Majesty's Ambassador out of the door. In the course of years an interpreter acquires a taste for grotesque situations; but I found nothing comic in this scene; it was extremely painful for the only spectator.

Fortunately, it did not come to wrestling. I went on scribbling in my notebook, heard more heavy breathing to my right and left, and then first Ribbentrop, and then Henderson, sat down again. I raised my head and could see from their expressions that the storm had blown over.

For a while the conversation proceeded in relative calm. Then Ribbentrop drew a paper out of his pocket: it contained Hitler's "League of Nations" proposals for the settlement of the Polish dispute. He read them out to Henderson in German, without, however, particularly hurrying over them as he was afterwards said to have done. On the contrary, he elaborated on some of the points. Then occurred the surprise.

Henderson asked whether he could be given the text of these proposals for transmission to his Government. According to normal diplomatic usage, that would follow as a matter of course, and I was rather surprised that Henderson should bother to ask at all. Expecting that Ribbentrop would hand him the paper with no more ado, I could scarcely believe my ears when I heard his answer. "No," he said with a rather misplaced smile, "I cannot hand you these proposals."

Henderson must have thought he had misheard, and he repeated his request. Again Ribbentrop declined. He threw, the document on the table, saying: "It is out of date, anyhowf as the Polish envoy has not appeared."

Now I, in my turn, became agitated. I suddenly saw the game which Hitler and Ribbentrop were playing. At that moment I understood that Hitler's high-sounding proposals had been produced only for show, and were never intended to be put into effect. The refusal to hand the document over to Henderson was made for fear that the British Government would pass on the proposals to the Poles, who might well have accepted them. Seldom have I so much regretted that, as interpreter, I could not intervene in the discussion. To say something on his own account is a mortal sin in an interpreter. By so doing he cannot but create confusion. So there was nothing for me to do but to sit by grinding my teeth while a chance of peace was deliberately sabotaged before my eyes. So this, I reflected, was what Hitler and Ribbentrop had been discussing at the Chancellery.

I made one last desperate attempt to transmit the contents of the document to Henderson, gazing at him fixedly and silently willing him to ask for an English translation of the German proposals. Ribbentrop could scarcely have refused this, and I would have translated so slowly that Henderson could have taken notes. But the British Ambassador did not react, and there was nothing left for me to do but to make a thick red mark in my book at the place where I had jotted down Ribbentrop's refusal, as a sign that in this hour the die was cast for war.

That I was right in the supposition I formed as to why Hitler's proposals were handled in so peculiar a manner was later confirmed by Hitler himself in my presence.

"I needed an alibi," he said, "especially with the German people, to show them that I had done everything to maintain peace. That explains my generous offer about the settlement of the Danzig and Corridor questions."

* * *

Next day, August 31st, late in the afternoon, I was present at one of the briefest interviews I have ever known. The Polish Ambassador, Lipski, called on Ribbentrop, and handed him a short communication stating that the Polish Government had accepted the British suggestion of direct negotiations between Germany and Poland, and would forthwith send the German Government a reply to its proposals.

"Have you authority to negotiate with us now on the German proposals?" asked Ribbentrop.

"No," answered the Polish Ambassador.

"Well then there is no point in our continuing this conversation," said Ribbentrop, and the interview was at an end.

Just before this Attolico had seen Ribbentrop to offer once again Mussolini's services as a mediator. Apparently our Foreign Minister too lacked authority to negotiate, for he said that he must ask Hitler. Attolico returned in half an hour for the reply; it was in the negative. Ribbentrop said that the next move must come from France and England; Germany's demands had been communicated to them.

Chancellery activity was again at high pressure. I was waiting about there, ready for further jobs, when I heard on the evening of August 31st that Hitler had finally given the order for the invasion of Poland, and that troops were to cross the frontier at 5.45 a.m. next day.

"By order of the Führer and Supreme Commander, the Wehrmacht has taken over the active protection of the Reich. In accordance with its instructions to check Polish aggression, troops of the German Army have counter-attacked early this morning across all the German-Polish frontiers. Simultaneously, squadrons of the Air Force have taken off against military objectives in Poland. The Navy has taken over the protection of the Baltic Sea"—so ran the first military communiqué of the Second World War, issued on September 1st, 1939.

"Last night Polish regular soldiers fired for the first time on our own territory," Hitler's hoarse and excited voice from the Reichstag rang from the loudspeaker on the morning of September 1st. "Once again I have donned the tunic which was to me the holiest and most beloved of garments," I heard him continue. "I shall take it off only after victory—or I shall not live to see the end."

That evening the British and French Ambassadors requested an immediate and joint interview with the Foreign Minister. Ribbentrop refused to see them together, and made an appointment for 9.30 for the British Ambassador, and 10 p.m. for the French Ambassador.

"Through its action the German Government has brought about a situation in which the Governments of the United Kingdom and of France must proceed to fulfil their obligations to support Poland. Unless therefore His Majesty's Government receives from the German Government satisfactory assurances that the German Government has ceased all aggressive action, and that it is prepared to withdraw its troops from Polish territory, His Majesty's Government will without delay carry out its obligations to Poland," I translated for Ribbentrop from the English Note Henderson had brought with him. Ribbentrop behaved as though he understood no English. He remained perfectly calm. Once again he was apparently not authorised to give any reply, and he confined himself to saying that he would transmit the communication to Hitler.

Directly afterwards Coulondre handed in an almost identical Note in French. This too I translated, for Ribbentrop was suddenly unable to understand French either. As had the British Ambassador, Coulondre asked for an immediate reply, to which Ribbentrop could only answer that he would submit the matter to Hitler.

The next day, September 2nd, the British and French wireless reported "General mobilisation ordered in England," and "Mobilisation in France."

On the morning of that day, Attolico hastened to the Foreign Office. "Mussolini has suggested to both the British and the French that he requests Germany and Poland to conclude an immediate armistice," he said breathlessly. Mussolini's proposal was that the fronts should be stabilised on the present positions and that an international conference should then meet to consider German-Polish questions and other frontier revision demands.

Half an hour later he was received by Ribbentrop, who put the single question: "Were the Notes which England and France handed in yesterday ultimata or were they not? If they were, the question of considering the Italian proposal is out of the question."

I can still see Attolico, no longer in his first youth, running out of Ribbentrop's room and down the steps to consult Henderson and Coulondre.

In my opinion the Notes in question had been ultimata, and I did not believe that my "school class" would meet again as the result of Mussolini's eleventh-hour intervention. To my surprise, however, only half an hour after he had left, Attolico came running back, as breathless as when he had left. "No, the Notes were not ultimata, but warnings."

Evidently the Western Powers also trafficked in ultimata which were not ultimata, as had Hitler the previous year, and again only a few days since.

In the afternoon Attolico came to see Ribbentrop once again, and I became more hopeful.

I have never been able to find out exactly how Hitler reacted to the Italian proposal. And, towards evening, we learnt that the British Government was insisting upon the evacuation of the Polish territory occupied by German troops. At 8 o'clock in the evening I was summoned to the Chancellery, where a crushed Attolico was informing Hitler that the British Government would not accept Mussolini's proposal unless Polish territory was evacuated. He added that the French Government had apparently hesitated for a long time whether or not to accept the Italian proposal, but finally adopted the British attitude.

* *
*

It was after midnight when the British Embassy telephoned to say that Henderson had received instructions from London to transmit a communication from his Government at 9 a.m., and that he asked to be received by Ribbentrop at the Foreign

Office at that time. It was clear that this communication could contain nothing agreeable, and that it might possibly be a real ultimatum. Ribbentrop in consequence showed not the slightest inclination to receive the British Ambassador personally next morning. I happened to be standing near him.

"Really, you could receive the Ambassador in my place," he said to me. "Just ask the English whether that will suit them, and say that the Foreign Minister is not available at 9 o'clock." The English agreed, and therefore I was instructed to receive Henderson next morning—that is, in five hours time, it being now 4 o'clock in the morning.

On Sunday, September 3rd, 1939, after the pressure of work over the last few days, I overslept, and had to take a taxi to the Foreign Office. I could just see Henderson entering the building as I drove across the Wilhelmsplatz. I used a side entrance and stood in Ribbentrop's office ready to receive Henderson punctually at 9 o'clock. Henderson was announced as the hour struck. He came in looking very serious, shook hands, but declined my invitation to be seated, remaining solemnly standing in the middle of the room.

"I regret that on the instructions of my Government I have to hand you an ultimatum for the German Government," he said with deep emotion, and then, both of us still standing up, he read out the British ultimatum. "More than twenty-four hours have elapsed since an immediate reply was requested to the warning of September 1st, and since then the attacks on Poland have been intensified. If His Majesty's Government has not received satisfactory assurances of the cessation of all aggressive action against Poland, and the withdrawal of German troops from that country, by 11 o'clock British Summer Time, from that time a state of war will exist between Great Britain and Germany."

When he had finished reading, Henderson handed me the ultimatum and bade me goodbye, saying : "I am sincerely sorry that I must hand such a document to you in particular, as you have always been most anxious to help."

I too expressed my regret, and added a few heartfelt words. I always had the highest regard for the British Ambassador.

I then took the ultimatum to the Chancellery, where everyone was anxiously awaiting me. Most of the members of the Cabinet and the leading men of the Party were collected in the room next to Hitler's office. There was something of a crush and I had difficulty in getting through to Hitler.

"What's the news?" anxious voices asked. I could only answer : "Classroom dismissed."

When I entered the next room Hitler was sitting at his desk and Ribbentrop stood by the window. Both looked up expectantly as I came in. I stopped at some distance from Hitler's desk, and then slowly translated the British Government's ultimatum. When I finished, there was complete silence.

Hitler sat immobile, gazing before him. He was not at a loss, as was afterwards stated, nor did he rage as others allege. He sat completely silent and unmoving.

After an interval which seemed an age, he turned to Ribbentrop, who had remained standing by the window. "What now?" asked Hitler with a savage look, as though implying that his Foreign Minister had misled him about England's probable reaction.

Ribbentrop answered quietly: "I assume that the French will hand in a similar ultimatum within the hour."

As my duty was now performed, I withdrew. To those in the anteroom pressing round me I said: "The English have just handed us an ultimatum. In two hours a state of war will exist between England and Germany." In the anteroom, too, this news was followed by complete silence.

Göring turned to me and said: "If we lose this war, then God have mercy on us!"

Gœbbels stood in a corner, downcast and self-absorbed. Everywhere in the room I saw looks of grave concern, even amongst the lesser Party people.

Coulondre handed Ribbentrop an identical ultimatum soon afterwards, which was to expire at 5 o'clock in the afternoon.

It was by an ironical stroke of fate that when I left a blacked-out Berlin that evening in the Foreign Office special train for the East, it was from the same platform of the same station as when I had left my native city in 1917 as a soldier.

CHAPTER VI

(1940)

As I travelled towards my secret destination, the Eastern G.H.Q., on the night of September 3rd, 1939, it seemed to me that my function as an interpreter had come to an end. The language of weapons which now must govern intercourse between the peoples of the world needed no translation. But in this I proved to be mistaken.

The H.Q. turned out to be in Pomerania, close to the Polish border. I was there not as an interpreter, but in the Minister's department of the Foreign Office. Some months previously I had been transferred from the Languages Service, in which I had worked since joining the Foreign Office in 1923. The move was made early in 1939, and was designed to ensure that I should be available exclusively to Ribbentrop as interpreter. Ribbentrop took jealous care that no other member of the Cabinet or Department should take part in foreign policy activities, and he therefore always declined to allow others to make use of my services, as the Foreign Office had done hitherto. "Unfortunately I cannot spare Dr. Schmidt from my Ministerial Office," was his invariable reply to such requests.

I much regretted my loss of freedom in being thus chained to the Ministerial Office, and also disliked having my work restricted to dealing with files. A wide range of confidential matters, it is true, came my way; but these were of no great interest to me. As an interpreter, I was familiar with all that was disclosed when the great men conferred, and I had become so indifferent to secrets that I no longer sought them out but expected rather that they would naturally find their way to my ears—as in fact they did. So my work lacked even this attraction.

If I was no conventional bureaucrat neither was the German Headquarters my idea of a conventional H.Q.. At the beginning

of the Second World War Supreme Headquarters consisted of
three trains: the so-called "Führer" train, the Wehrmacht
G.H.Q. train, and the "Heinrich" train which housed the
civilians who had to do with Headquarters. These included
Himmler (hence the "Heinrich"), Ribbentrop and Lammers.
"Heinrich" was a travelling exhibition of railway development.
It displayed the evolution of the railway coach, from ancient
decorated carriages "in which Charles the Great had travelled"
to Ribbentrop's newly built, streamlined saloon. It was made
up of almost every variety of model which had ever rolled on
German tracks. "That's a crazy kind of express," Hitler once
said when he saw the "Heinrich" steaming past, with its short,
high Grand Ducal saloon, the old wooden restaurant cars and
the super-modern Signals coaches which were in touch with
the whole world.

Had this arrangement gone on, conditions would have become
impossible, owing to the continual friction between Himmler,
Ribbentrop and Lammers. If the three had in later years
to travel together the train would doubtless have exploded
from the internal stresses, if the conflicting views of its occupants
about the political and geographical routes they wanted to
travel had not already wrenched it to pieces. In the early
period, however, they were all more or less going in the same
direction, and even used to pay visits in the evenings to each
other's saloons.

The little band from the Foreign Office which accompanied
Ribbentrop lived in a Mitropa sleeping car, and worked in
one of the wooden restaurant cars. The restaurant car accumulators were so weak with age that when the train stopped
anywhere, even for half an hour, the lights would slowly but
surely fade out. We then had to resort to candles stuck in
empty bottles, "as though we lived in the slums," said the less
warlike ones, or "as though we were dining at Savarin's," said
most of the "cowardly pacifists," as Ribbentrop designated
his diplomatic staff.

The Foreign Minister himself disturbed us but little. He sat
in his saloon-car office directing operations. This took the form
mostly of hour-long telephone conversations with the Foreign
Office in Berlin, in the course of which he became wildly

excited. His yells resounded far across the lonely railway siding on to which we were usually shunted.

Ribbentrop kept me on the run with jobs from morning till night, for I was then the only senior official from his office with him. I had to maintain routine communication with the Berlin office, and needed all my capabilities as an interpreter. Ministerial rebukes to the Under-Secretary in Berlin such as: "Tell that ox . . .," would have to be translated over the telephone into more suitable language. A rain of "cowards," "lazybones," 'dunderheads,' and " people who don't seem to know there's a war on" came from the Minister's coach, and had to be transformed before it reached its destination. It was all very exhausting.

One of my duties was to make a daily report on the military situation. Each morning I stumbled along the railway track to the "Führer" train a few hundred yards away, carrying a large general staff map rolled up under my arm. As I stood, rather helplessly, in front of the large-scale operational map, painfully drawing in the new front lines on my copy, one of my acquaintances on the General Staff usually took pity on me. He would draw in, with skilled accuracy, the red and blue arrows, racing forward or bent round (where attacks had been repulsed), all beautifully neat, with the necessary explanations. On my return to "Heinrich" I would feel my importance grow at each step over the sleepers, until I entered the Foreign Minister's office to give a situation report according to all the rules. I do not know what Ribbentrop got out of it—my colleagues seemed to be fairly impressed as I scooped in whole areas with the flat of my hand, shot out a finger to mark an advancing thrust or represented an encirclement with curved hand. For several days I was called nothing but Napoleon.

My martial glory was only short-lived, for a General Staff Colonel arrived to act as permanent liaison officer for our group. My activities were once again confined to telephone conversations with "idiots," or to brief written messages to the "idlers" and "halfwits" in Berlin.

For some time this Headquarters, on the side line of a small frontier station whose name escapes me, was an ideal target for air attacks. A heavy anti-aircraft battery had been sent up to protect us, and "Heinrich" had its own particular protection in the shape of two miniature anti-aircraft guns mounted on open goods trucks at either end of the train. Foreign Office staff were trained as gunners,—one night one of them fired his gun accidentally while loading.

In the latter part of September I got myself into hot water: the occasion was the entry of Soviet troops into Poland on September 18th, 1939, news of which we had been awaiting with some impatience.

One of Ribbentrop's main concerns was to see that the direction of foreign propaganda was in his, not Goebbels', hands. This led to constant friction between the two, and absorbed a large amount of Ribbentrop's time and nervous energy, even at the most critical junctures of the war.

On the night of September 17th Ribbentrop had kept us all busy till 2 a.m. At 5 a.m. I was instructed by telephone to inform him that Russian troops had entered Polish territory. I gave him the news at 8 o'clock in the morning. Ribbentrop was beside himself with rage that I had not woken him up at 5: "The German and Russian armies are rushing towards each other—there may be clashes—and all because you were too slack to waken me," he shouted. I tried in vain to calm him by pointing out that a demarcation line had already been agreed upon, and that the German and Russian military authorities were in direct communication. It did no good. Ribbentrop was shaving at the time in his sleeping compartment. He stood there with a lathered face, brandishing his razor, and clad only in his pants—a costume in which even a statesman of a great and victorious nation can look very funny. "You have meddled with the course of world history!" he thundered. "You have not enough experience for that!"

Shortly after I learned that the row had nothing at all to do with world history, but much with Ribbentrop's private war with Goebbels. It was Goebbels and not the Foreign Office Press Chief who had given out this item of news to the international Press in Berlin.

Headquarters were now transferred to the luxurious Casino Hotel at Zoppot, on the Baltic near Danzig. As we sat at breakfast on the hotel terrace, we could watch the bombardment of the Polish base at Hela, 18 miles away, by two old German cruisers. With their high funnels and superstructure, they made the whole scene look like some old picture of a naval engagement, especially when the Polish artillery retaliated and waterspouts shot up round the ships. Our hotel was beyond the range of the Polish guns, otherwise not much would have been left of that fine building. Punctually at noon the "naval engagement" was broken off, the ships withdrew and the whole performance was repeated at the same time next day.

On September 20th, 1939, Hitler made a big speech in the historic Artushof of the beautiful city of Danzig, where he was accorded an enthusiastic reception by the citizens of that town. "I stand for the first time," he said, "on ground which German settlers acquired five hundred years before the first white men settled in the present State of New York. For a further five hundred years this ground was, and remained, German. It will, let everybody be assured, always remain German."

This was the first and only occasion on which I heard a speech of Hitler's from start to finish without having something officially to do with it as an interpreter. I was particularly interested to see how events in which I had myself participated were put before the public. "I worked out the new plan," Hitler declared, referring to his proposals for the settlement of the Polish question, "it was communicated to the British Ambassador; it was read to him sentence by sentence, and, in addition, my Foreign Minister gave a detailed explanation." My mind went back to the stormy interview between Ribbentrop and Henderson, when the "explanation" had almost led to blows. Although I listened most carefully, I heard no indication of the fact that Henderson had been refused a copy of the proposals.

"Poland chose war, and now she has it . . . Eighteen days have passed. Never before in history could the saying be more exactly fulfilled: 'The Lord will break them in pieces, the horse and his rider, the chariot and his rider.' " So spoke the victorious Hitler describing the blitzkrieg on Poland. He was triumphant and uncompromising.

"Should the war last three years, the word 'capitulation' will not be heard—nor will it after four, five, six or seven years," I was horrified to hear him say. He continued in this boasting,

aggressive tone for some time.   I realised that there was certainly
no immediate prospect of my again interpreting between him
and Chamberlain, although this had been suggested, at Göring's
instigation, by a Swedish business man, in my presence, in a
conversation with Hitler which took place even after war had
broken out.

* *

On September 26th, 1939, we all returned to Berlin, though
Ribbentrop left next day by air for Moscow.

On October 1st Ciano appeared and had two long conversations with Hitler at the Chancellery and a further talk at the Foreign Office with Ribbentrop, now returned from his brief visit.

Nothing essentially new emerged at these lengthy conversations; the representative of "apostate" Italy was received
disdainfully by both Hitler and Ribbentrop—more especially
Ribbentrop.   Hitler was so elated by the success of his lightning
war in Poland that he was glad of a new audience, and went on
for hours recapitulating all the phases of the campaign and giving
detailed accounts of the prisoners and booty taken.   I could
not help being reminded by Ciano's expression of the refrain
of a popular song in Berlin in 1933: "We've heard enough of
that."   This was not the first or the last time that I was reminded of this song by the expression on the faces of Hitler's
and Ribbentrop's visitors.

Ribbentrop, too, was extremely pleased with himself—not
over the Polish campaign, but over his success in Moscow.
He raved enthusiastically about the Russians, as he had done
to me on his first visit to the Russian capital, until the Italians
"heard enough of that" too.   But, at a dinner he gave at his
Dahlem Villa, Ribbentrop really exceeded himself.   After
long and icy silences, during which Ciano addressed himself to
me, he remarked that he felt as much at home in the company
of the "strong-faced men" about Stalin as he did with old
Party members.   He had made this remark once before in my
presence—to a critical audience of long-standing Party members.
These men always had a contempt for Ribbentrop who only
joined the Party very shortly before it assumed power.

When I translated this remark Ciano gazed blankly at his

plate; no "ally" could have shown his displeasure more clearly. But Ribbentrop often displayed a considerable lack of diplomatic tact, and behaved on this occasion like a real *enfant terrible*. "The Russians at the Kremlin rather reminded me of the Duce's Guard of Honour at the Palazzo Venezia," he innocently added—and Ciano for the rest of the evening spoke only to me.

I had frequent opportunities of talking to Ciano on occasions other than this frigid dinner party. I came to know and have a regard for this man who, despite his frequently arrogant and somewhat uncivilised behaviour on official occasions, perceived the trend of events with great clarity, and did not allow himself to be blinded by Hitler's and Ribbentrop's fine words. He had come to Berlin on this occasion to improve Italo-German relations which had noticeably cooled off. His sceptical verdict on our opening successes in no way altered his opinion which he had expressed to me in August, that once England and France embarked upon war the end would not be swift nor the outcome by any means certain.

Soon after Ciano's departure the Languages Service entered on a period of great activity. Nominally, I was no longer attached to this important and busy service and was not its head. Now I was made responsible for everything to do with foreign languages, and was given absolute authority in this work. Hitler and Ribbentrop always saw to it that my requirements for any particular assignment were met. The Languages Service had been built up over a period of years, into a splendidly functioning, precision instrument, capable of handling the most difficult of translation jobs. Its existence was unknown to the public; within the Foreign Office it was looked at somewhat askance, owing to its mixed composition.

The Service was, even during the war, a miniature League of Nations. Its personnel included Englishmen, Frenchmen, Spaniards, Portuguese, Yugoslavs, Bulgarians and other nationals. In later years it had branches in Paris and other European cities. For a big assignment as many as 150 people would be employed. Secrecy was assured by a method similar to that employed by the Americans for the German currency reform of 1948, when the German experts were put to work under lock and key in an unknown place.

In October, 1939, the Languages Service occupied two floors of the Adlon Hotel hermetically sealed from the outside world. Here, as on a desert island, the "little League of Nations" could live and work days at a time; the telephone was disconnected, approach to the floors was guarded and outside the watchful eyes of the special police unobtrusively saw to it that the island remained an island.

It was here that the big speech which Hitler made at the Kroll Opera House on October 6th was translated into many languages. It was one of those speeches to the earlier part of which the refrain "we've heard enough of that" would have been very appropriate. This part of the speech consisted of a detailed account of the Polish campaign, of the story of the German attempts at a settlement, of attacks against England and the "Western Plutocracies," and had all the usual trappings of speeches of the kind—technical facts and statistical information alternating with lyrical declamation and furious tirades.

The end part of the speech, however, was of great interest to the Languages Service, from whose members one could often get an indication of the likely reaction of foreign countries.

These seemed to us the important points: "Clarification of the foreign policy of all European States;" "No further revision necessary except with regard to the return of the German Colonies . . . which is in no way immediate;" "Re-organisation of markets and a final settlement of currency problems;" "Reduction of armaments to a reasonable and economic level;" "A European statute which will give all peoples a sense of security and therefore ensure peace."

Reaction abroad, at least as far as the leading politicians were concerned, was nevertheless completely negative. Hitler's words, after the experiences of March and August 1939, were no longer taken at their face value.

"The position is now clear. England and France have rejected the Führer's proffered hand of friendship. They have shrown down the gauntlet and Germany has taken it up"—so taid an official statement emanating from Ribbentrop on October 21st, 1939, which we translated in the Languages Service. The Polish war was won, but the peace offensive had failed.

* * *

In a speech in the Italian Chamber in mid-December, Ciano avenged himself for the rough handling he had been accorded in Berlin. He said the so-called Pact of Steel, signed with so much ceremony in Berlin the previous year, provided that Germany and Italy should keep permanently in close touch in order to safeguard the peace of Europe for a period of from three to five years. In order to achieve this period of peace no political questions were to be raised which might provoke new crises. The Pact of Steel had been concluded in the same spirit as the Anti-Comintern Pact, and made no provision for the possibility of an agreement between Germany and the Soviet Union, about which Italy had first been informed as the German Foreign Minister was on the way to Moscow.

"The British Ambassador congratulated me on the speech," Ciano noted in his diary.

Ribbentrop was furious when he read this speech. And, in addition to these highly critical remarks about Hitler's action by Ciano, a letter from Mussolini was received in Berlin on January 4th, 1940. In this the Duce tried to suggest that Hitler should reach an understanding with the Western Powers, and hinted that he himself could act as mediator. He considered that a preliminary condition would have to be the continuance of an independent Polish State. He went on to point out that great powers fell not through attack from without but through lack of unity within. England and France would certainly never cause Germany to capitulate, but neither could Germany bring the democracies to their knees. To believe that was to suffer a delusion.

It was in this letter that I first noticed the tendency, later increasingly apparent in talks between Hitler and Mussolini, to want to come to terms with the West, and to turn against Soviet Russia. "I feel it my duty to add," wrote Mussolini, "that any further development of your relations with Moscow would have catastrophic results in Italy, where anti-Bolshevik feeling, particularly among the fascist masses, is unanimous and hard as granite." That this was a reference to Ribbentrop's slaverings over "the hard-faced men" in the Kremlin could not have been plainer. "The solution to your Lebensraum problem lies in Russia, not elsewhere."

I do not know what kind of reception Hitler gave to this critical letter from Mussolini. He cannot have been particularly pleased, for he took two months to reply to it. It was not until the beginning of March that the German Foreign Minister carried Hitler's answer to Rome. I accompanied Ribbentrop on this visit.

* * *

Early in March, before we left for Rome, there took place the strange interlude of the visit to Germany of Roosevelt's emissary Sumner Welles. His European tour which, apart from Berlin, included London, Paris and Rome, gave rise to all kinds of sensational rumours throughout Europe.

In Germany people felt a stirring of hope, although the Press hardly mentioned Sumner Welles's presence in Berlin. Hitler was well aware of the German people's craving for peace and had only very reluctantly agreed to receive Roosevelt's envoy. Neither Hitler, Ribbentrop nor the Foreign Office knew of a reason for this unexpected visit.

Hitler, Göring and Ribbentrop, in the long talks which they had with Sumner Welles were all on the defensive. They sought, with all varying degrees of skill, to demonstrate Germany's strength, power and determination to fight. They anxiously avoided showing any sign of a readiness to compromise, which Hitler, with his inferiority complex, always feared would be regarded as a sign of weakness.

I found Summer Welles an exceptionally intelligent man, if not a very imaginative diplomat. He showed no cordiality in his conversations with the Germans. He began each conversation by defining his mission—saying that America was interested in the creation of lasting peace in Europe, and not in a temporary truce; the Government of the United States had sent him to ascertain what were the possibilities of such a peace. He could, however, make no proposals, nor could he undertake any obligations on behalf of the United States. He reminded me of the present French Ambassador in London, René Massigli, who, on a similar mission during Franco-German negotiations in the 'twenties, opened the discussion with the words: "I am no more than a pencil with two ears."

Even if Hitler had been eager to start peace talks, the frigid, reserved attitude of the American envoy would scarcely have encouraged him. As the German attitude was in fact just the reverse, the only content of these conversations, which attracted so much interest, turned out to be the playing of a series of gramophone records. This analogy applied more especially to the German speakers, who all, Hitler, Ribbentrop, Göring and Hess, made almost identical speeches. As an interpreter, I was in a position to notice this, and it certainly lightened my work. There were, of course, differences in tone and minor detail.

It was the "diplomat" among these leading National Socialists who behaved most undiplomatically. "The most astonishing experience of my whole mission," Sumner Welles said, was his meeting with Ribbentrop, who received him "without even the trace of a smile and without a word of greeting," and who once again suddenly lost his ability to understand a word of English. In my opinion Göring, as on other occasions, was the most skilful and the most natural.

It would be pointless to relate the details of these conversations between the "pencil with ears" and the "gramophone records." One can only say that they bore no relation to the hopes of peace they aroused in Germany—and that hope was aroused I realised from the repeated, anxious questioning of my friends and acquaintances.

Sumner Welles was a good deal more friendly in personal conversation. On the long drive to see Göring at Karinhall, he told me much that was interesting about his experiences in South America. "I often had to use interpreters at conferences there," he said, "so I am in a position to know what a good interpreter you are." Sumner Welles left Germany on March 3rd, 1940.

Cordell Hull, at this time United States Secretary of State, makes the following interesting remarks in his Memoirs: "The President expressly stated to me that Welles had come to him

secretly on several occasions and pleaded to be sent abroad
on a special mission." Cordell Hull was opposed to this, as it
would be bound to arouse false hopes, but against his express
advice the journey was undertaken.

As I have already said, a few days after this American visit
I went with Ribbentrop and a large delegation to Rome to
deliver Hitler's reply to Mussolini's critical letter received in
January. Both the contents of the reply and what Ribbentrop
said personally to Mussolini showed that Germany was
determined to settle her problems by war and emphasised the
German view that Italy's place was at Germany's side.
Ribbentrop also dropped a hint of forthcoming military
operations against the Western Powers. "In a few months,"
he said, "the French army will be annihilated and those few
English who remain on the continent will be there as prisoners
of war." To Ribbentrop's highly coloured descriptions of
German strength and his urgings of the necessity of war Mussolini
listened at first with some reserve. Then, however, to my
astonishment, he came out with the remark that he too was of
the opinion that Fascism must fight side by side with National
Socialism.

In a second conversation, on the following day, Mussolini
had quite suddenly turned completely pro-war. He was
ready to plunge into the conflict by Germany's side, I
heard him say, only he must decide for himself when would
be the appropriate moment. Ribbentrop was obviously
reassured; for he had come to Rome very doubtful as to the
sentiments of the "disloyal" Axis partner. He felt the right
moment had come to put forward the suggestion of a meeting
between Hitler and Mussolini at the Brenner, which Hitler
had authorised him to make. Mussolini accepted with
enthusiasm.

The great event of this Rome visit, as far as I and most of
our delegation was concerned, was our audience with the Pope
which took place the following day. Mussolini was particularly
pleased about this—in his conversations with Hitler and

Ribbentrop he had frequently urged Germany to establish good relations with the Catholic Church, often citing his own success in the matter.

Three Papal cars took us, including Ribbentrop, to the Vatican City.   A Swiss guard, with ancient helmets and halberds, formed a cortege within the Pope's palace, and the whole audience took place with the solemn ceremony reserved for great occasions at the Vatican.   Pope Pius XII, better known to us as the Nuncio Pacelli, had represented the Holy See in Berlin in the '20s.   He had a long conversation with Ribbentrop in German, and then addressed some friendly words to the delegation, speaking very warmly of his time in Berlin.   He then dismissed us, without, it is true, giving the apostolic blessing, but with convincing good wishes for ourselves and our country. None of the statesmen whose acquaintance I have made during my long career has in so short a time, and through his appearance and bearing alone, made so deep an impression upon me as Pope Pius XII.   His tall, slim form with its narrow spiritual face as he stood before us in his Papal robes gave me the impression of a being who already in part no longer belonged to this world.

What Ribbentrop discussed when he was alone with the Pope, I do not know.   The Foreign Minister in any case appeared to have been quite impressed, and seemed not dissatisfied with the interview.   He had, on the other hand, got very annoyed with Cardinal Maglione, whom he had gone to see after the Papal audience.   "If he had continued to talk to me as he did," Ribbentrop told us, "I should have got up and walked out. I had already reached for my hat."

We were back in Berlin on March 13th, but a few days later we travelled south once again for the Brenner meeting of March 18th, 1940.   This was the first of a series of such rendezvous which took place periodically during the war. It was the fourth time Hitler and Mussolini had met for man-to-man talks.

***

The frontier station at Brenner, 4,500 feet above sea level, and within 300 yards of the then German frontier, is well known

to all German travellers to Italy. Snow was still lying deeply
when Hitler's special train drew in. Mussolini's train was
already there, and the Duce and Ciano met Hitler and Ribbentrop and escorted them to Mussolini's coach, where discussions
immediately began.

These Brenner conferences attracted much outside attention,
as they often appeared to herald some new development. All
traffic over the Brenner Pass had to come to a standstill, whether
it was a question of international expresses or urgently-needed
coal. The two dictators held up the whole traffic. These
conferences could never be described as discussions in the
proper sense of the word; "Hitler's Brenner Monologues" would
be a more appropriate term, for the Führer always spoke eighty
or ninety per cent of the time, and Mussolini was only able to
get a few words in at the end. The personal relationship
between the two appeared to be friendly enough, and continued
to be so right up to the last meeting before the fall of Mussolini
on July 20th, 1943. But they did not meet on equal terms;
already by 1940 Hitler had taken over the leadership and
forced Mussolini into the role of junior partner.

On this occasion a self-important Hitler gave the attentive
and admiring Italian a detailed description of his successful
Polish campaign and spoke of his preparations for the great
struggle with the West. Numbers and figures piled up. Hitler
had an amazing ability to carry in his head troop strengths,
casualty figures and the state of reserves, as well as technical
details about guns, tanks and infantry weapons. He seemed
less interested in the Air Force and the Navy. In any case,
he was able to smother Mussolini with facts and figures to such
an extent that the Duce goggled in wonder like a child with a
new toy.

I was particularly struck by the fact that Hitler avoided
giving Mussolini any precise information about his forthcoming
military plans. I knew that all preparations had been made for
an offensive in the West, the date for which had several times
been set, but always postponed. I also knew of the planned
attack on Norway and Denmark, which in fact occurred on
April 9th, that is three weeks later. But Mussolini was told
nothing of all this. Hitler had no confidence in the Italians

—indeed, he had worked out a theory that Italy was to blame for the outbreak of the Second World War. I heard Hitler say more than once: "The House of Savoy told the British Royal Family that Italy would not enter the war. As a result the British thought that they could without undue risk conclude the alliance with Poland which led to the war."

Mussolini used the few minutes left to him, to my surprise and, as I learned later, to the consternation of his associates, emphatically to reassert his intention of coming into the war.

Ciano's diary entry for March 19th, the day after this meeting, says: "He (Mussolini) resented the fact that Hitler did all the talking, he had in mind to tell him many things, and instead he had to keep quiet most of the time, a thing which, as dictator, or rather the dean of dictators, he's not in the habit of doing."

What caused Mussolini to change his mind about entering the war is not clear. As Ciano once said, and I had seen for myself, he undoubtedly allowed himself to be "fascinated" by Hitler's spate of words at the Brenner meeting. A contributory cause was that the Allies, with a clumsiness which seems incomprehensible, had a short time before cut off coal supplies to Italy by sea from Holland. In doing this they not only wounded Mussolini's pride, but put Hitler in the position o being able to allow these coal deliveries to be made overland through Germany.

Some three hours later the special trains drew out of the little station, and normal traffic could be resumed.

During the return journey I dictated my report on the conversation. Ciano, on Mussolini's instructions, had urgently asked me to let him have a copy, just as the train left. As had happened with Chamberlain at Berchtesgaden, so now there were difficulties about Mussolini seeing my report. Hitler was very much opposed to handing it over to the Italians. "One never knows," he said to me, "who may read this document on the Italian side, and what Allied diplomats may be told." For the next few days Mussolini kept asking the German Ambassador in Rome for my report, and in the end Hitler agreed to send it. But, as happened on many similar occasions, Hitler personally drafted an abbreviated version of the report.

In these cases, Hitler never interfered with statements made
to him. With regard to his own statements, he made no
alterations but only deletions. What remained contained no
inaccuracies but was nevertheless often incomplete at many
essential points. Thus often two versions of a report existed,
both of which bore my signature—the one for home, the other
for foreign consumption—and in most cases even I could only
distinguish between them by comparing them with the original
documents. Historians will later have to take into account
whether the document they are handling is the abbreviated
version prepared for Hitler's opposite number, the fair copy
corrected by Ribbentrop for the German archives, or the original
I dictated from my shorthand note as interpreter. When my
reports were not wanted by those with whom Hitler conferred,
he generally took no further interest in them, though Ribbentrop
usually went through them carefully.

The Italians noticed that my report on the Brenner meeting
had been abbreviated by Hitler. "Mackensen brings the
Brenner report from Berlin," Ciano notes in his diary on April
1st, 1940. "It is not in the verbatim style of Schmidt's other
reports; there has been a fairly considerable abbreviation."

Three weeks after the Brenner meeting Ribbentrop instructed
me to re-intern the Languages Service in the Adlon Hotel.
On the night of April 8th we translated the German
Memorandum to Norway and Denmark which preceded the
occupation of those countries. "The Government of the
Reich possesses irrefutable evidence that England and France
intend the surprise occupation of certain territories of the
northern States in the immediate future..."

As I translated with bitter feelings this document regarding
Germany's impending assault on the neutrality of the
Scandinavian countries, I looked on the statement about
British and French intentions as a mere pretext. What I did
not then know is recorded in Mr. Churchill's Memoirs: "On
April 3rd the British Cabinet implemented the resolve of the
Supreme War Council, and the Admiralty was authorised to

mine the Norwegian 'Leads' on April 8th. . . . As our mining of Norwegian waters might provoke a German retort, it was also agreed that a British brigade and a French contingent should be sent to Narvik to clear the port and advance to the Swedish frontier. Other forces should be despatched to Stavanger, Bergen and Trondheim, in order to deny these bases to the enemy."

We made a translation of the German Memorandum for Mussolini too; a short letter from Hitler accompanied it. This was the first information he gave his dictator colleague about the venture.

***

On the afternoon of May 9th, I was unexpectedly summoned to Ribbentrop together with the head of our Press and Radio section. "The attack against the West on the whole front from Switzerland to the North Sea starts early tomorrow," Ribbentrop told us. I was to pack up the Languages Service once again for the translation of a new Government Memorandum, and for Ribbentrop's statements to the Press. Ribbentrop went on to say: "If news of this offensive leaks out, the Führer will have you shot. I shall not be able to save you."

This time the Languages Service did not gather at the Adlon which was regarded as not safe enough, but in the staterooms of the former Palace of the President of the Reich. Ribbentrop had spent millions on modernising the Palace, which was now his official residence. He himself instructed me to collect the individual groups of the Languages Service in certain rooms of the Foreign Office as unobtrusively as possible, and then to conduct them personally through twisting passages and by the backstairs into his Palace in such a way that no one would know precisely where he actually was—"lest anyone should throw a note to an accomplice in the street," added the Foreign Minister, suddenly transformed into a master sleuth.

All this was duly done, and that night the staterooms of the Foreign Minister's Palace, with their costly candelabras, genuine gilding, luxurious furniture, paintings, Gobelin tapestries, and deep pile carpets, were transformed into busy offices.

The various language groups worked in separate corners; one could hear, above the rattle of typewriters, sentences of the Memorandum to Holland and Belgium being declaimed in English, French, Italian and Spanish: "In this battle for survival, forced upon the German people by England and France, the Government of the Reich declines to remain inactive and permit the war to be carried through Belgium and Holland into German territory. Accordingly it has now ordered German troops to safeguard the neutrality of those countries with all the military resources of the Reich." Thus ran Hitler's version of how to protect neutrality.

In the middle of the night there was great excitement when Ribbentrop was told that the Dutch military attaché had transmitted the news of the forthcoming invasion to his Government. "Has someone in the Languages Service made contact with the outside world?" Ribbentrop asked me nervously. "Go quickly through all the rooms and see if all the translators are still there." While I was making my count he sent his police adjutant on the same mission. "You'd better count too," he had told him. "Schmidt knows languages, but I don't know whether he can count accurately." No one was missing.

At dawn Ribbentrop lost a major battle in his private war. Gœbbels broadcast the proclamation which the Foreign Minister had intended to announce himself. "My whole broadcasting section is dismissed without notice for inefficiency!" screamed Ribbentrop, pale with anger, while through the loudspeaker in the background the mellifluous tones of his arch-enemy could be heard reading out the fateful Memorandum.

To complete the picture of utter confusion which our conduct of foreign affairs would have presented to an impartial observer, Ribbentrop handed the already broadcast Memorandum to the unfortunate Belgian Ambassador and the Dutch Minister, making a wordy statement as he did so. He also made a grotesque statement to the Press in which he said that we had anticipated a "new act of aggression and desperation whereby the present Governments in France and England seek to save the threatened existence of their Cabinets."

In the following weeks events succeeded one another at lightning speed. Within a few weeks Holland was occupied, the Belgian Army under King Leopold had capitulated, the British had succeeded in escaping at Dunkirk, and the French had been swept back by the German flood. Brussels and Paris were occupied undamaged, their Governments having sensibly declared them open cities.

Ribbentrop set up his "field headquarters" in the well known Château d'Ardenne Hotel, near Dinant. It was sad to see the luxurious furnishings of the famous hotel gradually buried under litter, and sad, too, to live in grand suites without light, water or any service.

On June 10th Ciano handed François-Poncet the Italian declaration of war—for Mussolini had hastened to come to his partner's aid. "You can probably guess," Ciano said to the French Ambassador, "why I have sent for you." "I have never considered myself particularly intelligent," replied François-Poncet who, even in this grave hour, did not lose his sarcasm, "but I have just enough understanding to grasp that you now want to hand me a declaration of war." This story went the rounds with us after Italian colleagues had passed it on with unconcealed joy at François-Poncet's ready answer.

The Spanish Foreign Office informed us on June 17th that the French Government at Bordeaux had asked the Spanish Ambassador to transmit to the German Government a request for an armistice.

That afternoon we flew with Hitler and Ribbentrop to Munich, where there was a short discussion between Hitler and Mussolini next day in the Führerbuilding—in the same room in which the conference with Chamberlain and Daladier had taken place in 1938. Hitler was surprisingly conciliatory; he was in favour of not subjecting France to oppressive armistice conditions. Mussolini wanted to demand the handing over of the French Fleet, but Hitler was emphatically against it. "If we make that demand," he said, "the whole French Fleet will go over to the British." Hitler also rejected Mussolini's suggestion of joint armistice negotiations. "I would not think," he said afterwards to Ribbentrop, "of burdening our negotiations with Franco-Italian animosity."

I noted with some surprise that Hitler's attitude to England seemed to have changed. He suddenly wondered whether it really would be a good thing to destroy the British Empire. "It is, after all, a force for order in the world," he said to the rather nonplussed Mussolini. Even his fanatical rage against the Jews seemed to have abated. "One could found a State of Israel in Madagascar," he observed to Mussolini when they were discussing the future of the French colonial empire.

* *
*

Directly the Munich talks were over we flew back to the Franco-Belgian frontier. On June 20th I was summoned to Hitler's headquarters and given the text of the armistice conditions; a French version had to be ready to hand to a French delegation at Compiègne next day. The small Italian language group was working in the vicinity of Hitler's headquarters, as they had to be available for the translation of letters to Mussolini, and I had arranged some time before that one of them should also be a good translator into French; fortunately, too, I had arranged for another translator to be flown out from Berlin. With this miniature Languages Service I worked through the night of June 20th in the little French village church. It was profoundly strange to be translating the conditions to be imposed on France in the tiny candle-lit church; below the draped altar the low voices of the translators mingled with the sound of the typewriters. What a contrast this was to the brightly lighted rooms of Ribbentrop's Palace where, not so long ago, among a babel of many languages and the monotonous run of duplicators, the documents were translated for a war whose last act was now being prepared in this quiet church.

"The French Government orders the cessation of hostilities against the German Reich in France, in French possessions, colonies, protectorates and mandated territories, and at sea. It decrees the immediate laying down of their arms by those French units now surrounded by German forces." So ran Point I of this historic document. "French territory to the north and west of the line shown on the attached map will be occupied by German troops." The French for such phrases as "demobilisation and disarmament," "transport material and transport routes," "prohibition of radio transmission," "resettlement of the population" echoed in the church.

"The German Government solemnly declares to the French Government that it does not intend to make use of the French Fleet during the war. . . .   It further solemnly and emphatically declares that it does not intend to make any demands on the French Fleet on the conclusion of peace."   This was Hitler's decision which Mussolini had contested at Munich.

But we also had to translate some ominous conditions: "The French Government undertakes to hand over on demand all Germans in France named by the German Government"—I immediately thought of my former colleague, Jacob, whose voice, after he had emigrated to France, I used to hear reading the news on Strasbourg wireless.   I hoped he had got out of France in time—and so he had, for I later heard the voice I knew so well on the Boston short-wave German programme.

"Members of the French armed forces who are in German captivity will remain prisoners of war until the conclusion of peace."   All the misery of long captivity which I so well remembered from the period after the First World War came back to me as I translated this condition.

From time to time Keitel, and occasionally Hitler himself, came to see us in the church in order to make sure that the work would be finished in time, or to make last-minute alterations in the German text.   Somewhere nearby must have been the conference room where, as we translated them, the armistice conditions were subjected to a final scrutiny.   It was not until after midnight that the last sheet was sent over to us, and by dawn the task was completed, and a fair copy for the French had been made.

I hurriedly drove back to the Château d'Ardenne in order to get a little rest after the strenuous night's work, for I was on duty at the armistice negotiations which were to start the same day —June 21st, 1940.   After two hours sleep I was called by an orderly.   I was to drive at once with Ribbentrop to Compiègne, as fog made flying impossible.   I hustled into my uniform like a fireman going to a fire and rushed out of the house to the car in which the impatient Foreign Minister was already waiting for me.

"Drive as fast as you can," said Ribbentrop to the chauffeur. "The interpreter musn't be late for armistice negotiations!"

We sped along "regardless" at more than 75 miles an hour, over the fortunately excellent motor roads of Northern France, through the battlefields of the First World War and the villages and towns on which the Second World War had now laid its destructive hand in a tragic repetition of that event. For the first time since 1918 I saw once more the outward manifestations of war. It was a depressing sight; the clock seemed to have been put back, and the hopes I had cherished in the 'twenties in my work for Stresemann, Briand and Austen Chamberlain —hopes to which I had still clung at Munich in 1938, now seemed finally dissipated. Nevertheless, hope stirred again on this journey through areas devastated by the new war. Was I not, I reflected, on my way to armistice negotiations? That afternoon the shedding of blood would come to an end—between France and Germany at least. Perhaps it was the beginning of a better peace, I thought.

At two o'clock, as we were slightly ahead of our time-table, we stopped on a little hill near Compiègne to eat a lunch consisting of a sandwich and a bottle of mineral water. Thus fortified, we drove into the historic forest where in bright sunshine in the well-known clearing stood the famous wooden restaurant car in which the Armistice with Germany had been signed on November 11th, 1918. I had often seen this car in Paris, where it was on show in the 'twenties, and I naturally never dreamt then that one day I should sit in it among the conquerors facing a French delegation.

Shortly after three o'clock in the afternoon I went alone to the restaurant car, which was empty. In the middle, where travellers had dined before the First World War, a long, plain table had been set up with five or six chairs on either side for the two delegations. My place was at the head of the table, so that I could see and hear both the French and the Germans.

Soon afterwards Hitler arrived with Göring, Raeder, Brauchitsch, Keitel, Ribbentrop and Hess, and sat on my right; a few minutes later there appeared the French General Huntziger, Ambassador Noël, Vice-Admiral Leluc and General of the Air Force Bergeret. Hitler and his associates stood up without a word; both delegations made brief bows; then they sat down at the table and negotiations began.

Keitel read out the preamble to the armistice conditions. "After heroic resistance . . . France has been vanquished. Germany does not therefore intend that the Armistice conditions should cast any aspersions on so courageous an enemy." I translated to the French from the text we had prepared during the night. "The aim of the German demands is to prevent a resumption of hostilities, to give Germany security for the further conduct of the war against England which she has no choice but to continue, and also to create the conditions for a new peace which will repair the injustice inflicted by force on the German Reich."

When I had finished reading the French text Hitler and his companions rose. The French stood up too, and, after perfunctory bows on both sides, the Germans left the room. The first act of the Compiègne drama had lasted exactly twelve minutes. During this time the French and Germans had sat opposite each other with frigid faces like wax figures.

Of the Germans only Keitel and I remained in the coach. Then a few more German officers came in, and the second act opened. The actual armistice conditions were handed to the French by Keitel in both the French and the German texts. The French read them carefully, and asked for a short interval in which to consider them. Everybody left the coach. A small conference tent had been set up at the edge of the wood for the French; we Germans contented ourselves with a little clearing in the trees. After a time the French sent someone over to say that they were ready to continue negotiations. When we were all in the coach once more the French stated that they would have to transmit the conditions to the Government at Bordeaux before they could comment upon or sign them.

"Absolutely impossible!" said Keitel. "You must sign at once."

"In 1918 the German delegation was allowed to make contact with its Government in Berlin," Huntziger replied, "and we ask for the same facility."

A lively discussion amongst the Germans followed. Keitel asked the German officer sitting next him whether telephonic communication with Bordeaux was technically possible. The German officer did not know. The two countries were, after all, still at war and divided by a front of iron and steel. Eventually it was discovered that it would be possible to speak to Bordeaux on an improvised line, and Keitel then said he was prepared to allow the French to telephone. Negotiations continued for two hours. An orderly then reportedt hat the connection could now he made: a line had been laid from the wood to the coach, and a telephone apparatus set up in the former kitchen of the restaurant car.

"We'll have Bordeaux on the line in five minutes," a signals officer reported. The German delegation withdrew to allow the French to telephone to their Government from the kitchen undisturbed. I myself was instructed to listen in to the conversation from a signals coach in the wood.

A corporal had set himself up on the ground in front of this coach with a couple of accumulators, some dry batteries and a simple field telephone, as an improvised telephone exchange. He kept shouting something into the instrument. At first I did not understand what he was saying, but then it dawned on me. The soldier was talking French with a Berlin accent. "Ici Compiègne," I at last made out. "Ici Compiègne," he repeated at least twenty times, in the process making prodigious progress in the French language. Suddenly he started; the other end had answered. "Oui, mademoiselle, je vous donne la délégation Française," I heard the corporal say, intelligibly enough, though still with a very pronounced accent. Once again, there was the extraordinary contrast. Here, from the heart of a French forest, in the middle of a new war, someone was suddenly telephoning to a "mademoiselle" in Bordeaux as though it was the most natural thing in the world. It would be difficult for anyone to realise now, years afterwards, how unreal that scene in the forest of Compiègne seemed to me at the time.

I quickly came back to earth and put on my earphones. "Yes, General Weygand speaking," in the far distance but quite clearly I heard the French commander-in-chief say from Bordeaux.

"Huntziger here," I heard loud and clear from the restaurant-car kitchen, which I could see through the branches. "I am telephoning from the coach"—a pause—"from the coach you know." (Weygand had been present in 1918 at the armistice negotiations as A.D.C. to Foch.)

"Have you got the conditions?" Weygand asked somewhat impatiently from distant Bordeaux.

"Yes," answered Huntziger.

"What are they like?" Weygand quickly asked.

"Les conditions sont dures, mais il n'y a rien contre l'honneur," ("The conditions are hard but they contain nothing dishonourable") answered the head of the French armistice delegation.

During the next few hours there were several telephone conversations between Compiègne and Bordeaux; in the intervals between them discussions proceeded in the restaurant-car.

The negotiations went on until dusk; Keitel grew impatient, but there were further technical questions to be dealt with. Next morning the discussions were resumed at ten o'clock and lasted nearly the whole day. Keitel was getting more and more irritable. At about six o'clock, during an interval, I went to the French tent and issued an ultimatum from him. "If we cannot reach agreement within an hour," I read, "the negotiations will be broken off, and the delegation will be conducted back to the French lines."

Great excitement ensued among the French. There were further conversations with Bordeaux, again with Weygand, who was evidently attending a Cabinet meeting in the next room. Huntziger, no doubt in order to cover himself, had repeatedly asked for authorisation to sign: this the French Government now finally accorded him. At 18.50 on June 22nd, 1940, Keitel and Huntziger then signed the terms of the German-French armistice, in the presence of the other delegates. Some of the French had tears in their eyes.

The French then took their leave, and only Keitel, Huntziger, and myself remained in the historic coach. "I do not want to forgo the expression to you as a soldier of my sympathy for the grave moment you as a Frenchman have just passed through," Keitel said to Huntziger. "Your painful position will be alleviated by the knowledge that the French troops fought bravely—a fact I expressly desire to state to you." The German and the Frenchman stood silent: both had tears in their eyes.

"You, General," Keitel added, "have represented your country's interests with great dignity in these difficult negotiations." He shook hands with Huntziger.

I accompanied the French General out of the coach, and was the last German to bid farewell to him and his delegation. I had been deeply impressed by the attitude which the French had maintained throughout this most difficult situation.

I can still remember every detail of those memorable June days of 1940. The only reason I regret not having been present as interpreter at the surrender negotiations of 1945, in Rheims and in Berlin, is that I am thereby unable to compare the respective victors and vanquished on the two occasions.

* *

On July 6th, 1940, Hitler entered Berlin as a conquering hero. On the following day, a Sunday, he met Ciano at the Chancellery.

Hitler seemed to have abandoned the sober thoughts which had played a part in his conversations with Mussolini shortly before the Armistice, and which had their offect in the framing of the conditions of the Armistice itself. He was again the trumpeting, victory-conscious German dictator, ready for battle, as I had known him during the negotiations immediately preceding the outbreak of war, and especially in his conversations with Ciano in August of the previous year, when he had been utterly convinced that France and England would not fight.

A completely changed Ciano sat facing him at the Chancellery. The lightning victory over the French and British armies had obviously had its effect, and he seemed to have shed his earlier misgivings about the Western Powers. He now went to the opposite extreme, at any rate for the time being. Ciano behaved as though the war was already won. He almost fell over himself in making open or hinted demands on behalf of his country. He wanted to annex Nice, Corsica and Malta, make Tunis and the greater part of Algeria into an Italian Protectorate, and occupy strategic bases in Syria, Transjordan, Palestine and the Lebanon. In Egypt and the Sudan, Italy simply wanted to step into Britain's place, and Somaliland, Jibuti and

French Equatorial Africa were to become Italian territory. Ciano was not in the least shy about expressing such wishes. Hitler paid no attention to them at all but simply uttered a long victory monologue.

Ciano left to visit occupied France, and we met him again on July 10th in Munich, where Hitler and Ribbentrop received him together with the Hungarian Premier, Count Teleki, and the Hungarian Foreign Minister, Count Csaky. The conversation took place at the Führerbuilding, and dealt with disputes between Hungary and Rumania. These were settled a month later at Schloss Belvedere in Vienna in the so-called Second Vienna Arbitration Award.

* *

"The Führer is going to make a very magnanimous peace offer to England," Ribbentrop told me in Berlin some days later. He added: "When Lloyd George hears of it, he will probably want to fall on our necks." He had evidently discussed this offer in great detail with Hitler, and he seemed to be fully confident of its effect upon the British. "I would not be surprised," he said in conclusion, "if we are not all soon seated at a peace conference."

I recalled Hitler's words to Mussolini in June, and the way in which he had just recently ignored Italy's exaggerated demands, and I began to feel some hope that in this hour of victory he might after all prove himself one of those statesmen who have produced a lasting peace by their magnanimity.

"Make sure that the offer is translated into English as perfectly as possible," Ribbentrop enjoined me as he went away. I would certainly do my utmost if an end to blood-letting was the issue at stake. I had been informed that Germany's enemies often translated German statements very inaccurately and capriciously, and I decided to combat this by getting in first with my English version.

On July 19th, while Hitler addressed the Reichstag, I sat in a small studio of the Berlin broadcasting station with the English text of his speech before me. A colleague sat beside me, listening to Hitler's speech through earphones, and indicating with his pencil on my text exactly where Hitler had got to. I remained silent for the first two or three sentences, so that Hitler's words were first of all heard in German on the British and American wavelengths. Then I pressed a button which connected my microphone to the transmitter, and proceeded to read the English text. I was speaking more quickly than Hitler, who was often held up by the applause, etc., and as soon as my colleague's pencil showed me that my translation had overtaken the original, I disconnected my microphone and Hitler's voice could be heard for another two or three sentences; then I switched myself on again. In this way, from the moment that Hitler left the tribune in the Reichstag, the whole English-speaking world was in possession of the full and correct English text.

This new transmitting technique was a smash hit in America, where my English translation was carried by a large number of stations. Many newspapers marvelled at my achievement; the fact that they could hear Hitler making his speech in German led them to assume that the translation was impromptu. Others were puzzled as to how it was achieved technically. The London *Times* wrongly stated that the B.B.C. had already used this system for some time.

Gratified though I was at my technical success, I was profoundly disappointed in the content of the speech. It was interminably long, and enlarged upon the favourable course which events had taken for Germany—to such an extent that even many Germans, not to mention foreigners, said: "We've heard enough of that." I had looked in vain for Ribbentrop's magnanimous peace offer, which was to induce Lloyd George to "fall on our necks." It was contained in a single passage, high sounding but completely bereft of substance: "In this hour I feel I owe it to my conscience to make another appeal to reason in England. I believe I may do so because I do not speak up for reason as one who has been conquered and then pleads, but as a victor. I see no reason that makes the continuation of this struggle necessary." Nothing more. Not the slightest hint of any concrete suggestion. I had often noticed at negotiations that precision was not a strong point of Hitler's. Nevertheless it was incomprehensible to me that he should believe that such a meaningless, purely rhetorical, observation would have any effect upon the sober British.

I was then of the opinion that, between telling Ribbentrop about his peace offer and making the speech, Hitler must for some reason have changed his plan. As far as I could see, the only reason why he should was his grievance and annoyance at the adverse reaction of the British Press to the very first rumours of a peace offer. This, I presumed, was inspired by the British Government, and I assessed it as the sign of a certain amount of war weariness, much more evident among all the combatants in the second world war than it was in the first, which, in the event of a tempting offer from Hitler, might possibly lead in England to consequences which would endanger the prosecution of the war. Part of Churchill's letter to Roosevelt of June 14-15, quoted in the second volume of his war history, seems to hint at this:—

"A declaration that the United States will, if necessary, enter the war might save France. Failing that, in a few days French resistance may have crumpled and we shall be left alone.

"Although the present Government, and I personally, would never fail to send the Fleet across the Atlantic if resistance was beaten down here, a point may be reached in the struggle where the present Ministers no longer have control of affairs, and when very easy terms could be obtained for the British Isles by their becoming a vassal state of the Hitler empire. A pro-German Government would almost certainly be called into being to make peace, and might present to a shattered or a starving nation an almost irresistible case for entire submission to the Nazi will. The fate of the British Fleet, as I have already mentioned to you, would be decisive in the future of the United States, because if it were joined to the Fleets of Japan, France and Italy and the great resources of German industry, overwhelming sea-power would be in Hitler's hands. He might of course use it with a merciful moderation. On the other hand, he might not. This revolution in sea-power might happen very quickly, and certainly long before the United States would be able to prepare against it. If we go down, you may have a United States of Europe under the Nazi command far more numerous, far stronger, far better armed than the New World."

It was from sheer pique, then, that Hitler refrained from making the generous offer which might have weakened British resistance.   When, in the little studio, I read into the microphone sheet after sheet of the English text as it reached me from the Languages Service, I realised with growing concern that the peace offer so bombastically predicted by Ribbentrop was proving to be a provocative, vainglorious speech which would further strengthen the British will to fight.   I was later able to form a very good idea of the British reaction, when, some years afterwards, I observed a similar situation in my own country. When Roosevelt, at the Casablanca Conference in 1943, to the surprise of his own Foreign Minister, unexpectedly demanded unconditional surrender, he gave renewed vitality to the German will to resist, instead of undermining it by offering to negotiate.

During the following weeks two new subjects—South-East Europe and Spain—cropped up in the conversations which I interpreted at Berchtesgaden, Vienna and Rome.   Henceforward they were to play an important part in my work.

Relations between Hungary and Rumania became more and more strained each month, until finally Hitler, who wanted at all costs to avoid complications in South-East Europe, intervened.   He summoned Ciano and Ribbentrop to the Obersalzberg on August 28th and directed them to settle the dispute between the two countries by an arbitral award.

I was particularly interested in Hitler's reason for wishing to prevent a conflict between Hungary and Rumania.   "I must at all costs secure the supply of oil from Rumania for carrying on the war," he told Ciano.

"Bad weather alone has so far prevented us from proceeding vigorously against the British Isles," he remarked on this occasion.   "We need at least two weeks of good flying weather to put the British Fleet out of action and leave the way free for a landing."

On August 30th I again sat in the Golden Chamber, the little round room at Schloss Belvedere in Vienna where the arbitral award between Hungary and Rumania, as decided by

Ciano and Ribbentrop, was to be announced. As before, it was a matter of delineating a new boundary. The new frontier between Hungary and Rumania divided the ethnographically complex Rumanian Transylvania, half of this territory being restored to Hungary, which had possessed it all before the first world war. It was just as problematic an arrangement as the thickly pencilled boundary fixed a year before between Hungary and Czecho-Slovakia.

Eight men sat at the round table, listening attentively as I read the award. On my right were Ribbentrop, and next to him Ciano, and then the Minister Vitetti; on my left, the Rumanian Foreign Minister Manoilescu, and the Minister, Valer Pop; opposite me sat the Hungarian Prime Minister, Teleki, and his Foreign Minister, Count Csaky. When I spread out the map of Transylvania on the table, with the new boundary line marked on it, the Rumanian Foreign Minister fainted at the sight of it. The new boundary had claimed its first victim—it was not to be the last.

"With effect from today, Germany and Italy undertake to guarantee the integrity and inviolability of Rumanian territory," I read, when my neighbour, thanks to medical aid, had recovered. This was the guarantee to which Molotov was to react so angrily in Berlin some months later.

Next day Ciano and Ribbentrop went hunting.

The question of Spain was discussed three weeks later, on September 10th and 20th, by Mussolini and Ribbentrop at the Palazzo Venezia in Rome. The German Foreign Minister put forward the view that they could count with fair certainty upon Spain entering the war in a short time. He was indulging in exaggeration, just as in his statement that a landing in England was imminent and could easily be carried out. "A single division will suffice to bring about the collapse of the whole British defence system," he told Mussolini, who watched him with incredulous amusement. It was a typical Ribbentrop remark. I had to translate hundreds of the same sort and in time got the impression that his listeners no longer took him seriously.

On September 23rd we were back in Berlin, where the following morning the Spanish question appeared at close quarters in the shape of Serrano Suñer, Franco's brother-in-law. He was then Minister of the Interior, and became Foreign Minister a month later. It was perfectly clear from the conversation which took place with him, that Ribbentrop's remarks in Rome had been exaggerated. Germany naturally wished to bind Spain more closely to the Axis; I knew, too, that plans were in existence for taking Gibraltar, which could only be done if permission was granted for German troops to march through Spanish territory. Only oblique references were made to all this in the Berlin conversations, even when, on September 25th, Suñer was received by Hitler himself.

I can still clearly visualise one further remarkable scene in Ribbentrop's office. Hanging by the window, which overlooked the old park behind the Wilhelmstrasse, was a map of the French colonial empire in Africa. Suñer and Ribbentrop were standing in front of it. "Help yourself" was in effect the gist of Ribbentrop's high sounding words. And the Spaniard did help himself. He took the port of Oran; he wanted the whole of Morocco and large areas of the Sahara, and needed French West Africa to "round off" the Spanish West African colony Rio de Oro. Ribbentrop eagerly sold the goods which did not belong to him; apparently no price was too high for Spanish collaboration.

Incidentally it is of interest that Franco has recently stated that Churchill offered him French territory in North Africa during the war with the same object. Answering a question in the House of Commons by Mr. Stokes on June 22nd, 1949, Mr. Eden replied that he was in a position to state in the most categorical terms that no such assurances had been given.

In the conversation with Suñer Ribbentrop, for his part, confined himself to making certain economic requests with regard to Morocco, and asked for U boat bases in Rio de Oro and on the island of Fernando Po opposite the Cameroons. In response to Ribbentrop's magnanimity, however, the Spaniard was quite niggardly; about Morocco, Suñer looked thoughtful. Without in any way committing himself, he seemed to think that the U boat bases might perhaps be conceded in Rio de Oro, but he definitely declined the request with regard to Fernando Po "for historical reasons" and "on account of Spanish public opinion."

This brought the first chill to the warm friendship between Franco and Hitler. The real change came in October, in the sunny South, when the two dictators met to discuss matters on the Franco-Spanish frontier, and could not agree. We know from Ciano's diary entry of October 1st, 1940, that Suñer complained to him "drastically" of the tactlessness with which the Germans treated Spain. Hitler and Mussolini, for their part, referred to Suñer as a "crafty Jesuit." The warm friendship which has reputedly always existed between the Spanish and German peoples was not in evidence here.

* *

"Japan recognises and respects the leadership of Germany and Italy in the creation of a new order in Europe," ran Article I of the Three Power Pact between Germany, Italy and Japan which I read out on September 27th. The reception room of the new Chancellery had been dressed up as though for a musical comedy film signature of the treaty by the representatives of the three countries, Ribbentrop, Ciano and the Japanese Ambassador, Kurusu.

"Germany and Italy recognise and respect the leadership of Japan in the creation of a new order in greater Asia," ran Article II. Article III, meant as a broad hint to the United States, read: "They further undertake mutually to support one another with all political, economic and military means if any of the three contracting parties is attacked by a Power which is not at present involved in the European war or in the Sino-Japanese conflict."

"A military alliance between the three most powerful States on earth!" said Ribbentrop. Then the Foreign Ministers appended their signatures, the Japanese Ambassador using a brush to form elegant Japanese characters one below the other. Immediately above the signatures stood the words: "Done in triplicate original texts, in Berlin, on September 27th, 1940, in the XVIII year of the Fascist era— corresponding to the 27th day of the 9th month of the 15th year Syowa."

*_**

A week later, on October 4th, 1940, international traffic across the Brenner was again suspended for three hours. Hitler held forth in the Duce's saloon. His main theme was France, which he wanted somehow to mobilise against England. Spain was hardly mentioned, not so much because of the coolness caused by Suñer's visit, as because of tactical considerations of which I only became aware some days later. The battle against Britain in the Mediterranean also played a large part in this Brenner monologue, and I got the impression that the invasion of England itself was to be given up in favour of a Mediterranean offensive. Mussolini looked very interested. He was obviously pleased that Hitler should thus enlighten him as to his future plans, at any rate in broad outline. This did not happen often, and even on this occasion he found little opportunity to contribute to the conversation himself. At last Hitler's flow of words ceased, and the flow of international traffic was once again resumed.

*_**

"Drive quickly to the station; there'll be an air-raid warning directly," the Foreign Office exchange told me on the evening of October 26th. I was starting on a long journey, in the course of which I was to cover more than 4,000 miles in a few days. My first destination was Hendaye, on the Franco-Spanish frontier. From there I was to go to Florence, and then back again to Berlin. At that time British air attacks on Berlin were still pretty harmless. They did little damage, and caused only very few casualties; but they usually lasted all night. The English would send over only two or three planes at a time, at short intervals. In this way they succeeded in depriving four million persons of their night's rest.

The R.A.F. were overhead when I entered our special train

at the Lehrter station, but we stayed in the train, and awoke next morning in Hanover. The following night we stopped at a small station in Belgium near a tunnel in which the train was to shelter in case there was an air raid—a very well thought out scheme, which, however, by no means always functioned. I once had the experience during an air raid of being in a train whose engine was so weak that it could only just drag itself into the tunnel and left the rest of the train outside, while huge clouds of steam billowing from the tunnel drew attention to the target. The British, however, had flown on contemptuously, "regarding a gasometer as more important than the Reich Foreign Minister," as one of our junior members remarked.

We made a wide circuit round Paris, and reached Montoire, in central France, next evening. Meanwhile, Hitler had arrived in his special train, and he had a short conversation in his saloon with Laval, who was then Vice-Premier. It was the first time that I had worked for Laval since the conversations at the Berlin Chancellery in 1931. He greeted me very warmly, with obvious relief at seeing at least one familiar face; and during the conversation with Hitler called on me as witness to the fact that as early as 1931 he had favoured a policy of closer association with Germany. Nothing new of any significance emerged during this talk at Montoire, in which Ribbentrop also participated, and the atmosphere was fairly friendly. It dealt almost exclusively with arrangements for a meeting with Marshal Pétain, which took place at the same place two days later, on our return from Hendaye.

We travelled on toward the Spanish frontier that same night, our two special trains arriving at the little station the next afternoon. I had stopped here on a previous journey—in 1928, when I accompanied Stresemann to the League of Nations Assembly at Madrid. As at the Brenner conversations, the negotiations were to take place in Hitler's saloon. Franco's train, which was to arrive on the wider Spanish gauge at the next platform, was a full hour late, but as it was a lovely day no one minded; Hitler and Ribbentrop stood chatting on the platform.

I heard Hitler say to Ribbentrop: "We cannot at the moment

give the Spaniards any written promises about transfers of territory from the French colonial possessions. If they get hold of anything in writing on this ticklish question," he continued, "with these talkative Latins the French are sure to hear something about it sooner or later." He added the interesting reason: "I want to try, in talking to Pétain, to induce the French to start active hostilities against England, so I cannot now suggest to them such cessions of territory. Quite apart from that if such an agreement with the Spaniards became known, the French colonial empire would probably go over bodily to de Gaulle." These few sentences showed me, more clearly than any long memoranda could have done, the whole nature of the problem underlying the forthcoming meeting between the dictators, and they revealed one of the reasons why it was a fiasco.

The Spanish train appeared on the international bridge over the Bidassoa river, which forms the boundary, at about three o'clock in the afternoon. Military music, inspection of guards of honour—all the familiar ceremonial of a dictators' meeting took place, and immediately afterwards the fateful discussion began which was to end all sympathy between Hitler and Franco.

Short and stout, dark skinned, with lively black eyes, the Spanish dictator sat in Hitler's coach. In the pictures I had seen of him he had always looked much taller and slimmer. If he were wearing a white burnous, it occurred to me, he might be taken for an Arab, and as the discussion proceeded, his hesitant, tentative way of putting forward his arguments seemed to confirm this impression. It was at once clear to me that Franco, a prudent negotiator, was not to be nailed down.

Hitler began by giving a most glowing account of the German position. "England is already decisively beaten," he said, concluding that part of his exposé which dealt with German prospects of victory, "only she is not yet prepared to admit the fact." Then came the clue word—Gibraltar. If the English lost it, they could be excluded from the Mediterranean and from Africa. Hitler now played his trump. He proposed the immediate conclusion of a treaty, and asked Franco to come into the war in January 1941. Gibraltar would be taken on

January 10th by the same special units which, by new methods, had won the Eben Emael fort of Liége with such surprising speed. The German methods of attack, of which an important part was the exploitation of "dead ground" (ground that the traverse or elevation of the guns prevents them from firing on), had in the meantime been brought to such technical perfection that the operation was bound to succeed. As I had already heard, German units in southern France had an exact model of the fortress of Gibraltar and were in fact carrying out exercises for taking it by this method.

Hitler, there and then, offered Gibraltar to Spain and, somewhat more vaguely, colonial territories in Africa also.

At first Franco, sitting huddled up in his chair, said nothing at all. From his impenetrable expression I could not make out whether he was taken aback by the proposal or whether he was just quietly thinking out his reply. He then undertook evasive action similar to that of his Italian colleague at the outbreak of war. Spain was in sore straits for food. The country needed wheat—several hundred thousand tons immediately. Was Germany in a position to deliver this? he asked with what seemed to me a slyly watchful expression. Spain needed modern armaments. For operations against Gibraltar heavy artillery would be required; Franco mentioned a very large figure for the number of heavy guns which he wanted from Germany. Then too he must protect his long coastline against attacks by the British Navy. In addition, he was short of anti-aircraft guns. How was Spain to insure against the loss, which would have to be expected, of the Canary Islands? Apart from this, it was not consistent with Spanish national pride to accept Gibraltar, taken by foreign soldiers, as a present. The fortress could be taken only by Spaniards.

I was much interested in an observation Franco made in reply to Hitler's statement that Panzer units from the Gibraltar bridgehead could clear the British out of Africa. "To the edge of the great deserts, very possibly," said Franco, "but central Africa would be protected against major attacks by land by the desert belt, in the same way that an island is by the open sea. As an old African campaigner I am quite clear about that."

Hitler's high hopes, amounting almost to a certainty, of

being able to conquer Britain were also discouraged. Franco was of the opinion that England might possibly be conquered, but that then the British Government and Fleet would continue the war from Canada with American support.

As Franco made these remarks in a quiet, gentle voice, its monotonous sing-song reminiscent of the muezzin calling the faithful to prayer, Hitler became more and more restless. The conversation was obviously getting on his nerves. Once, he even got up, saying there was no point in continuing the discussion, but he immediately sat down again and renewed his attempt to win Franco over. Franco finally said that he was ready to conclude a treaty, but this was subject to so many reservations regarding the supply of food and armaments and the time of his active intervention in the war that the agreement amounted to nothing more than a façade.

The meeting was then adjourned. Ribbentrop and Suñer continued discussions in the Foreign Office train. The change in the German attitude, about which Hitler had spoken to Ribbentrop before Franco's arrival, did not escape the notice of the sharp-witted Suñer. "Spain will receive territory from French colonial possessions," was what the formula advanced during Suñer's visit to Berlin had amounted to. But "Spain will receive territories from French colonial possessions to the extent that France can be indemnified from British colonial possessions" was the formula offered by Ribbentrop at Hendaye as the utmost concession. The logical Spaniard rightly objected that Spain might then get nothing—that is, if it proved impossible to offer France compensation from British possessions.

The Spaniards were given a dinner that night in Hitler's great banqueting car, specially brought from Germany, which was superbly illuminated by indirect lighting. After dinner Hitler and Franco were to depart and leave their Foreign Ministers to work out a formula on which they could agree. After the meal, however, the two dictators plunged once more into discussion which delayed the departure of their trains for two hours, but brought them no nearer to a mutual understanding. Indeed, the feelings of both had completely changed.

Right up to the following morning Ribbentrop continued

bit by bit to dismantle what remained of German-Spanish friendship. He systematically plagued the increasingly recalcitrant Spanish Foreign Minister trying to high-pressure the Spaniards into formulae for agreement which they persistently rejected. Finally Ribbentrop sent the Spaniards back to San Sebastien as though they were schoolboys who had to write out lines. "The text must be here at eight o'clock tomorrow morning," said the stern schoolmaster. "I have to leave then, as we are meeting Marshal Pétain." But his pupils did not re-appear next morning. They sent their "imposition" instead through the Under-Secretary of State, Espinosa de los Monteros, a friendly, gentle man, one-time Ambassador in Berlin, who spoke German like a Viennese, having been educated in that city. The schoolmaster described the work as "unsatisfactory." Just before we left Hendaye another draft was concocted. This provided for Spain's entry into the war after mutual preliminary consultation, but contained no expressly stated reservations regarding deliveries of food and weapons. The friendly Spaniard promised, in his charming Viennese German, to lay the draft before Franco, and to report his decision to Germany.

Spluttering with rage, Ribbentrop drove off with me to Bordeaux, which was the nearest aerodrome. As on the drive to Compiègne, we had to drive hell for leather in order to reach Montoire in time for the conversation with Pétain. All the way Ribbentrop cursed the "Jesuit" Suñer and the "ungrateful coward" Franco "who owes us everything, and now won't join in with us." The car springs seemed to join in the abuse.

We flew to Tours in very bad weather. Any other navigator than Bauer would probably have been unable to make a landing in the rain and fog, but he brought us safely to earth, and we were in Hitler's saloon at the Montoire station on time when the old Marshal of France was shown in.

In spite of his advanced years the smartly uniformed Marshal sat up very straight as he faced Hitler. His attitude was self-

confident rather than servile, and he listened with calm indolence
to my translation. I spoke fairly loudly because I had been
told that the Marshal was hard of hearing. Beside him, a
vivid contrast, sat small, dark Laval, with the inevitable white
tie, gazing alternately at Hitler and Ribbentrop with searching
eyes as I translated.

Hitler enumerated a long list of French sins without, however,
showing any harshness. He repeated what he had said at
Hendaye: "We have already won the war; England is beaten,
and will sooner or later have to admit it." He went on to say:
"It is obvious that someone has to pay for the lost war. That
will be either France or England. If England bears the cost,
then France can take the place in Europe which is her due,
and can fully retain her position as a colonial power." If
this was to happen, however, it was essential that France
should even now protect her colonial empire from attack and
should reconquer the central African colonies which had gone
over to de Gaulle. An indirect suggestion to join in the war
against England was implied when Hitler asked Pétain what
France would do if she were again attacked by England, as
she had been, for instance, when the French warships at Oran
had refused to obey the orders of the British Fleet.

Pétain understood the implication at once, for he replied
that France was not in a position to conduct a new war. He
put a question of his own to Hitler about a final peace treaty
—"so that France may be clear about her fate, and the two
million French prisoners of war may return to their families
as soon as possible."

Here Laval intervened in the discussion, pointing out the
readiness with which France had met Germany's request for
collaboration in other than purely military matters. The
French were a peace-loving people. They had gone to war
unwillingly, and had never really fought properly, as was shown
by the large number of prisoners.

Hitler did not answer what must naturally have seemed
to Pétain and Laval the most important questions, and the
French said not a word about Hitler's hint that they should
enter the war against England. The great stake for which
Hitler had played had been lost as a result of the prudent

reticence shown by Pétain and Laval. Pétain's monosyllabic
utterances during the Montoire discussion had clearly been
meant as a rebuff, nor had any better progress been made with
Laval. Knowing the French as I did, my sympathies during
that discussion were entirely with the vanquished. I believe
that on such occasions one is particularly sensitive to any
false notes struck by the other side. I felt then, and feel today,
that France had no occasion to feel ashamed of the attitude to
the conqueror displayed at Montoire by these two Frenchmen.
My impression was confirmed by the fact that I observed that
Hitler that evening seemed profoundly disappointed by the
French aloofness. In the following months this disappointment
continued to increase and culminated in an outburst of rage
against Admiral Darlan, Laval's successor, at Christmas time.
Hitler then upbraided Darlan for an hour, in the same coach
in which the discussion with Pétain and Laval had taken place
at Montoire.

* * *

The atmosphere in the two special trains as Hitler and Ribbentrop returned to Germany was not exactly cheerful. Neither
at Hendaye nor at Montoire had Hitler got what he set out for.
But there was to be another failure: soon after we reached the
German frontier our Rome Embassy reported that the Italians
were about to invade Greece. Hitler was beside himself; he
regarded Mussolini's undertaking as quite unsuitable at that
time of the year. Ribbentrop, "his master's voice," said
to us at dinner: "The Italians will never get anywhere against
the Greeks in the autumn rains and winter snows. Besides, the
consequences of war in the Balkans are quite unpredictable.
The Führer intends at all costs to hold up this crazy scheme of
the Duce's, so we are to go to Italy at once, to talk to Mussolini
personally." In the tense atmosphere prevailing in our train
on receipt of this news one could almost feel the swerve of the
train as it turned southwards away from Berlin. "The police
hastened to the scene of the crime," as they say in detective
stories.
We passed through a prematurely snowy landscape, as chilly

as our mood, and arrived at 10 o'clock in the morning on
October 28th at the festively decorated station of Florence. We
already knew that we were too late, for two hours before we
had received word that the Italians had marched into Greece.
Mussolini greeted Hitler with a self-satisfied smile. He did
not wait to leave the platform before announcing, in our own
style on similar occasions: "Victorious Italian troops crossed
the Greco-Albanian frontier at dawn today." It was Mussolini's revenge for the innumerable *coups* about which Hitler had
never informed him until the last moment, when the Prince of
Hesse, the royal courier, left by special plane for Rome in the
grey dawn.

Hitler controlled himself surprisingly well. He was a good
loser, as the English say, on that occasion, and there was not
the slightest sign of his mental gnashing of teeth in the friendly
words he exchanged with Mussolini at the Palazzo Pitti.

Hitler went north again that afternoon, with bitterness in his
heart. He had been frustrated three times—at Hendaye,
at Montoire, and now in Italy. In the lengthy winter evenings
of the next few years these long, exacting journeys were a constantly recurring theme of bitter reproaches against ungrateful
and unreliable friends, Axis partners, and "deceiving" Frenchmen.

* * *

During the remaining months of 1940 I got no rest. Early
in November Ribbentrop and Ciano met for hunting at Schoen-
hof near Karlsbad. I found that kind of fancy sport most out
of place in wartime. In the evenings I translated the political
talks in the little castle Ribbentrop had "rented." "We have
already won the war", the "gramophone record" endlessly
repeated—a refrain I translated with growing repugnance.

Ten days later, on November 12th, Molotov arrived in Berlin.
I shall relate in greater detail in the next chapter the fateful
and highly interesting discussions that Stalin's envoy had with
Hitler during those November days.

On November 18th and 19th I was working at Berchtesgaden,
where Hitler received first King Boris of Bulgaria and then Ciano

and Suñer. The Italian and Spanish Foreign Ministers had already had long but quite fruitless conversations with Ribbentrop.

Another king required my services as interpreter: Leopold of Belgium, held prisoner of war in his own country, had an interview with Hitler on November 19th. A few weeks earlier the Crown Princess of Italy, King Leopold's sister, had been received at the Berghof, and during an informal tea party she had mentioned not only a number of Italian questions but also the difficult situation of her native country, Belgium. As was natural in a woman, she had dwelt on the more human problems; in particular she interested herself for the fate of the Belgian prisoners of war, and pleaded eloquently that they should be allowed to return to their homes. She painted a gloomy picture of the situation in Belgium as regards food supplies.

Hitler's attitude was most evasive. Had he been talking to a man, his replies to both questions would probably have been a curt refusal; but he was always very much milder with women, especially if they were young and elegant, and advanced their cause with as much feminine charm and diplomatic skill as did the Princess of Piedmont. After a time she naturally became aware of Hitler's evasive tactics.

"If you will not discuss these matters with me," she said finally, with true feminine ingenuity, "because I am a mere woman and don't understand politics, couldn't you talk to my brother Leopold some time about them? All these hardships which his people undergo weigh very heavily on his mind."

I saw at once that Hitler was not in the least interested in such a meeting; an irritable frown showed that he felt he had been trapped. He hesitated, then his brow cleared and he said that he was prepared to receive King Leopold—but he assented in such a way as to suggest that nothing would come of the matter. The Crown Princess was satisfied with her success. On the journey back to Munich she made me recapitulate the whole conversation; I formed the impression that she wanted to give her brother a very exact report on it.

As I fetched King Leopold, a little time later, from the small inn below the Berghof for his interview with Hitler, I felt it to be unlikely that he had known beforehand about his sister's move.

As he walked beside me, tall and slender, he seemed to me like a student who goes to extra tuition to please his parents, though he sees no point in it himself. He mounted the famous Berghof steps with slow reluctance, showing none of the expectancy of such visitors as King Boris, Lloyd George, Chamberlain and the Duke of Windsor.

I could see that Hitler had to force himself to assume the air of somewhat frosty friendliness with which he received Leopold. The King's expression as he sat down in Hitler's office was an odd mixture of displeasure and expectancy, and I felt that he secretly regretted his sister's initiative. Hitler tried to improve the atmosphere by a few personal questions. The companionable phrases he used to use on these occasions gave away his Austrian upbringing. "I regret the circumstances under which you have to visit me here. Have you any personal wish that I could grant?"

"I have no wishes at all for myself personally," replied Leopold, with the condescending tones of a monarch addressing the revolutionary dictator from the people—though the dictator now faced him as conqueror. By this remark he clearly indicated that he intended to make other, non-personal, requests. To begin with, though, he took pains to get Hitler into a more amenable mood to receive them by thanking him for what he had already done. He expressed gratitude among other things for the permission granted by the Germans for the return home of the Belgian refugees, and added his personal thanks for the favours accorded to him—especially over the return of his children from Spain. But Leopold was not a good diplomat; he spoke his words of gratitude, but they did not sound very convincing.

Hitler then began one of his long monologues about the political situation. But the conversation developed better than I had at first feared. In the middle of his exposition Hitler rather unexpectedly asked Leopold how he envisaged future relations between Belgium and Germany. Leopold adroitly replied with a counter-question: would Belgium recover her independence on the conclusion of peace? Hitler, who disliked all definite questions, embarked on a long dissertation about the future of Europe. King Leopold stuck to his point: he asked

for a more precise definition of Belgian independence, adding
that he was thinking in particular of independence in internal
affairs (a clear reference to German support of the Flemings).
By this time Hitler was visibly annoyed at such persistence, and
he launched a fairly violent attack on Belgium's previous attitude, her violation of her obligations as a neutral, and so on.
Belgium must, in the future, orientate herself politically and
militarily towards Germany.

"Am I to understand that Belgium's political independence
would be guaranteed as a quid pro quo for a military and
political agreement between Belgium and the Reich?", asked
Leopold. In his immediately following remarks he laid such
stress on Belgium's love of independence that he at once cast
doubts on the feasibility of this solution. He demanded
unconditional independence, giving as his reason that Britain
had long ago formally acknowledged their independence, and
that the Belgians would, out of sentiment, turn to the side
which guaranteed their independence under all circumstances.
This was more than ever so then, when the British radio was
persistently working on Belgian public opinion on this
vulnerable point.

From this moment Hitler was deaf to Leopold's requests. He
was obviously annoyed that the Belgian King, unlike other heads
of states, had not willingly agreed to the suggestion of collaboration with Germany. Foremost among Leopold's requests
was the return of Belgian prisoners of war. "We need their
man-power ourselves," said Hitler. "The officers will naturally
remain in captivity until the end of the war." Leopold made
further desperate efforts to get some small concession from
Hitler over the matter of food supplies and with regard to the
internal administration of Belgium. On both these points Hitler
was obdurate. They now became mutually antagonistic.
Leopold became more and more monosyllabic and sometimes
seemed to be no longer listening properly, after the rejection of
his requests. He let Hitler's flood of words flow over him with
a disdainful expression, offering no more than an occasional
formal gesture. As I had seen happen so often before, the
conversation became empty of all content.

Hitler would probably have liked to put an end to the visit

at once. But arrangements had been made to give the King and his entourage tea, so although the conversation was broken off long before the appointed time, Leopold was kept for tea. This was served in the room in which a few weeks before the King's sister had pleaded hopefully for this interview, which had now proved so unsatisfactory to her brother and so disappointing to Hitler.

At tea Hitler produced a final inducement in order to persuade the King to reconsider his suggestion for closer collaboration between the two countries. In the course of a long monologue about the new order in Europe he indicated that if Belgium turned to Germany he would not only guarantee her complete military protection, so that she would scarcely require an army of her own in future, but that Belgium might also acquire certain extensions of territory, as far as Calais and Dunkirk. I interpreted this conversation as it took place, naturally being very careful over the translation of this suggestion. But the King remained silent. Had he even been listening? Had he lost interest in the conversation? I could not make out. I saw only a completely apathetic, disappointed man sitting before me, who seemed like a boy longing for school to be over. But this was not to be, for Hitler had got into his stride and went on for a considerable time, repeating what he had already said again and again.

My impression of this conversation was borne out by later developments. Hitler never saw Leopold again; everything in Belgium remained as it had been. The administration was not changed and the position regarding foodstuffs remained as bad as ever; Belgian prisoners of war were not liberated until the end of the war; Leopold himself remained a prisoner, and was even taken to Germany, despite his protests, shortly before the end of the war. Hitler never forgave him for having refused his offers at Berchtesgaden. "He is no better than the other kings and princes," I heard him say occasionally, although before the visit he had sometimes spoken of him appreciatively—"King Leopold prevented useless slaughter in 1940."

My report on this conversation played a part in 1945 in the discussions in Belgium about the King's return to the throne. It was known as the "Schmidt Report." I learnt about this only much later, almost by accident. It turned out that only one of my reports on the actual conversation had been found by the Allies, and that what was perhaps the more important report—the one which contained Hitler's offer at the tea party—had apparently been lost. I was indeed questioned by a Belgian representative about the conversation between Leopold and Hitler, but owing to the mystification which was sometimes practised in 1945 in regard to the interrogation of German officials I neither got a sight of my own report, nor was I told what was really at issue. I could easily have cleared up any obscure points had I known what it was all about.

Later I learnt that the accuracy of my report had been questioned. I was supposed to have reported some of the King's words so as to please Hitler, and not as they had actually been spoken. This is completely misguided, in the first place because Hitler in the ordinary way no longer saw my reports at that time, and secondly because there was not the slightest reason for me to take a clairvoyant part in 1940 in the dispute about the Belgian throne in 1945. As far as I am concerned, I had the impression then, as I have today, that Leopold yielded nothing to Hitler, and I reported accordingly. All that anyone need do is to take the trouble to read my report, with the necessary political understanding, in the German original.

* *
*

From Berchtesgaden I went with Ribbentrop to Vienna. There, on November 20th, Hungary joined the Three Power Pact. The customary ceremonies were observed at Schloss Belvedere—signatures were once again written and painted in Japanese characters, and I again had to read out the complicated conclusion with the dates given in the German, Fascist and Japanese manner.

Two days later we were back in Berlin. General Antonescu, the Rumanian head of state, had his first interview with Hitler on November 22nd. This Rumanian, though his appearance suggested a Prussian staff officer, had been educated in France; he was to become in later years one of Hitler's closest intimates, and was even kept more closely in the picture than Mussolini.

He was the only foreigner from whom Hitler ever asked for military advice when he was in difficulties.

Antonescu was anti-bolshevik, and anti-slav, to the marrow, and made no attempt to conceal his attitude when in Berlin. He was fanatically opposed to the Vienna arbitration award which had given Hungary Transylvania, which he called "the cradle of Rumania." Before he saw Hitler, it was drummed into him that he must not say a word against the award. He spoke for two hours about nothing else. "That always impressed me," Hitler frequently said in my presence on later occasions. To me, as interpreter, Antonescu, with his French way of speaking, was a kind of rhetorical counterpart to Hitler. He made long speeches just like Hitler, usually starting off at the creation of Rumania, and somehow relating everything he said to the hated Hungarians, and the recovery of Transylvania. This hatred of Hungary, too, made him congenial to Hitler, for the Führer despised the Magyars.

The actual occasion for Antonescu's visit was the great show which was put on, with the usual theatrical effects, to celebrate Rumania's accession to the Three Power Pact. This was followed two days later, on November 24th, by another performance in the great chamber of the new Chancellery to celebrate the accession of Slovakia.

The year which had been such a turbulent one for me ended true to form. On the afternoon of Christmas Eve I was unsuspectingly crossing the Wilhelmsplatz to go to my celebrations at home. Just before I reached the underground a colleague shouted out: "Good journey!" I asked him in surprise what he meant. "Why, don't you know that you are to fly to Paris today?" he answered. I hurried back to the office. My namesake, the pilot, was on the telephone. "We must start soon if we are to reach Le Bourget before dark," he said. Half an hour later the crew of three and I were flying over the Havel lake. "Quite the wrong direction to be taking on Christmas Eve," we told each other with annoyance.

The purpose of my journey was to interpret between Hitler and Admiral Darlan in Hitler's train, somewhere north of Paris. Hitler showed none of the Christmas spirit; for half an hour reproaches hailed down on the French admiral. "Why was Laval dismissed?" shouted the German dictator. "It is the work of anti-German intriguers around Marshal Pétain."

Hitler complained bitterly about Pétain, who had declined his invitation to attend the interment of the remains of the Duke of Reichsstadt, Napoleon's son. Hitler, as a big gesture, had had these brought from Vienna to Paris. The reason for Pétain's refusal had somehow come to the Führer's ears—the old Marshal feared that the Germans would kidnap him. "It is contemptible to credit me with such an idea," Hitler roared, beside himself with rage, "when I meant so well."

Darlan scarcely had a chance of saying three sentences in reply, but what he did say was not without interest. Before the German armistice conditions were made known, he had considered whether to sink the French Fleet, to take it over to Africa or America, or even to place it at the disposal of the British. When he heard the armistice conditions, he felt that France could still play a rôle in Europe, and for this reason he had decided to serve under Pétain. Darlan, incidentally, impressed me with his marked hostility towards England on this and other occasions.

Hitler abruptly terminated the interview. I travelled back to Paris with the French admiral, and noted, with inward satisfaction, that the whole scene had slid off the back of this creator of the modern French Navy like a breaker off the oily skin of an old walrus. On the journey he entertained me in radiant manner with the most delightful stories, as though nothing at all had happened; his complete indifference impressed on me.

The day after Christmas, I flew back in the old AMYY, unrecognisable in new war paint. They had been strange Christmas celebrations with which to bring an eventful year to a close. The intense diplomatic activity of 1940 represented the final flare up of National Socialist foreign policy before the end; during the following years matters of foreign policy gradually receded into the background of my sphere of activity as an interpreter. I had to acquire a new vocabulary, and learn to speak in foreign languages about tanks, assault, guns, corvettes, types of aircraft and fortifications. The increasing gravity of the situation slowly but surely pushed the political phrases into the background.

CHAPTER VII

(1941)

I must go back a few weeks, to November, 1940, to include Molotov's Berlin discussions with Hitler in this chapter, where they have their proper context. These discussions were the prelude to the conflict with Russia in 1941 just as clearly as the march on Prague in March, 1939, had been the decisive event that led to the break with the West. To the failure of Hitler's approaches to Spain and France, at the meetings with Franco at Hendaye and with Pétain at Montoire, was added, in November, the infinitely more consequential fiasco of the talks with Molotov.

Some days before Molotov's arrival a discussion was proceeding as to whether the Soviet national anthem—then still identical with the Internationale—should be played to greet him at the Anhalt Station. Ribbentrop looked at me very severely when I jokingly said that a large number of German spectators might join in with the German version, which no doubt many of them could still remember from not so very long ago. However, caution prevailed, and only the usual march of welcome was played at the station, which had more flowers and greenstuff decorating it than Russian flags and hammers and sickles. The train bearing the Soviet delagation arrived on the morning of November 12th, 1940.

The ceremony of welcome was identical with that of other state visits. There were the same handshakings, introductions, inspection of guards of honour, and driving in open cars to the guest apartments at Schloss Bellevue in the Tiergarten. But there was one difference which struck me greatly as I drove with "my" Russian through the streets of Berlin; the populace remained perfectly silent. This might perhaps have happened on the occasion of other visits, had not welcoming applause been organised by the Party—especially in the "Via Spontana," as some of us liked to call the Wilhelmstrasse on these occasions.

Little time was wasted on formalities. The discussions began soon after the Russians arrived. Before the two heavyweights, Hitler and Molotov, entered the ring there were some preliminary rounds between Molotov and Ribbentrop. In neither case, however, was it just shadow-boxing with phrases, and mutual assurances of friendship that had no real substance, as at many another meeting I had recorded. The representatives of Germany and Soviet Russia went in for hard, expert boxing in Berlin that November. True, there was no knock-out, but at the end of those two fateful days peace between the two countries was left severely battered.

Ribbentrop had vacated Bismarck's historic office at 76 Wilhelmstrasse some time ago. He had probably never felt quite at home there. The Foreign Minister's new office in the former Presidential Palace was fairly comfortable compared with some of the other elaborately decorated rooms, which looked as though they had been designed for some Hollywood production. In this office, on November 12th, the People's Commissar for Foreign Affairs of the Soviet Union, Molotov, and the Foreign Minister of the Greater German Reich sat opposite each other at a circular conference table. Dekanosov, Deputy People's Commissar for Foreign Affairs, who has been frequently mentioned since the war in connection with German affairs, was also present. A younger member of the Soviet Embassy staff in Berlin, "little Pavlov," as we called him, acted as Russian interpreter. I have seen photographs of him standing by Molotov and Stalin at many conferences since the war. Hilger was the German interpreter, and I was present only as an observer, to draw up the report. Thus I was able to observe everything in peace and to make my notes in comfort on both days of the negotiations.

Ribbentrop was at his most forthcoming with "the men with the strong faces." Ciano would probably have rubbed his eyes if Ribbentrop had ever smiled at him in the friendly way he did at the Soviet Foreign Minister. Only at long intervals did Molotov reciprocate, when a rather frosty smile glided over his intelligent, chess player's face. This rather short Russian with his lively eyes, behind old-fashioned pince-nez, constantly reminded me of my mathematics master. It was not only his appearance; Molotov had a certain mathematical precision and unerring logic in his way of speaking and of presenting his arguments. In his precise diplomacy he dispensed with flowery phrases, and, as though he were taking a class, gently rebuked the sweeping, vague generalities of Ribbentrop and later even of Hitler. Dekanosov sat huddled up, listening to the discussion, to which he contributed nothing, with rapt attention and a completely expressionless face.

"No power on earth can alter the fact that the beginning of the end has now come for the British Empire." Ribbentrop turned on his usual record to open the conversation, having chosen a particularly loud needle that day, so that after a few bars my ears began to hurt. A little later Molotov ironically replied to Ribbentrop's exaggeration, referring to "that England which you assume is already beaten." "England is beaten and it is only a question of time before she admits her defeat," Ribbentrop boomed on. "If the British do not decide to admit their defeat at once, they will certainly beg for peace next year. . . . ." "Owing to the extraordinary strength of their position the Axis Powers are not considering how they can win the war, but rather how they can most swiftly terminate a war that is already won." He went on for quite a while in this way. What does Molotov think of it, I wondered as I saw him attentively listening with a blank face to Hilger's translation.

After this beating of the drum, Ribbentrop turned to the practical subjects which were to be discussed. The first of these was Japan. Ribbentrop was still at that time warmly advocating closer relations between Russia and Japan. Four months later he and Hitler, during the highly significant discussions with the Japanese Foreign Minister Matsuoka, had already made a complete about-turn, and warned Matsuoka in most emphatic terms against any closer relationship. I deduced from that that between November 1940 and March 1941 Hitler made the decision to attack Russia, which sealed Germany's fate.

Ribbentrop now introduced a broader theme, which I shall for the sake of brevity call the "Southern Motif." Its general drift may be described as follows: "Everything turns towards the South," said Ribbentrop, and he assumed the statesmanlike expression which he reserved for great occasions. "Japan has already turned her face to the South and will be occupied for centuries in consolidating her territorial gains." I noticed how he linked the southern motif to Japan, for if Japan was kept busy for centuries in the south, she could not be a menace to Russia. "For her *Lebensraum* Germany, too, will seek expansion in a southerly direction, that is in central Africa, in the territories of the former German colonies." Here the southern motif was combined with a note of reassurance. "With regard to Russia, Germany has set boundaries to her spheres of influence," Ribbentrop added soothingly. Then he swerved south again. "Italian expansion also tends to the South, to the African Mediterranean coast"—and now he had reached the point to which his motif was leading. "Will not Russia also finally turn southwards in order to acquire the natural outlet to the open sea in which she is so much interested?" It was clear to me that Germany was endeavouring to divert to the South Russia's century-old demands for access to the sea in the West, and was trying to liberate the Europe of Hitler's New Order from the threat now again prevalent in present day Europe.

"What sea did you mean just now, when you spoke of access to the open sea?" asked Molotov with an innocent expression. Thrown somewhat out of his stride by this interruption, Ribbentrop, after a long diversion about "the great changes which will take place throughout the world after the war," and "the new ordering of affairs in the British Empire," finally reached "the Persian Gulf and the Arabian Sea," and an unmistakable reference to India. Molotov sat opposite him with an impenetrable expression. He made no reference to these hints, at any rate not in Berlin at the time. Only after his return on November 26th did a telegram arrive from the German Ambassador in Moscow stating that Molotov agreed with the proposals regarding a Four Power Pact, "subject to the condition that the territory south of Batum and Baku in the general direction of the Persian Gulf is recognised as a focal point of Soviet aims." This was only one of four conditions.

The next subject Ribbentrop touched upon was the question of the Dardanelles; he wanted a pact between Russia, Turkey, Italy and Germany to replace the old Montreux Convention.

His fourth theme dealt with of Russia's accession to the Three Power Pact. "Could we not envisage some agreement between Russia and the Triple Pact Powers, whereby the Soviet Union would declare itself in agreement with the aim of the Three Power Pact—that is the prevention of an extension of the war, and the early conclusion of world peace?" Ribbentrop suggested a further visit to Moscow for discussion of this question. "Perhaps the presence of the Italian and Japanese Foreign Ministers at the same time would be useful. So far as I know both would be prepared to go to Moscow."

In conclusion, Ribbentrop also brought China into the discussion, cautiously letting it be understood that he would like to mediate between Chiang Kai-Shek and Japan. "I have by no means offered Germany's mediation, but . . . merely informed Marshal Chiang Kai-Shek of the German view.

Molotov was obviously conserving his forces for the main battle. He scarcely went into the points raised by Ribbentrop, who in any case had not chosen his themes at random, but only touched on the main questions the Russians had already raised at Moscow with the German Ambassador. They had expressed some criticisms and alleged various grievances. The methodical Molotov confined himself to asking some questions of his own.

"What does the Greater Asian area actually mean?" he wanted to know.

"This concept has nothing to do with the spheres of influence vital to Russia," Ribbentrop hastened to reply.

"Spheres of influence must all be more precisely defined," retorted the Russian. "First we want to reach an understanding with Germany," he said, "and only then with Japan and Italy." He added immediately: "After we are exactly informed about the significance, the nature and the aim of the Three Power Pact."

The gong sounded. It announced lunch and the end of the preliminary bout.

In the afternoon the heavyweights entered the ring, and the first round between Hitler and Molotov began. Those taking part were the same, with Hilger and Pavlov acting as linguistic seconds. Hitler set out first to anticipate certain Russian complaints, which he knew of from conversations between Molotov and the German Ambassador. Molotov himself also took care to draw attention to them pointedly later in the discussion.

"Germany is at war, Russia is not," said Hitler. Many of the measures taken by Germany were explained by the necessities of war. For instance, in the struggle with England, Germany had found it necessary to advance into far distant territories in which, fundamentally, she had neither a political nor an economic interest.

Hitler then spoke in very general terms (as he always did) about Germany's non-political economic interests, especially with regard to the supply of raw materials. He recognised Russia's efforts to gain access to the open sea, without bringing in Ribbentrop's southern motif, and spoke of the need for Russo-German collaboration. To this Molotov heartily agreed. Hitler went on to call for battle against the United States, who "not in 1945 but at the earliest in 1970 or 1980 would seriously imperil the freedom of other nations."

With Hitler Molotov was no silent observer, as he had been with Ribbentrop; in his own way he entered very actively into the discussion. He wanted much more precise information than Hitler had given him on matters that concerned Russia; he wanted the i's dotted. In a tone of gentle remonstrance he said that Hitler had made general statements to which he could, in principle, agree. He then proceeded immediately to ticklish points of detail.

He took the bull by the horns. "Does the German-Soviet Agreement of 1939 still apply to Finland?" "What does the New Order in Europe and in Asia amount to, and what part is the U.S.S.R. to play in it?" "What is the position with regard to Bulgaria, Rumania and Turkey, and how do matters stand with regard to the safeguarding of Russian interests in the Balkans and on the Black Sea?" "May I be given information about the boundaries of the so-called Greater Asia area? How does the Three Power Pact stand with regard to it?"

The questions hailed down upon Hitler. No foreign visitor had ever spoken to him in this way in my presence. I remembered how indignant Hitler had been at Eden's May, 1936, questionnaire—which he had simply left unanswered—and was intensely curious to see how he would now react to Molotov's questionnaire.

Hitler did not jump up and rush to the door, as he had done in September, 1939, when Sir Horace Wilson brought him Chamberlain's letter; nor did he say that there was no point in continuing the discussions as he had done to Franco just three weeks before at Hendaye. He was meekly polite.

"The Three Power Pact will regulate conditions in Europe according to the natural interests of the European countries themselves," he said, almost apologetically, "and that is why Germany now approaches the Soviet Union—so that she can express her views on the territories which are of interest to her." In no case would a settlement be arrived at without Russian collaboration. That applied not only to Europe, but also to Asia, where Russia, by the very definition of the Greater Asia area, would be brought in and could substantiate her claims. "Here Germany plays a mediating rôle; in no circumstances will Russia be faced with a *fait accompli*." In addition they were concerned to oppose any attempt by the United States to make capital out of the affairs of Europe. "There is nothing for the United States in Europe, Africa, or Asia."

Molotov eagerly agreed with this last remark. But he was less prepared to commit himself on the other matters; first of all he wanted to know more details before expressing himself about Russia's accession to the Three Power Pact. "If we are to be treated as equal partners, and not mere dummies, we could, in principle, join the Triple Pact," he said cautiously. "But first the aim and object of the Pact must be more closely defined, and I must be more precisely informed about the boundaries of the Greater Asia area."

Hitler avoided answering any more of Molotov's insistent questions by having recourse to the British.

"I fear we must now break off this discussion," he said, "otherwise we shall get caught by the air-raid warning." On parting, he assured Molotov that he would go into his questions the next day.

Hitler's reference to the air-raid warning was not only a

means of escape. I often noticed that he was much concerned for the safety of official visitors during air-raids. He had, for instance, had the cellars of the Adlon Hotel, where Suñer was to stay, specially strengthened in preparation for his visit. The big deep shelter under the Pariser Platz, next to the Adlon, which enabled us to carry on emergency office work for the Ministerial Office during the heavy raids of '44 and early '45, was originally intended for use by official guests of the Government.

That evening, however, Berlin was not attacked by the British, and the reception which Ribbentrop gave for the Soviet delegation was held unmolested.

During the second conversation between Hitler and Molotov, on the following day, Molotov insisted on pinning the debate down to concrete subjects. The first flurry arose over the question of Finland.

"We ourselves, in taking over territory, have always strictly adhered to the secret clause of the Moscow agreement delimiting the German and Russians spheres of influence," Hitler began. "This is more than one cansay about Russia in every case." This remark referred to the unforeseen occupation of Bukovina by the Russians. "The same goes for Finland," Hitler continued. "We have no political interests there." But Germany needed nickel and timber from that country during the war, and she could not therefore allow any military complications with regard to Finland which might give England the opportunity to involve Sweden, and thereby endanger the Baltic Sea. "Germany has a life and death struggle with England on her hands," Hitler said emphatically, "and therefore cannot tolerate anything like that."

"If good relations are maintained between Russia and Germany," Molotov replied calmly, "the Finnish question can be settled without war." He then added somewhat tartly: "But in that case there must be no German troops in Finland, and no demonstrations against the Soviet Government there."

"I need not deal with your second point," Hitler replied quietly but emphatically, "for that has nothing to do with us." He went on sarcastically: "In any case, demonstrations can be staged, and one never can tell who in fact instigated them."

Hitler did not mince words, as in talks with his Western partners. With regard to German troops who had crossed Finnish territory in transit to northern Norway, he said that he could give Molotov assurances on this point when general agreement on the whole question had been reached.

"When I mentioned demonstrations, I was also referring to the sending of Finnish delegations to Germany and the reception of leading Finns in Berlin," said Molotov. "The Soviet Government considers it its duty to make a final settlement of the Finnish question." No new agreement was necessary for this purpose, since the existing Russo-German agreement had quite clearly assigned Finland to the Russian sphere of influence.

"We must have peace in Finland, because of their nickel and timber," Hitler was now getting cross. "A conflict in the Baltic would put a severe strain on Russo-German relations— with unpredictable consequences."

"It's not a question of the Baltic, but of Finland," Molotov snapped back.

"No war with Finland," Hitler repeated.

"Then you are departing from our agreement of last year," Molotov answered obstinately.

This rally never became violent, but the debate was conducted on both sides with singular tenacity. Even Ribbentrop felt himself called upon to intervene soothingly. Then Hitler, too, began to speak about the southern motif, endeavouring to change the Russian drive to the West into a drive to the South. He spoke of the British Empire's "bankrupt's estate," which had to be divided up, and though he did not mention India by name he referred fairly unmistakably to "a purely Asiatic territory in the South which Germany already recognises as part of the Russian sphere of interest."

Molotov refused to be fooled. He said that he preferred to deal first with matters of more concern to Europe. "You have given a guarantee to Rumania which displeases us," and he turned to Hitler. "Is this guarantee also valid against Russia?"

"It applies to anyone who attacks Rumania," Hitler declared flatly; but immediately added: "This question should nevertheless not become acute in your case. You have just made an agreement with Rumania yourselves."

"What would you say," Molotov asked, "if we gave a guarantee to Bulgaria similar to the one you have granted to Rumania, and on the same terms—that is, with the despatch of a strong military mission?" Bulgaria, he said, was an independent country lying very near the Dardanelles, and therefore important to Russia.

"If you want to give a guarantee on the same terms as we did to Rumania," Hitler remarked, "then I must first ask you whether the Bulgarians have asked you for a guarantee, as the Rumanians did from us?"

Molotov's reply was in the negative, but he expressed the view that Russia could certainly reach agreement with Bulgaria, and emphasised that they had no intention of interfering in that country's internal affairs. He would be grateful if Hitler would reply to his question.

"I must talk it over with the Duce," Hitler said evasively.

But Molotov stuck to his point, and again asked for a reply from Hitler "as the man who decides all German policy." Hitler said nothing.

In connection with Bulgaria the question of the Dardanelles was also discussed. As Ribbentrop had done on the previous day, Hitler wanted to take the opportunity of getting, a revision of the Montreux Convention. Molotov, on the other hand, wanted "more than a paper guarantee against any attack on the Black Sea through the Dardanelles;" he wished for an agreement on the matter between Russia and Turkey alone. Flanking cover would be provided through the guarantee to Bulgaria, who would receive "an outlet to the Aegean."

Some days later, on November 26th, 1940, our Ambassador in Moscow informed us that Molotov was demanding "military and naval bases in the Bosphorus region and the Dardanelles, secured on a long term agreement," and proposed the conclusion of a protocol "regarding the military and diplomatic measures to be taken in the case of Turkey's refusal."

Thus the subjects of chief importance to Russia, then as now, were broached.

In the afternoon of this day Hitler and Molotov exchanged

a further series of ill-tempered remarks upon such questions as Salonica and Greece, and Hitler, like Ribbentrop, advocated Russo-Japanese rapprochement.   Once again the English came to his aid in enabling him to put an end to the uncomfortable conversation by pointing out that there would soon be an air-raid warning.

Molotov gave a banquet that evening at the Russian Embassy which Ribbentrop, but not Hitler, attended.   In the unaltered (except for a bust of Lenin) magnificent rooms of the Czarist Embassy in Unter den Linden, the most excellent Russian products, especially, of course, caviar and vodka, were served. No capitalist, or plutocratic—to use the word then current in the Third Reich—table could have been more richly spread. Everything had been most tastefully arranged.   The Russians proved perfect hosts, so that in spite of language difficulties it was a very good party.   Molotov proposed a friendly toast, and Ribbentrop was just about to reply when the English intervened once more and broke up the harmony of the Russo-German banquet.   The guests left the Embassy hurriedly on receipt of the preliminary warning, as most of them wanted to get home quickly by car.

Ribbentrop escorted Molotov to his air-raid bunker.   I did not take part in their conversation, as I had only just reached the Adlon when the English arrived, but Hilger told me about it next day.   As I had expected, it was in essentials a repetition of the other discussions, although Molotov, on this occasion, had been more communicative, and had shown an interest in Rumania, Hungary, Yugoslavia, Greece and Poland, as well as in Turkey and Bulgaria.   Ribbentrop had been really shaken by a remark about Russian interest in the Baltic.   Hitler and he constantly referred to this remark in many future conversations with other visitors, in which I took part, when they sought to prove that it was quite impossible to get on with the Soviet Union.   Molotov, on this occasion, had also described the approaches to the Baltic as a matter in which Russia was not uninterested, and mentioned the Kattegat and Skagerrak.

Molotov and the Russian delegation left next day.   I had not been present at such sharp interchanges as those which took place during the conversations between Hitler and Molotov since the conversations with Chamberlain during the Sudeten crisis. I am convinced that it was during those days that decisions were taken which led Hitler to attack the Soviet Union. This was the last time that outward form and inner content bore any relation to each other. I attended many another discussion, under a political sky that darkened with the gathering storm, but all were unreal and shadowy compared to the Hitler-Molotov conversations.

There was, however, to be one exception—the conversations which Hitler and Ribbentrop had four months later with another envoy from the East, the Japanese Foreign Minister, Matsuoka.

The musical name of the Foreign Minister, who came to Berlin on a state visit from Japan, was then on everybody's lips. It was notable that the Berliners pronounced his name clearly, without changing it into Berlinese, as they had done for instance at the time of the Kellogg Pact, when President Coolidge and Kellogg were nicknamed *Kulicke* and *Kellerloch*. I often had occasion to drive through Berlin with Matsuoka during his visit in March, and could thus observe the Berliners' reaction to the little man from Japan. "Look, there's Matsuoka!" the crowd would shout. "Watch out that the little man doesn't slip away under the car!" a fat Berliner once called out to me as I alighted. Matsuoka took this as a compliment and raised his top hat with Asiatic solemnity.

I had known Matsuoka since 1931, when he was chief of the Japanese delegation at Geneva, representing Japanese interests at the League Council during the Manchukuo conflict. When I saw him again in Berlin, I immediately remembered the scene when he had thundered "anarchy in China" in the crowded League of Nations hall.

On March 26th I waited at the Anhalt Station "with the leaders of the Party and the State" for the arrival of the special train bringing Matsuoka. Such a "Bahnhof" (station), as we of the Foreign Office used to call these grand receptions, was always a sort of music hall spectacle on the diplomatic stage.

With the officials and Party members all in uniform—and

what richly decorated uniforms they were!—the whole scene looked more like a film set than a meeting of diplomats. A long red carpet spread over the platform set the tone. Ranged along it were grouped the officials, according to their department and rank; at their head stood the Foreign Minister of the Reich, looking like a bored film star, acting out the part of a statesman. Next to him stood the immensely tall *chef de protocole*, von Dörnberg, who, like a Furtwängler, was the expert conductor of the diplomatic orchestra at such a station meeting. He was responsible for seeing that the soloists did not miss their cue. Above all, he had to arrange that the Reich Foreign Minister should be properly floodlit when East and West shook hands at the exactly fixed moment just after the train had stopped. Another condition had to be fulfilled if the scene was to come off exactly as laid down in the "shooting script"—the front door of the guest's saloon coach must be exactly opposite the red carpet when the train stopped. As any engine driver knows, that needs some skill with a train of twelve to fifteen coaches; but at each of the innumerable "stations" in which I took part, this trick was faultlessly performed by the Reichsbahn. For the purpose the whole train had to be carefully measured at the last station before Berlin; it was then necessary to calculate how much the buffers of the individual coaches would be compressed at a given brake pressure—and there were other problems as well. But it always worked, even if sometimes, as on one of Mussolini's innumerable visits, the train stopped with such a jolt that the foreign VIP's knocked their heads against the window frames, and the smile prescribed at this point in the script was intermingled with an expression of pain.

There was no jolt for Matsuoka. His train, with Matsuoka visible at the window, slid in quietly and stopped dead opposite the red carpet, so that the representative of the Far East could step on to the platform according to programme. The Reich Foreign Minister and his suite stepped forward solemnly to greet him. There followed the mutual introduction of colleagues—flashlights of press photographers—floodlights for newsreels—applauding crowds—singing children—a short respite in the so-called "princes' room" (the waiting room for state visitors at the Anhalt Station). Then more shouting on the station square—the military bands—national anthems—and an inspection of the Guard of Honour by the two Ministers. The comic effect created by their differences in height was grotesquely accentuated by the height (over six-foot tall) of the *chef de protocole* who stood by them.

The dapper little Japanese with his solemn face, his short little black moustache, and golden spectacles, made one think of him as a child who has lost his parents at a fair. One felt tempted to take him by the hand and lead him gently away from the noise and bustle. What a different effect he made here, surrounded by the tall figures of the Germans, who literally looked down upon him, to that occasion in Geneva when I had looked up as he stood on the speakers' tribune snarling about "anarchy in China!"

The enthusiasm of the populace had been carefully organised along the streets we had to drive through to reach Schloss Bellevue, as was fitting in a dictatorship. The producers, on this occasion Party members, had thought of everything, including thousands of little paper Japanese flags which, rushed up at the last moment, were distributed among the crowd in the "Via Spontana." Someone had seen it in the weekly newsreel, and had thought this a particularly delightful Japanese custom, and so Berlin promptly went Japanese.

To start with the Berliners' enthusiasm for Matsuoka was indistinguishable from that they accorded to other state visitors—from Mussolini to the Croat leader, the Poglavnik, as he was called. But during the days after his arrival when people in Berlin, through newsreels, radio and seeing him, had got a clearer idea of their little guest from East Asia, interest became more human. With his instinct for comical situations, the Berliner saw the light opera effect in all these scenes, and the longer the visit lasted the more pronounced was the Gilbert and Sullivan atmosphere in the streets through which Matsuoka drove.

The first meeting with Hitler took place the day after Matsuoka's arrival. The ceremony surrounding such receptions has often been described. In many particulars it was like a "station." The props were the same. The most notable feature of a reception was the walk along the five-hundred-foot-long hall of the new Chancellery; one could immediately see whether the visitor was at home on polished parquet.   Here, it is true, there were marble tiles, not parquet, but they were so smooth that they compelled the visitor to cover the five hundred feet to the great swing doors of the ante-room to Hitler's office with short, prudent, courtly steps.   When these doors opened only very few persons were admitted by Minister of State Meissner, Hitler's High Master of Ceremonies who ruled here.   Anyone else, however fine his uniform, was politely but decisively intercepted by Meissner's staff and diverted into other ante-rooms, where they were kept more or less under observation.

Thus on this occasion there were, apart from Hitler and Matsuoka, only the two Ambassadors—Ott, our Ambassador in Tokyo, and Oshima, the Japanese Ambassador in Berlin, when the conversations began on March 27th, 1941.

News had come in that morning that in Yugoslavia Zvetkovitsch and the Prince Regent Paul had been overthrown by an opposition *coup d'État*, and that Belgrade was in a state of siege. This news had caused Hitler to set back the meeting with Matsuoka, at short notice, to a later time than had been originally arranged.

I had witnessed Yugoslavia's adherence to the Three Power Pact only a few days before, at the Schloss Belvedere in Vienna. Only after considerable German pressure had Yugoslavia been prepared to sign.   Experts had advised against insisting on it, as the Yugoslav Government, in view of prevailing sentiment, probably would not survive this unpopular measure.   Foremost among those who advised against it was von Heeren, the German Ambassador, but, as happened so often on these occasions, the opinions of the "weakly diplomats" were thrown into the wastepaper basket.   Pressure was intensified, Zvetkovitsch signed at Vienna, and only a few days later the disaster occurred just as the "weaklings" had predicted.   I must add that after the solemnisation of the treaty I succeeded in drinking a slivovitch with Zvetkovitsch, and in doing so won a bet that I would achieve this Balkan rhyme.

While Hitler, gasping for revenge, had been making arrange-

ments for the attack on Yugoslavia, Ribbentrop had preliminary discussions alone with Matsuoka.   Almost as a matter of
routine he played over the old records of Germany's enormous
military supremacy.   True, he no longer said that the war was
already won.   Since the Molotov visit he played his records
with a softer needle; in place of the refrain of the war already
won, there was now the statement that Germany would bring to
naught any attempt by England to land on the Continent and
establish a footing there.   In addition, Germany, he said, now
had an enormous army reserve "which can be committed at any
time and at any place the Führer considers necessary.

To anyone with acute ears, especially one who was aware
of Hitler's abiding intention of attacking the Soviet Union, the
Russian motif could be heard in these words for the first time.
With many different variations it ran through the whole Matsuoka series of conversations.   Combined with a modified
southern motif, now changed into an endeavour to persuade Japan
into attack on England in East Asia, it constituted the main
theme of the talks.

"Strictly between ourselves, Mr. Matsuoka," said Ribbentrop
at the end of this discussion at which he substituted for Hitler,
"I should like to inform you that present relations between the
Soviet Union and Germany are correct, but not exactly very
friendly."   This was a very mild understatement of the position
as I knew it after the Molotov conversations.   "After Molotov's
visit," Ribbentrop continued more outspokenly, "during which
we offered Russia accession to the Three Power Pact, the
Russians suggested unacceptable conditions to us.   We were to
sacrifice German interests in Finland, to leave the Russians
strongly influential positions in the Balkans, and to grant them
bases in the Dardanelles.   The Führer will not enter into such
arrangements."

Matsuoka sat there inscrutably, in no way revealing how
these curious remarks impressed him.

In the course of further conversations both Hitler and Ribbentrop constantly returned to this subject.   They were obviously
much concerned to eradicate Matsuoka's impression that
harmonious relations existed between Germany and the Soviet
Union, lest Japan should be inclined to work for closer friendship

with Russia. In view of the impending conflict with Soviet Russia this would not have fitted at all into the political framework as Germany saw it. I was especially interested to note how their statements gradually pointed more and more openly to the coming conflict with the U.S.S.R., although they never actually mentioned such a thing. Thus, in another context, Ribbentrop complained quite openly about the increasingly unfriendly attitude shown by the Soviet towards Germany "Since Sir Stafford Cripps has been Ambassador in Moscow relations between Russia and England have secretly been very actively cultivated." Matsuoka pricked up his ears, and Ribbentrop continued in the rather overbearing tone he sometimes assumed: "I know Stalin personally, and do not believe that he is inclined to adventures, though naturally I do not know for certain." He had come to the point he had in mind from the start, and now broached it with a frankness which surprised me: "If the Soviet Union should one day adopt an attitude which Germany regards as a threat, the Führer will destroy Russia."

Even the inscrutable Matsuoka blinked at these words, such was his surprise at the prospect this opened up. Ribbentrop must have thought he looked rather concerned, for he decided to administer a sedative: "Germany is absolutely convinced," he said, stressing each word, "that a war against the Soviet Union would result in a complete victory for German arms and the total destruction of the Russian army and the Russian state."

Ribbentrop gathered from the alarmed expression on Matsuoka's face that he had accidentally administered the wrong dose, and gone too far in his revelations. He therefore quickly added: "I do not, however, believe that Stalin will pursue a foolish policy."

The southern motif was now brought in. "The Three Power Pact can best achieve its true aim of preventing an extension of the war—that is, by frightening the United States from taking part in it," said Ribbentrop, "if its partners decide upon a common plan for the final conquest of Britain," and he combined this fairly obvious hint with the suggestion that Japan should capture Singapore.

At this point the discussion was interrupted. A messenger

called Ribbentrop to a discussion with Hitler.   At this discussion they decided on war against Yugoslavia.

I made use of the interval to have some words with Matsuoka, telling him with what interest I had followed his activities over the Manchukuo question at the time, and how I still remembered the Japanese delegation walking out of the League of Nations.

"Just so," he replied.   "I was not very successful on that occasion; if we could have remained in the League and got the Japanese view accepted by the member states, my mission would have been a success.   As it is, I regard our having left the League as a failure."

I should have liked to answer: "Not only *Japan*'s leaving the League"—but that was a private opinion and irrelevant to the discussion.

The talks with Hitler which had been postponed because of the Yugoslav crisis began that afternoon.   Hitler was again confident of victory, speaking of the successes of the German U boats and the supremacy of the Luftwaffe.   "I advise you," he told Matsuoka, "to take a look, while you're in Berlin, at the negligible damage done by British air attacks, and compare it with the devastation we have wrought in London; that will give you an idea of our supremacy in the air."   Although his Foreign Minister now showed more reserve in the matter, Hitler still maintained that England had already lost the war.   "It's now only a question of England being sensible enough to admit her defeat.   Then we shall see the collapse of the persons in the British Government who are responsible for Great Britain's senseless policy."   Britain had only two hopes left: American help—"but if it reaches England at all it will be too little and too late"—and the Soviet Union.

This remark brought Hitler to one of the two main themes. He treated it on the same lines as Ribbentrop had done, but not so clumsily.   From time to time he used the same stock phrases as Ribbentrop had done; these were later repeated to Matsuoka by Göring and others.   I was reminded of the stereotyped speeches on the occasion of Sumner Welles' visit.

In discussing the second main theme, the southern motif, Hitler observed that it seemed to him highly desirable to keep the United States out of the war. This was obviously a matter of grave concern to him, for he was to make the point constantly in the course of his conversation with Matsuoka. One of the most appropriate ways of attaining this object, he suggested, would be a resolute attack on England—for instance, the surprise capture of Singapore by Japan. Another such opportunity would not soon occur, therefore Japan should act quickly. "And she need have no fear of Russia with regard to this enterprise in view of the strength of the Germany army."

All these weighty hints were given in a setting of magnificent rhetorical fireworks. Hitler himself no doubt took a rosy view of the military and political situation. As he often did, he juggled with facts and figures, seeming to carry in his head all the details of armament production and strategy.

The little Matsuoka sat quietly opposite Hitler; so far, like many others who "conversed" with the German dictator, he had not been able to get in a word. At last, however, Hitler stopped talking, no doubt feeling that he had prepared the ground adequately, and looked challengingly at Matsuoka. The English words came slowly and deliberately from Matsuoka's lips—he had mastered the language fairly well during his long stay in the United States. He answered Hitler's suggestion about Singapore evasively; personally he was convinced that the German view was the right one. "But," he added with some emphasis, "I can give no firm promise on behalf of Japan at the moment."

Hitler's expression plainly showed his disappointment at these words. Matsuoka said soothingly that he himself was for quick action, but that he could not yet put his view across in Japan. He continued with a surprisingly outspoken lament, highly unusual in such a conversation, about the opposition he had to overcome in Japan to his energetic, all-out policy. This opposition came from the intellectuals, from the Japanese who had been educated in England or America, and in whom pure tradition had been corrupted by association with the Western world. Commerce—court circles—everyone apparently conspired to hamstring Matsuoka. I felt, as I took notes, that I was hearing one of Gœbbels's leading articles on difficulties inside Germany.

Matsuoka's remarks would have seemed to me even more intriguing had I known, as we do now, that at almost the same moment another Japanese envoy was complaining about him in a conversation with President Roosevelt on March 14th, 1941. I refer to Nomura, the Japanese Ambassador in Washington, who said quite openly that his Foreign Minister talked too big because it had a good effect at home and he was actuated by personal ambition. Nomura said that Japan could not commit herself to ambitious plans such as Matsuoka devised. Conditions in Europe were becoming worse and worse, and therefore Japan and the United States must work together for the preservation of peace! With regard to Matsuoka's Berlin journey, Nomura said that it was no more than a gesture of courtesy to the German Government, and that the belligerent remarks Matsuoka had made while on his way to Berlin were not to be taken too seriously. This did not quite satisfy the American Secretary of State Cordell Hull. He has told us that he replied to Nomura: "You must understand that Matsuoka's dallying with the Axis and his noisy statements on the way to Berlin, taken in conjunction with the concentration of Japanese naval and air forces in the neighbourhood of Indo-China and Thailand, have made a very bad impression here in America."

As I have said, these interesting conversations were taking place in America, without our knowing anything about them, at about the same time that Matsuoka was conversing with Hitler at the Chancellery.

Despite his disappointing reaction to Hitler's suggestion of an attack on Singapore, Matsuoka did tell us that such an undertaking had been the subject of detailed examination by the Service Departments, who regarded three months as the necessary time in which to complete the operation. Being a cautious Foreign Minister, he had preferred to reckon on six months. These long periods of time put forward by Japan were a further severe disappointment to the impatient Hitler.

Hitler's conversations with Matsuoka thus achieved nothing on the essential point of interest to Germany—Japan's part in the war against England. In further discussions Ribbentrop frequently tried to extract a binding statement from Matsuoka, but Asiatic caution proved more than a match for the thick-skulled Westphalian.

In the course of his visit Matsuoka went to see Göring at Karinhall, and duly heard the same line of talk as he had in his conversations with Hitler and Ribbentrop, though it was, perhaps, more skilfully expressed.

Karinhall had been further enlarged. Among its rambling passages one sometimes got the impression of being in a small museum. In Göring's study, with its vast seats and mighty writing table, and especially, of course, in the huge hall with its heavy beams, the little man from Japan seemed even more diminutive than he had in Berlin. When we sat down in the magnificent dining room, one whole wall of which was a window, one was almost surprised that Matsuoka, sinking into his seat, could see over the edge of the vast table, with its heavy silver and floral decorations. His surroundings seemed rather to oppress Matsuoka. He gazed meditatively at the snowy landscape outside the enormous window. Looking at the snow-covered pine trees of the Schorfheide, which stood out like filigree work against the grey March sky, he said to me: "That reminds me of the pictures we love in Japan. The marvellously delicate drawing makes me feel quite homesick. And it reminds me too of my name, for Matsuoka, you know, means pine hill."

Mr. "Pine Hill" was also greatly interested in the marvellous floral decorations on the dining table. I had never yet known a State visit where the guests showed such a fond concern for these things. His love of nature was revealed in another way: he told me that he enjoyed his quarters at Schloss Bellevue so much because, though the Schloss was in the heart of the city, it stood in a great park, and "one could even hear birds singing." "In the evenings I sometimes used to make the men on guard outside the house rather uneasy," he naïvely told me, "when I walked in my nightshirt on the terrace to listen to the birds." I had to smile inwardly at this picture of the Foreign Minister of powerful Japan, who was expected in Berlin to hurl himself precipitately on Singapore!

Matsuoka's remarks to me that afternoon were not confined to the beauties of nature. He suddenly leant towards me so as not to be heard by the others, and said: "Do you know that abroad they say that he" (indicating our host), "is mad?"

I naturally knew of these stories, but adopted the astonished expression prescribed by diplomatic custom for such situations— as illustrated in comic papers by question marks drawn above the astonished face. He must have seen my question marks, for he drew his chair a little closer and said, " Oh yes, it's true enough. There are mental institution papers shown around with his name on them," and he tapped his left hand with two tiny fingers, as apparently is the Japanese custom, to drive home the point.

I said nothing, being somewhat embarrassed in my efforts to remain serious at the gratuitous comedy of this situation. Words such as these, spoken by the guest of honour amidst the festive surroundings and seated opposite his host at the, fortunately, very large table, could indeed only have been adequately rendered by Walt Disney in a Mickey Mouse film with suitable saxophone accompaniment. My somewhat prolonged silence, and my expression which appeared pained, owing to the considerable effort I had to make to keep a straight face, aroused the sympathy of good Mr. Pine Hill, who sought to reassure me by saying: "But that need not mean anything.—There are many people in Japan who say the same thing about me. They say 'Matsuoka is crazy!' "

Misfortunes seldom come singly: this weighty remark by the envoy from the East coincided with one of those silences which occur fairly often at such gatherings, when no one can think of anything more to say to his neighbour. Into this silence there dropped the vehement words "Matsuoka is crazy!" Naturally everyone asked me what he had been talking about, and I had to exchange the office of interpreter for that of diplomat, saying with a smile that we had been discussing the withdrawal of the sons of the Rising Sun from the hall of the League of Nations —and I was relieved that I could now laugh openly.

Matsuoka was naturally taken on a tour round the house by Göring. The master of the house, like a big boy showing his possessions to a younger playmate, displayed with pride the treasures he had collected, the pictures, Gobelin tapestries, art antiques, sculptures, and valuable old furniture. Göring took him through the whole house, starting at the cellar, where once he had shown the Duchess of Windsor how Elizabeth Arden's massage apparatus worked, and which now contained in addition an excellent swimming bath. "I hope that one of these gentlemen in their beautiful uniforms doesn't slip on the tiles and fall in!" Matsuoka whispered to me with a grin. Then we came to the large room on the ground floor, where a model railway had been set up.

"There's three hundred square yards here," said Göring, and he went to the control station and released a Flying Dutchman, a perfect model of a German express. The train seemed to run as steadily as a main line train. The Duke of Windsor would not now have had to stand on tiptoe to pick up the trains which had run off the line. "The track is 1,000 yards long and there are 40 electric points and signals," the big boy told the small boy, who was shyly admiring this splendid toy.

There were further conversations with Ribbentrop during the next few days. The subjects were the same as before, and so were the results. The only matter of interest was that Ribbentrop had continually to reassure Matsuoka, who pointed out the danger that if Japan attacked England America would come into the war.

"We have no interest in a war against the United States," declared Ribbentrop. But this statement did not completely reassure Matsuoka, who constantly argued that the English-speaking peoples must be reckoned with as a single unit.

Matsuoka went from Berlin to Rome, and on his return stayed again for a short time in the German capital, where he had further conversations with Hitler and Ribbentrop. These conversations produced nothing new, and in no way altered the fact that Hitler's endeavours to bring Japan into the war against England had failed.

When Matsuoka bade Hitler farewell I had, once more, to translate for his benefit: "When you get back to Japan, you cannot report to your Emperor that a conflict between Germany and the Soviet Union is out of the question." I was fully conscious of the significance of these words, and repeated them slowly twice to make certain that Matsuoka also wholly understood their import. He looked at me very seriously and intently, and I felt sure that he realised what Hitler had meant.

I felt less sure of this a few days later, when I heard of the neutrality treaty concluded with Stalin by Matsuoka on his return journey. But perhaps he took this step just because he had realised in Berlin how critical the situation between Germany and the Soviet Union was, and wanted reinsurance in case a conflict did arise.

We were much impressed when we heard of a scene which occurred when Matsuoka left Moscow. Contrary to his usual practice, Stalin had been at the station, and after Matsuoka's departure he had turned demonstratively to the German Ambassador, Count von der Schulenburg. Putting his arm round the Ambassador's shoulders he said: "We must remain friends, and you must do all you can to further that end." A few moments later Stalin turned to the assistant German military attaché, Colonel Krebs, and said to him: "We shall remain friends with your country—whatever happens."

While Matsuoka was in Moscow the British, also, as we now know, made an endeavour to influence Japan. Mr. Churchill sent a letter to the Japanese Foreign Minister in Moscow, in which he warned Japan against entering the war on the side of the Axis Powers. The Anglo-Saxon Powers, the letter stated (bearing out what Matsuoka had himself maintained in Berlin) would always act together. The final victory of the Anglo-Saxons was absolutely certain. Churchill, like Hitler, sought to influence Matsuoka by facts and figures. England and America produced ninety million tons of steel annually, the Axis less than half that amount, and Japan scarcely ten per cent of it, Churchill pointed out.

While Matsuoka was still in Europe efforts were also made by the Americans, with the support of certain circles in Japan, to detach Japan from the Axis. The United States stated that they were prepared to act as mediators between Japan and China, and even to recognise the independence of Manchukuo. Manchukuo, as we know, had been the occasion for Matsuoka's demonstrative departure from the League of Nations in 1931. The United States, it seemed, was prepared to forget the whole incident and to fall in with Japan's requirements.

* *
*

After the highly significant conversationswith Matsuoka,
in which the coming disaster was quite clearly evident, there
followed for me some weeks of rather superficial, routine activity.
This took place against the background of the war in the Balkans
and preparations for the forthcoming attack on Russia, of
which I had been aware for some time.

Early in May, 1941, I was sent with Ribbentrop on a hasty
journey to Rome, to give the Duce an explanation of Rudolf
Hess's surprising flight to England. Hitler was as appalled
as though a bomb had struck the Berghof. "I hope he falls into
the sea!" I had heard him say in disgust. When we reached
Rome Hess had arrived in England. "He's mad," Ribbentrop
told Mussolini—using the word seriously, unlike Matsuoka.
"Did you know that we are ruled by lunatics?" an old work-
man who helped me look after my garden asked me, on my
return to Berlin.

On June 2nd I interpreted again at an interview of several
hours duration on the Brenner. "The German U boats will
force England to capitulate," was now Hitler's refrain. Not
the faintest hint did he give his dictator colleague of his intentions with regard to Russia. Hitler's complete silence about
his plans for attacking Russia, of which I now knew a good deal,
particularly impressed me.

Hitler had more confidence in Antonescu. On June 12th,
at the Führerbuilding in Munich, he let him into the secret of the
forthcoming action against the Soviet Union, almost going so
far as to tell him zero hour. Antonescu was delighted. "Of
course I'll be there from the start," he said, after Hitler had
promised him Bessarabia and other Russian territory. "When
it's a question of action against the Slavs, you can always count
on Rumania."

On June 15th the newly-created Croatia joined the Tripartite
Pact amidst great celebrations in the Doge's Palace at Venice.
The lagoon city and the old Venetian Palace which, despite the
removal of art treasures for safe keeping, was redolent of centuries
of Mediterranean history, constituted a dreamlike background

to which the insignificant and theatrically staged accession of the little state formed a fantastic contrast.

* *

The next scene was dramatically different. In the early hours of June 22nd, 1941, I waited with Ribbentrop in his Wilhelmstrasse office for the Soviet Ambassador, Dekanosov. Dekanosov had, since the afternoon of the previous day, a Saturday, been ringing up the Foreign Office every other hour, saying he had pressing business to settle with the Foreign Minister. He had been told, as was usual on the eve of great events, that the Foreign Minister was not in Berlin. Then at two o'clock in the morning Ribbentrop gave the sign, and Dekanosov was told that Ribbentrop wanted to see him at four o'clock that morning, June 22nd.

I had never seen Ribbentrop so excited as he was in the five minutes before Dekanosov's arrival. He walked up and down his room like a caged animal. "The Führer is absolutely right to attack Russia now," he said to himself rather than to me; he repeated it again and again as though he wanted somehow to reassure himself. "The Russians would certainly themselves attack us, if we did not do so now." He went on walking up and down the large room in a state of great excitement, his eyes flashing, and kept repeating these words. At the time I attributed his attitude to the fact that he looked on himself as the creator of Russo-German understanding, and now found it hard to have to destroy his own work. Today I can almost believe that on that day he felt, subconsciously at any rate, that disaster would result from the decision he now had to communicate to the Russian Ambassador.

Dekanosov was shown in punctually and, obviously not guessing anything was amiss, held out his hand to Ribbentrop. We sat down, and with "little Pavlov's" assistance Dekanosov proceeded to carry out his mission, which was to put on behalf of his Government certain questions that needed clarification to Ribbentrop. But he had hardly begun before Ribbentrop, with a stony expression, interrupted, saying: "That's not the question now. The Soviet Government's hostile attitude to

Germany and the serious threat represented by Russian troop concentrations on Germany's eastern frontier have compelled the Reich to take military counter-measures." Ribbentrop did not mention the word "war" or "declaration of war;" perhaps he thought it too "plutocratic", or perhaps Hitler had instructed him to avoid the word. "As from this morning, the relevant counter-measures have been taken in the military sphere." He then recited a short but fiery list of misdemeanours, referring especially to the Pact concluded by Soviet Russia with Yugoslavia just before the outbreak of war between that country and Germany. "I regret that I can say nothing further," he concluded, "especially as I myself have come to the conclusion that, in spite of serious endeavours, I have not succeeded in establishing reasonable relations between our two countries."

Dekanosov recovered his composure quickly; he expressed his deep regret that developments had taken such a course. "It is entirely due to the non-cooperative attitude adopted by the German Government," translated Pavlov, while I took notes for my report. "Under the circumstances there is nothing more for me to do but to make the necessary arrangements with your *chef de protocole* for the transport home of my mission." He rose, bowed perfunctorily, and left the room with Pavlov, without shaking hands with Ribbentrop.

"It's how Napoleon's Russian venture may well have started," I reflected, and felt ashamed of my imperfect knowledge of history. I telephoned to the Languages Service and released them from the incarceration in which they had again been working all night at the old Hindenburg Palace.

For the next few weeks all attention was concentrated on military events on the eastern front, and I was able to have a brief period of respite. But I was soon very busy again. To start with, there were conferences at Hitler's Headquarters, which were in a wood near Rastenburg, in East Prussia. He talked to Antonescu, early in August, almost exclusively about military questions, and for the first time I had to use the technical vocabulary I mentioned. During the latter part of August,

Mussolini paid a visit of several days to the front, which I shall describe later, and in October Ciano came. Somewhat later Hitler received Dr. Tiso, the President of Slovakia. It was strange to see Hitler greeting this Catholic priest with friendliness; the short, stout Church dignitary stood facing a man who could hardly be called a friend of the Catholic Church. But when Tiso wanted something for Slovakia, he would have visited the devil himself. He once told us: "When I get worked up I eat half a pound of ham, and that soothes my nerves."

In November I was working at high pressure in Berlin where, to celebrate the anniversary of the Anti-Comintern Pact of 1936, Hitler had assembled numerous leading statesmen of the countries under German influence. These celebrations were held on November 24th and 25th, and provided the greatest show yet put on in the reception hall of the new Chancellery. On the afternoon of November 25th Ciano, Antonescu, and Serrano Suñer, as well as the Foreign Ministers of Hungary, Bulgaria, Croatia, Finland and Denmark, sat at a very long polished table laden with microphones in front of a magnificent Gobelin tapestry. Facing an invited audience of notables, they made a series of high sounding, meaningless speeches. This was Hitler's great review of his allies and vassals. He received each one individually, and gave each his special injection of courage. By the end of these two days I had almost lost my voice.

At the beginning of December I went with Göring to France, for a meeting with Pétain at St Florentin-Vergigny, a little town north of Paris. The Marshal, who appeared much aged since Montoire, was even more reserved than he had been previously. I could see no reason why this meeting had been held at all.

While I was observing these meaningless activities from my interpreter's post at Headquarters and in Berlin, the really decisive events were taking place elsewhere. During the night of December 7-8th, 1941, the foreign broadcast monitoring service got the news of the Japanese attack on Pearl Harbour, and when a second report to the same effect seemed to confirm the news, Ribbentrop was informed. He was extremely angry at being disturbed with these unverified reports. Next day I was told that Ribbentrop had said it was "probably a propaganda trick of the enemy's for which my Press Section has fallen," but he had at the same time given instructions that further enquiries should be made and the results reported to him in the morning.

The event was duly confirmed. Hitler and Ribbentrop had been taken by surprise by the Japanese, just as they had surprised their ally Mussolini on similar occasions, only enlightening him at the very last moment. We "fault finders" commented: "It seems to be the fashion among Dictators and Emperors."

On December 8th the United States declared war on Japan. Cordell Hull relates how Roosevelt and some members of the Cabinet, including himself, discussed, on the preceding evening, whether or not to declare war on the other Axis Powers. They assumed, however, that Germany would certainly declare war on the United States, having gathered from an exchange of telegrams between Berlin and Tokyo that there was a definite understanding on this point. They therefore decided to wait and to leave it to Hitler and Mussolini to take the initiative. They did not have to wait long.

In point of fact, I know of no understanding with Japan which compelled Hitler to declare war on the United States. From what Ribbentrop said at the time I got the impression that, with his inveterate desire for prestige, Hitler, who was expecting an American declaration of war, wanted to get his declaration in first.

On December 11th, at noon, I was once again in Ribbentrop's office in the Wilhelmstrasse, only this time, six months later, we were expecting the U.S. Chargé d'Affaires. When he came in he was not asked to sit down, and Ribbentrop, also standing, read out a statement accusing the United States of breaches of neutrality and of making overt belligerent attacks on German U boats. "The Government of the United States of America, beginning with violations of neutrality, has finally proceeded to overt acts of war against Germany . . . Under these circumstances, brought about by President Roosevelt . . .

Germany regards herself as from today as in a state of war with. the United States of America." Having with sweeping gesture handed the document to the Chargé d'Affaires, who obviously felt his position keenly, Ribbentrop indicated with a stiff bow that the audience was terminated.

I saw the American diplomat, whom we all liked at the Foreign Office, to the door, shook his hand and gave him a friendly smile. The *chef de protocole* was waiting for him outside, and I was pleased to see him behave as I had done, seeking, as far as possible, to alleviate this unpleasant situation.

During this year the East had spoken twice to us in Berlin, and twice in Ribbentrop's office I had seen the start of a new war, directly or indirectly connected with the East. Seldom did I leave the Foreign Office so depressed as after this second declaration of war. At the time I underrated America, and I did not believe that the war between Japan and the United States, separated as the two countries were by the thousands of miles of the Pacific Ocean, could be over as quickly as proved to be the case. My first reaction was: "The war will now be endlessly protracted," and then I went on to think that victory was now impossible for Germany who, as in the First World War, would again be fighting on two fronts. But, in spite of these premonitions, I had no conception of the scale of the catastrophe to which the Reich was heading under Hitler's leadership.

CHAPTER VIII

(1942-1943)

SOON after the memorable morning of June 22nd, 1941, when Ribbentrop notified the Russian Ambassador of the "military counter-measures," the surroundings in which I did my interpreting became very different. Instead of working in magnificent palaces or at banquets, I was now stationed to an increasing degree at Hitler's Headquarters in the East. He regarded his presence among his military colleagues as so important tha even his foreign visitors were summoned to see him theret

Hitler's General Headquarters, where most discussions now took place, were in East Prussia, hidden in a gloomy wood near Rastenburg which reminded one of the fairy tale of the wicked witch. They were aptly known by the code-name 'Wolf's Lair."

The quarters occupied by Hitler and his military staff were in the heart of the forest, miles from any human habitation. They consisted of comfortable hutments, built partly of stone, with wood panelling inside, and were furnished quite simply and in fairly good taste. The whole encampment was naturally fitted with all the most up-to-date telephone and wireless installations, and there was even a cinema which showed, in addition to the latest news reel, British and American films, otherwise strictly forbidden in Germany, in order to alleviate in some degree the monotony of this sort of existence. Anyone coming from the sunny expanses of the surrounding countryside to this encampment in the gloomy East Prussian forest found the atmosphere oppressive. The electric light in Hitler's rooms often had to be on all day. Hitler himself seldom went out—it was as though even the dim light of the forest was too bright for him—and his entourage only rarely emerged from the dark wood.

"It's dreadful to be surrounded by trees the whole time,"

Hitler's liaison man with the Foreign Office once said to me, "and never really to get out into the open." I could well appreciate the oppressiveness of this twilit atmosphere at Headquarters, although I rarely spent more than one or two consecutive days there, and always breathed a sigh of relief as I escorted foreign visitors away from the dark forest. I sincerely commiserated with the many whose duties tied them to Hitler and his entourage, and who had to live for weeks, even months, like prisoners in the great wood. Most of them would gladly have exchanged this strange artificial existence for life in the front line.

Conditions became even worse when, owing to the increasing danger from air attacks, H.Q. offices were transferred to surface bunkers. Camouflaged grey and green, with 15-ft thick walls of reinforced concrete, they squatted in the wood like primeval monsters. Low corridors, like galleries in a coal mine, ran through these "montagnes synthétiques," as Antonescu once very aptly called them. The rooms were very small, and one felt cramped in them, and the dampness from this mass of concrete, the artificial light and the perpetual buzzing of the ventilating machinery increased one's sense of unreality. It was in this milieu that Hitler, growing daily paler and more puffy, received his foreign visitors. The general effect was of the lair of a legendary evil spirit. Observers less grimly inclined felt themselves to be in a film studio. A witty colleague once said to me: "The wood used in the Hansel and Gretel films we've just finished will be taken down tomorrow, and the day after tomorrow we'll start shooting Anthony and Cleopatra; the pyramids are up already."

In the course of the years my activities had varied considerably, but one thing was always the same, and that was the way I was sent on journeys suddenly without any warning. On these occasions a voice on my office telephone would tell me: "You must go to Headquarters at once. The courier plane leaves Staaken aerodrome in an hour."

These courier planes were a crazy means of transport. They

were not fitted up for passengers; one sat on a chest or a packing case, or, later on, one would have to balance oneself on a primitive wooden bench. There was a frightful draught and a smell of petrol, and the noise was deafening. The pilot was usually an Air Force man, less interested in his passengers than in flying quickly to his destination. Closely following the straight line marked on his pilot's map he would hurl his passengers and freight through the storm clouds and the hail showers. Even the strongest of men were apt to lose their breakfasts when using this spartan form of transport.

The speed of my movements was materially increased in 1941. Scarcely had I arrived at Headquarters when I was told that I was to fly to the Ukraine next day with Hitler. He was meeting Antonescu, to confer an Order on him, and to have a further discussion with him on the military situation. We took both breakfast and lunch in East Prussia, having in the meantime flown from Rastenburg to Berdichev, conferred the Order, had a political conversation, and discussed the military situation with Rundstedt.

I also at this time established long-distance records for interpreters: in the second half of August I travelled 3,750 miles in a few days. It differed from my long journey of 1940 in that this time I travelled in an easterly direction, and with Mussolini. Owing to the shortage of staff, which was very noticeable in the Foreign Office as elsewhere, I had sometimes to come to the assistance of my friend the *chef de protocolé*, and act for him; and on several occasions I combined the two capacities quite conveniently.

It was in the course of these varied duties that I was detailed to meet Mussolini at the Brenner (in my capacity of Chief of the Ceremonial Service), and to remain with him until, a week later, I handed him back to his countrymen at Tarvisio in Carinthia on the Reich frontier. From the Brenner we went direct to East Prussia, where we met Hitler, then spent the following day in Brest-Litovsk, returning that night to East Prussia. We left the same night in the Italian special train for Hitler's southern Headquarters, near Cracow, flew from there next day to Uman in the Ukraine, where we jolted along in an old car looking for an Italian division which Mussolini wanted to see, found it in the end, and then hurried back to Cracow by plane. Here the special trains awaited us in a kind of cement tunnel, where they were protected from air attacks, and I left that evening with Mussolini for Vienna, whence I was to take him on to Tarvisio.

It is obvious that this programme scarcely allowed time for any serious discussion. The two dictators did not even use the same special train, and met only in the plane, in the jolting car, and during short stays at Headquarters. Meetings such as this one therefore were only a fantasy staged for the outside world. When Hitler and Mussolini were together, Mussolini expressed his own opinions even less frequently than he had at the Brenner meetings; when the two dictators sat opposite one another for an hour, Hitler played off a favourite gramophone record—about our forthcoming victory, or the strength of our position and the weakness of Russia and England, or the inevitability of final victory; overwhelmed his visitor with figures and technical details; called for Kluge or Rundstedt to give military dissertations, and exhibited the newest giant gun. I was surprised to see that the final effect was always to produce a strengthening of morale in Mussolini, or in his visitors who were treated to a shortened version of the same programme. Of the lasting effects of these high-powered vitamin treatments I had considerable doubt, even at the time. My own confidence would weaken markedly after I parted with one of these visitors, and I would reflect that back in his own country the visitor would share my pessimistic views, as indeed he must have done, since the general situation from 1941 onwards persistently grew worse.

These meetings called for a vast amount of organisation. Everything had to be worked out to the minute; Mussolini's shaving time, during which his special train would stop, had to be accurately allowed for by the Reichsbahn; a number of locomotives, and they were already becoming scarce, had to be requisitioned, and special personnel detailed; staffs behind the front who had the misfortune to be visited had to waste their time in preparing shows and lectures, when there were much more urgent things to do; and all this vast amount of futile activity was eventually condensed into stereotyped communiqués about "comradeship," "carrying the war to its victorious conclusion," "the new European order," and so forth. Indeed, I often had the feeling that all these elaborate arrangements were carried out only for the sake of the communiqués, whose purpose was to impress the German public and, even more, the outside world. Fantastic incidents sometimes occurred over their preparation.

On my way back to Tarvisio, for instance, at a station where our train was linked up to the Reich telephone network, I got a curt message for transmission to Mussolini: "The German Foreign Minister has withdrawn the agreed communiqué." Immediately after receiving this, the train started off again and communication was broken off. Having regard to the time it would take to encode a telegram, to reach Hitler and Ribbentrop in their special trains, and for the telegram then to be deciphered, I suggested dealing with the matter when we got to the next place where we could telephone. The Italians did not dare agree, and immediately reported the message to their Duce. He exploded with rage, and said to me in the greatest excitement: "Have the train stopped at once. I shall not leave German territory until Ribbentrop's shameless conduct has been dealt with." I had the impression that he would have liked to pull the communication cord straight away. "We'll stop at the next station, and you'll telephone!" he commanded me, with a look worthy of the Caesars. I explained that I could only speak on the through line, and that we must wait till we reached the next station which would give us a link to the main network. When we got there I was able to find out what had happened, and relate it as typical of the fantasy of these years.

After Mussolini's departure Hitler and Ribbentrop had also left in their respective trains. Ribbentrop had then read through the communiqué again, and noticed that the concluding paragraph went: "In the military and political conversations there also took part, on the German side . . . General Field-Marshal Keitel and Reich Foreign Minister von Ribbentrop." In a fury that his name was put after Keitel's (one of his many enemies), Ribbentrop rang through to my namesake Schmidt, the head of the Press Section, and told him to have the order changed. At the next station Schmidt dashed into Hitler's special train to report Ribbentrop's complaint to Hitler, whereupon Hitler began to rage about his Foreign Minister's vanity. Ribbentrop's disputes with Gœbbels, Keitel and others had often infuriated Hitler, but he always inexplicably gave in, and Ribbentrop became more and more arrogant. This time, too, Hitler in the end said that he would allow Ribbentrop to be named first in the communiqué. Much relieved, Schmidt returned to Ribbentrop's train at the next station, and reported his success.

"What did the Führer say?" asked Ribbentrop rather anxiously, and when Schmidt gave him a toned-down version of the Führer's displeasure he suddenly declared: "I withdraw my request. It shall stay as it was."

As the communiqué was to be issued in Berlin within an hour and announced over the wireless, the matter was most urgent, and Schmidt decided to use the wireless telegraph. His message reached Berlin and was retransmitted to me for communication to Mussolini.

Rather less unreal were the discussions Hitler had with Antonescu, who came for the first time to the Headquarters in East Prussia in February, 1942. I have already related how he always began with a long-winded dissertation upon the creation of Rumania, which he described as "the rock which has withstood the Slavonic flood throughout the centuries," and whose "cradle is Transylvania." On each visit he indicated pretty plainly his firm intention of one day recovering the whole of Transylvania by force of arms. Hitler took a secret pleasure in Antonescu's outbursts against the Hungarians, and even went so far as to hint that he might perhaps give him a free hand later in his plans of conquest.

"History never stands still," Hitler said, by way of mollifying Antonescu, who was complaining most emphatically about the "injustice of the Vienna Award." To make his meaning plainer, Hitler added: "You, perhaps, will be able to turn over another new page of history." Antonescu understood him well enough, for in later years he more than once reminded Hitler of his "promise" about Transylvania.

On other matters, too, Antonescu never minced his words at these conversations. On one occasion, when Hitler wanted to blame the Rumanians, as well as the Hungarians and the Italians, for the Russian break-through that led to the encirclement of the Stalingrad army, Antonescu contradicted him emphatically, and proceeded to a vehement criticism of German leadership—Hitler by implication—using what seemed to me the very telling arguments of a former General Staff officer. For in military matters Antonescu refused to be hoodwinked. As far as I could judge he was an outstanding strategist. He always turned up at these meetings well supplied with volumes of statistics and charts in which all operational details were set out, from casualties, neatly indicated in various colours to show categories and age groups, to ammunition requirements and artillery reserves.

Antonescu followed with attentive and critical eyes the daily conference on the situation at the front as indicated on the big map in the room in which the attempt on Hitler's life took place later. Army, naval and air experts successively described the position, and I translated their accounts into French. Antonescu was always given a general survey, but, as the real position at the fronts grew worse, I heard the officers more and more often refer to these situation reports as "show pieces"—that is the foreign visitor was given a picture which showed things in a better light than they really were. I could not gather whether Antonescu, a professional soldier, saw through these tactics or not. At all events, he asked very few questions, and always seemed to leave Headquarters in better spirits. However, I often heard a few days later, from Bucharest, that on his return to Rumania he showed no signs of any good effects from Hitler's pep talk, having in the meantime learnt from his own reports from the front that matters had been too favourably represented to him at Headquarters.

* *

Even if the communiqués were dated "From the Führer's Headquarters" the meetings had not always taken place in the simple setting of the forest encampment in East Prussia or at one of Hitler's other Headquarters in the East.

In the spring of each year there was a sort of Salzburg Season when, as far as the public was concerned, the meetings took place "at the Führer's Headquarters," although actually they were held at the baroque Schloss Klessheim, which had formerly belonged to the Prince Bishops of Salzburg, and had been used by Max Reinhardt during the Salzburg Festivals before the *Anschluss*. One can say without exaggeration that, especially after it had been completely renovated inside by experts, this Schloss was an architectural jewel—quite different from what the general public pictured as the Führer's Headquarters.

Mussolini and Ciano were at Salzburg on April 29th and 30th, 1942, during the "Salzburg Season," and had discussions with Hitler and Ribbentrop in the apartments of the former episcopal residence, sometimes in pairs and sometimes all four of them together.

When they paired off I translated for Ciano as he did not know any German, and Mussolini and Hitler conversed alone. As is of course known, the winter of 1941-1942 brought the first difficulties of the Russian campaign. We were held up in front of Moscow, and there was rising popular indignation about the inadequate supply of winter clothing for the army. Quite suddenly furs had to be collected from civilians, and skiers had to give up their equipment, so that any unprejudiced person got an extremely bad impression of the lack of foresight shown by the German leaders. In their conversations with the Italians Hitler and Ribbentrop had somehow to gloss over these and similar misfortunes. For this purpose a new gramophone record was put on and played over-loudly by Ribbentrop. "The Führer's genius has overcome the Russian winter." Germany would press on to South Russia, and force the Soviets to capitulate by depriving them of their oil resources. Then the British too would realise that they had better sue for peace. "America is one big bluff," "France is unreliable." Such were the themes of the Salzburg fantasy.

In his dary entry dated April 29th, 1942, Ciano vividly describes the scene: "Hitler talks, talks, talks. Mussolini, who is accustomed to speak himself and must almost be silent here,

suffers. On the second day, after the meal, when everything
had already been said that could be said, Hitler went on talking
for an hour and forty minutes about war and peace, religion
and philosophy, art and history. Mussolini looked mechanically at his watch, I followed my own thoughts . . . After
struggling manfully against sleep, General Jodl nodded on a
sofa. Keitel was a bit unsteady, but managed constantly to
keep his head up, sitting too near to Hitler to be able to follow
his inclination. Those poor Germans, they had to endure this
every day, and there was certainly no word, pause or gesture
that they did not know by heart." As interpreter I can certainly
confirm this last pronouncement, since my work was materially
lightened by the playing off of the seasonal records.

At the following year's Salzburg "performance" Ciano did
not have to be bored. He had been demoted by Mussolini
and sent as Ambassador to the Holy See, to the great joy of
Hitler and Ribbentrop from whom Ciano had not concealed
his increasingly critical attitude towards German policy. He
was condemned to death, in one of those political trials which
became the fashion, for the part he played in Mussolini's over-
throw, and was executed on December 23rd, 1943.

Mussolini appeared, in early April 1943, with his new diplomatic adviser, Bastianini, who was the complete opposite of
Ciano—serious, almost grim, and quiet and reticent when he
spoke. The scenes of the previous year, so aptly described by
Ciano, were repeated; the only new element was the interesting
fact that Mussolini now emphatically advocated coming to
terms with the Soviet Union. "To conquer Russia seems to
me impossible," was, in effect, what he said. "Therefore it is
better to make a compromise peace with the East, and have our
hands free for the West."

Antonescu, who met us at Klessheim two days after Mussolini's departure, held exactly the opposite view. "All our forces
against the East," was his advice. He therefore advocated
concluding a separate peace with the Western Powers.

Four days after Antonescu's visit, on April 16th, 1943, Horthy
appeared. I have little information about his conversation
with Hitler, as I did not have to interpret, and Horthy objected
to my presence as a reporter. Before his talk with the Regent,

Hitler had said to me: "I want to have you there today when
I talk to Horthy, so that we can have an independent report
made; otherwise Horthy distorts what I say." But when the
Regent arrived he looked at me rather disapprovingly, and said
to Hitler: "I thought we should be talking alone, without
witnesses"—and I was sent out. I was never sorry to be
spared a tedious job.

Before the end of the month we had two more visitors at
Klessheim—Tiso ("When I'm worked up I eat a pound of
ham"), and Pavelitch the "Poglavnik," that is, the leader of the
Croats. "Never was a local mayor received with such honours
by the Head of State of a great Power" was the comment on
this visit in the corridors of Schloss Klessheim; for by this time
the partisans already had such a hold in Croatia that the
Poglavnik's authority scarcely extended beyond the city of
Agram.

* *

In the summer of 1942 Hitler's Headquarters were transferred
to the Ukraine. Two hours away were the "Field Headquarters" of Ribbentrop, who always thought he had to be near
Hitler after the launching of the Russian campaign. Hitler
saw to it that Ribbentrop did not get too near "so that he
doesn't always come bothering me about his affairs."

In East Prussia, too, Ribbentrop had had to accommodate
himself some distance from Hitler's Headquarters. He had
stayed at Schloss Steinort, near Angerburg, which belonged to
the Lehndorf family, and a large part of his staff lived and
worked at the opposite end of the Schwentzeitsee in the Hotel
Jägerhöhe, which had been built for the ice yachting regattas
of the winter Olympiad. This distance between the two staffs,
both in East Prussia and in the Ukraine, was responsible for a
lot of lost time.

Ribbentrop, who had no experience in running a department,
summoned the Foreign Office officials to East Prussia or to the
Ukraine for the most trivial reasons, and then used to leave
them hanging around for days with nothing to do. It was a
fantastic waste of time, valuable man-hours, and petrol.

Foreign Ambassadors, too, were often summoned to Headquarters, and, as many of them did not speak German well enough, I had to make many a journey to the Ukraine. A special sleeping-car train, the so-called Service Train, was made available for this purpose, and left Berlin every evening. It went earlier in the winter, to avoid air-raids. The Service Train reached Warsaw next morning, Brest-Litovsk at noon, and the former Russo-Polish frontier in the evening. From there on, because of the partisans and frequent damage to the track, this luxury train proceeded at a snail's pace to Vinnitsa, where it arrived the following morning. But the foreign diplomats had to turn out at Berdichev, at three in the morning, and make a two hours drive to Ribbentrop's Field Headquarters. He received them at eleven o'clock, lunched with them at noon, and flew with them at one o'clock to Hitler's Headquarters. Here the conversation took place at about three or four o'clock, and lasted an hour or two. They then had to return by car to Ribbentrop's Field Headquarters, where they dined, leaving at midnight for Berdichev and catching the Service Train back to Berlin at 2 a.m. They arrived in Berlin at 8 a.m. two mornings later. Thus, for a short discussion with Hitler, on what were nearly always trivial or irrelevant matters, Ambassadors or other important persons spent three days and four nights travelling. This example is characteristic of the methods favoured by Hitler and Ribbentrop. Not only the Ambassador and I, but also usually an escort from the protocol section were set in motion. On some occasions, as for instance when the new Turkish Ambassador presented his credentials, a whole saloon coach with attendants was attached to the Service Train, and Minister of State Meissner, as Hitler's Master of Ceremonies, had personally to escort the guest.

Hitler made several attempts to induce Turkey to come into the war on the side of the Axis Powers. One of the baits he proffered was the hint that Turkey might take over Turkish-speaking territories held by Russia. Neither Gerede, nor his successor Arikan, would discuss such a suggestion; both stated bluntly that Turkey had enough to do in fully developing her own country, and had not the slightest interest in any acquisition of territory.

Hitler's efforts were also directed at preventing Turkey from joining the Allies. The Turkish Ambassador always denied this possibility, but our Intelligence Service kept us well informed of the Allies' efforts to induce Turkey actively to join the war against Germany. For some time our Intelligence Service had succeeded in getting photographs of documents from the desk of the British Ambassador in Ankara, and these gave us remarkably useful information about the Allies' negotiations with Turkey. They were of particular interest to me, because Turkey seemed to evade the Allies' vigorous efforts by methods very similar to those I had seen employed by Franco at Hendaye, when Hitler had tried to get him to enter the war on Germany's side.

* *

In April and again in August I went to France to interrogate Canadian prisoners of war who had recently spent some time in Great Britain and had been captured in the Dieppe raid, and British prisoners of war taken at Saint-Nazaire. I was, in particular, attempting to get information about the food situation, the effect of German wireless propaganda, and the general mood prevailing in England. The military authorities were very reluctant to let Foreign Office civilians have access to "their" prisoners, and we were expressly forbidden to put any questions to them on military matters.

We had elaborated a system whereby, in the course of conversation with the prisoners of war, we touched on selected points and drew our conclusions from the prisoners' reactions and answers. In this way we ascertained that the food situation in England, despite our U boats, could not be anything like as bad as wishful thinkers in Germany—prominent among them our own Minister—said they knew it was. We learnt that the English language broadcasts from Germany were listened to attentively, and we were told the best time to give them. "If you want to, you yourselves can give your family the news of your capture over the German radio," we told the English. Despite the strict ruling against broadcasting, almost all of them were prepared to do so.   To the question of when their families in England would be listening, so that their personal messages could be sent over the German wireless at that time, most of them answered: "Our people listen first to the nine o'clock news, and then to the news from Germany at nine-thirty." When we went on to ask whether they believed what they heard from Germany, they all answered "No!"   They added: "But we don't believe all we hear on our own wireless either; probably the truth lies somewhere between the two."

We were interested to find out that people in Canada were unlikely to hear our propaganda.   When the Canadians who had been captured at Dieppe wanted to send personal messages, we asked them whether their families had short-wave sets so that they could receive messages from Germany.   They said they had not, and explained that personal messages from prisoners of war were relayed by local transmitters.   If this was so, it was a brilliant way of making our attempts to exploit such messages for the purposes of propaganda of no avail, because the local transmitters relayed the greetings and cut out the propaganda.

All the prisoners made an excellent impression, and behaved splendidly.   I found it a melancholy experience to see these men with whose language and history I was so thoroughly familiar, and whose peoples had always been so congenial to me, behind barbed wire.   I sometimes thought of my conversations with the Englishmen of Saint-Nazaire and the Canadians of Dieppe, when, after 1945, I myself sat behind barbed wire, and now and then divined a similar feeling of commiseration in those who interrogated me, especially among some of the members of the American State Department.   In the course of this brief assignment in France I had naturally learnt a good deal about methods of interrogation, and later could make interesting comparisons. It was not without amusement that I discovered that the civilians of the other side were regarded with the same suspicion by the American military as we diplomats had been by the German military authorities in 1942.

At Saint-Nazaire and Dieppe the other ranks and the senior officers were the easiest to talk to; the young English lieutenants were the most difficult to draw.   Only when one went on saying that Germany would certainly win the war, it would draw a hot denial. "I should say the same in your place," we would reply, "but I can explain why Germany will win the war, whereas you cannot tell me why England will win." This method never failed and always got the conversation going, usually with very interesting results. I was greatly impressed by the complete confidence of all, from private to General, expressed in their prospects of victory, and by the absence of any fanaticism or any suggestion of hatred of Germany.

We had almost insuperable difficulties with the Canadians, not on account of their obstinacy, but because these huge, hearty backwoodsmen, with their friendly blue eyes and the jolly laughs which revealed their perfect teeth, knew practically nothing about Europe, let alone Germany.

I once asked one of these splendid lads: "Have you ever heard of any Germans?"

He thought deeply for a long time, and then said: "Yes. General Rommel and Lilli Marlene."

As a matter of purely personal interest—at Saint-Nazaire one of the prisoners looked at me closely, and said: "Why, you are the Dr. Schmidt, who is always interpreting," and explained that he had often seen my photograph in illustrated accounts of conference meetings. The same thing happened at Dieppe with a French-Canadian Major to whom I was talking in French. "I have followed your career in the Press," he said, "and would have given quite a lot of money to have had a chat with you!" The Major escaped eight days after our conversation, and two months later an article by him about our talk appeared in England. I was glad that he did not repeat some of the rather indiscreet remarks I had made on the assumption that he would remain a prisoner until the end of the war. But he had taken remarks I had made on the theme of winning the war at their face value—I had only made them to draw him out.

These conversations also showed me how good were underground communications between France and England during the war. As did the other members of the delegation, I always drew up a report on the interrogations which, as far as I know, was never used, since it stated facts which did not fit in with the official view.

I used to write these reports in a room at the Hotel Bristol in

Paris, and now and then the head waiter brought in drinks. Only a short time after my August visit to Paris, a London newspaper reported that certain orders, ostensibly found on a British officer who fell near Dieppe, and used for propaganda purposes by Germany, "had in reality been forged by Dr. Schmidt, the English expert of the German Foreign Office, and a large staff in Paris." Remembering the head waiter, I could see how this story had arisen, and I was rather gratified that my knowledge of languages was rated so high in England that I was thought capable of fabricating even official documents convincingly.

* * *

While the political world receded further into the mists of unreality, my work in Berlin was carried on under increasingly warlike conditions as British air-raids were gradually intensified. I had been deeply grieved in the autumn of 1940 when I read the jubilant accounts in the Gœbbels Press of the air-raids on London, where I had a large number of friends. I knew London as well as I knew Berlin, and the many months I had spent there, and in Paris too, in the years before the war, made me look on it as a sort of second home. "How on earth shall I be able to look my English friends in the face again?" I used to think sadly, when I read in the papers of "great conflagrations," "widespread destruction," and the like, and heard Hitler and Ribbentrop give gloating accounts of the raids to foreign visitors. I rejoiced at heart when I heard on the wireless of the courage with which Londoners behaved, and read in the English papers, which I saw throughout the war, that they stood up to all their trials with the equanimity and humour that seemed to be characteristic of the folk of all capital cities in all countries. I cursed the Hitler regime for forcing on me this battle with my conscience, for in the midst of war my heart was with "the enemy," whom I could not regard as my enemy.

In the years that followed I went through almost all the major air-raids that Berlin had to endure, as I always seemed to be at home when the big raids were on. When, on raid nights, I sat in the cellar with other anxious people, and we heard the bombs drop near our inadequate shelter, and waited with bated breath for it to collapse, when the cellar doors sailed through the room, the lights went out, and the house swayed, and everyone ran out because we expected next moment to be buried under the ruins, when all this went on, with my fear for my personal survival I felt a paradoxical sense of satisfaction. During those nights I knew that I could look my English friends in the face. The burning districts of Berlin seemed to me to square the account, at any rate as far as the war in the air was concerned. Another result of these air-raids was my feeling of pride in my fellow Berliners. In 1940 I had always heard with mingled satisfaction of the "we can take it" of the Londoners; now I knew that we Berliners did not lag behind. Here was a link between the citizens of the capitals.

The Foreign Office was badly damaged early in 1943. But it was not only a question of the building gradually being reduced to rubble; Ribbentrop had long anticipated the structural damage done by enemy action by his organisation of the department. He had not the slightest notion of how to run a department of state, creating new departments and posts and appointing "special commissioners" in the same manner in which the bomb-damaged buildings were propped up by crude repairs.

In these symbolic and actual ruins of our Ministry the permanent officials of the Foreign Office lived and worked. They the had the weary and laborious task of trying to extinguish both incendiary bombs of Allied origin, and the "incendiaries" hurled by Ribbentrop from his "Field Headquarters" upon the German Foreign Office, which had once had a good name. Here and there they might succeed in putting out a fire, but just as they could not catch the bombs before they reached the ground, so they were not in a position to check the catastrophe to which Hitler's amateurish policy was leading. Several were killed by bombs; some of the best fell victims of Hitlerian justice. The survivors were reproached after the war had ended with having failed to extinguish all Hitler's and Ribbentrop's incendiaries.

So firm was the structure of the Foreign Department that it withstood Ribbentrop's bombardment for a very long time. It was not until 1940 that a purge of a hundred and fifty higher officials was ordered; as they were all specialists, they were irreplaceable and had willy-nilly to be allowed to remain in the office; many were individually "dismantled" a good deal later.

The clamp which held the structure of the Department together was the Under-Secretary of State, Freiherr von Weizsäcker. He enjoyed the high esteem both of his own officials and of all foreign diplomats, and combined the highest moral integrity with the greatest diplomatic competence. With a word, a gesture, or a significant silence at the right moment, he could let us know what he wanted in a manner that could be understood neither by the receiving apparatus of such minds as Hitler's or Ribbentrop's, nor by his later accusers at Nuremberg. The two former had such primitive sets that they could not pick up transmissions from a man as moral as was Weiszäcker, and the latter were ignorant of the whole waveband, never having lived under a dictatorship. All the old, and some of the new, Foreign Office staff looked for guidance to the Statssekretär, or "Staats," as we called him. With his quiet but all the more persuasive manner, it was his moral authority which strengthened our resolution to maintain Western European mental and moral standards in so far as we could under the Ribbentrop regime.

This Foreign Office, as administered by Weizsäcker, with which Ribbentrop in his Field Headquarters would have nothing to do, which he repudiated and despised, was for me a relic of the old Germany which I had valued, and which was respected abroad. In these three houses of the Wilhelmstrasse, though they in the end were but ruins, I definitely did not feel myself a "stranger in my own country." Here I could talk freely about everything with my colleagues, here prevailed a true community of spirit, here no one betrayed another, either under Hitler or at other times. The old Foreign Office opposed the manifold assaults of Hitler and Ribbentrop with tough resilience, with the intention of making itself available, after the foreseen and inevitable catastrophe, as an expert salvage team.

Like all Foreign Ministries, the German Foreign Office was

divorced from home politics. Political parties might fight at home, but the officials of the Foreign Office service had only their country's interest at heart. Governments came and went, Foreign Ministers changed, but, however the scene shifted, there was no change in Foreign Office representation of the interests of the Reich abroad. It was therefore quite natural that German diplomats should regard the National Socialist Government as a phenomenon just as transitory as its predecessors, and allow themselves to be ruled only by the idea of serving their country as before. Any notion that the Third Reich might be a permanency evoked only a smile amongst us at the Foreign Office.

As soon as it became clear that, in the realm of foreign affairs, the conduct of policy by the National Socialists did not promote the general interest, indeed, to a constantly increasing degree, ran counter to it, considerable opposition was aroused. By reason of its whole tradition and training the Foreign Service found itself in ever sharper opposition to National Socialist foreign policy and its exponents, as that policy became more reckless. The Hitler regime's mistakes and dilettantism in foreign affairs were first evident to German diplomatists, and so it was amongst them that an opposition, varying according to individual temperament from passive to the most active resistance, was aroused.

As an old member of the Service, if something of an outsider, since I was only a technical official and not a diplomatist in the strict sense of the word, I shared the diplomatist's view of one's duty to one's country, especially as this attitude corresponded with my personal convictions. I was fairly well informed about the activities undertaken by the more energetic members to avert from our country the misfortunes accruing from Hitler's foreign policy, and with my accurate knowledge of the conversations between statesmen, I was in a position to give some helpful advice. I had heard from my friends about Halder's command to the troops at Potsdam at the end of September 1938 to march on Berlin in case of a general mobilisation—an order which was withdrawn when the Munich Conference was summoned. I knew that the British statements of 1939 (given in detail in my description of that period), which left nothing to be desired as to outspokenness, could largely be ascribed to the influence of friends of mine in Berlin and London, diplomats who made every effort to bring home to the English that they would be understood by Hitler only if they spoke blunt words without beating about the bush. I also knew to what an extent Weizzäcker and Attolico worked together with the object of doing everything they could to prevent war. I have given a notable example of this in my account of the events preceding the Munich Conference. I had shared in a great many of the disappointments which these sincere men had again and again experienced, as their efforts, made at great personal risk, were frustrated by Hitler's fanatical obstinacy and blindness, and by the compliance and lack of understanding of other countries. I witnessed the human tragedies enacted during the war and thereafter; their extent will be revealed only when all those events which lie outside the scope of this book are one day described in greater detail. Much has already become known to a number of people both in Germany and abroad through political writings, especially in connection with the Nuremberg Trials. I am convinced the whole truth about the part played by the best men of our Foreign Office under the Hitler regime will soon become known, and I can therefore confine myself to these brief observations.

The incendiaries also descended on my smaller circle, the Ministerial Office. Quite early on, a high-ranking official was summoned for personal interrogation by Heydrich, and dismissed; after the events of July 20th, 1944, he lost his life. Another member, who was a good friend of mine, was banished in 1941 to East Asia by Ribbentrop, who was no doubt aware of his critical attitude, although unable to make any concrete allegation. At the same time I, for similar reasons, was excluded from close collaboration with Ribbentrop and "promoted" to be Head of the Ministerial Office—but only of the Berlin section. "It's better for you to rest a little in Berlin between conferences, after your strenuous work as interpreter," said Ribbentrop's stooge, the notorious Under-Secretary of

State Martin Luther, who had formerly run a transport business. He was later to be sent to a concentration camp for "disloyalty" to Ribbentrop. If anyone talks to me about a rest, I always agree, as I did then.

I always felt that I enjoyed to some extent a jester's licence, and expressed my views on the monstrous events I was living through in the various languages at my disposal, in no way concealing my sympathy for the customs of the Western peoples whose languages I had mastered. Until the spring of 1945 I wore the international uniform of non-authoritarian Foreign Offices—a black homburg and the despised umbrella which Chamberlain had first widely publicised in Germany. I was practically the only civilian to be seen in the Wilhelmstrasse. It was not until after 1945 that I learnt that these matters had not passed unnoticed.

I caused considerable worry to our Personnel Section, which constantly exhorted me to be prudent, and at least to join the Party, as, if I did not, it might give rise to scandal. In view of my work at the highest levels of National Socialism, my remaining outside the Party might justly be deemed proof of disloyalty. I had decided to remain outside till 1940. Actually, I succeeded in postponing my entry into the Party until 1943. It was then high time to join, and when the purge set in after July 20th, 1944, I was glad that in the end I had followed the kindly advice of the Personnal Section.

***

The gramophone records were being changed; instead of "We have won the war," foreigners now heard "We shall win the war," and finally "We cannot lose the war."

In January 1942 I went to Rome with Göring, who was to reassure Mussolini about the Russian campaign; this was when we had come to a standstill outside Moscow. "Nothing more can be done this winter," Göring told the thoughtful-looking Duce. Soon afterwards Mussolini switched the conversation to his plans for the conquest of Malta.

I also had business once more at the Führerbuilding in Munich. After the American landing in North Africa, Hitler,

Laval, Ciano and Ribbentrop met together on November 9th, 1942, in the Munich Agreement conference room. Hitler spoke at great length, Ciano listened with boredom. Laval could contribute little as he was brought into the discussion only right at the end. Finally, as in 1938, Keitel entered the room with a large map. This time it was wanted in connection with the occupation of hitherto unoccupied France, which Hitler had ordered as a reply to the landing in North Africa. The conference was nothing more than a briefing. "It is the desire of the German Government and its soldiers," I translated for Laval's benefit, from the appeal to the French people which Hitler was to make on the following day, "not only to protect the French frontiers together with the members of the French forces, but above all to assist in preserving for the future the African possessions of European peoples from piratical attacks." At the same time Hitler announced the occupation of Corsica and Tunis. Laval left Munich the next day very much depressed; he had endeavoured in vain to restrain Hitler from occupying the whole of France.

Laval was already the subject of much controversy both in Germany and in France. As far as I could see during the conversations he had with Hitler and Ribbentrop, he justified Hitler's distrust, in so far as he sought to gain time for France by delaying tactics. As I have mentioned, I was the only one of the Germans whom he had known before, and I always enjoyed talking to him; I always believed that, despite his tactical manœuvring, he was just as honestly concerned for a Franco-German rapprochement as he had been in Brüning's time; and, too, I felt a certain sympathy for him in the infinitely difficult position in which he was placed. Besides, he was often fearless in what he said to Hitler, and did not hesitate to express his opinion openly.

Laval often advocated the calling of a big conference— even during the war—of all the states of continental Europe, to deliberate upon their common interests and common action. No doubt he hoped on such an occasion to be able to improve in some degree the position of France. I still recollect a very telling remark he made to Hitler in this connection: "*Vous voulez gagner la guerre pour faire l'Europe — mais faites donc*

l'Europe pour gagner la guerre!" he exclaimed emphatically.
Hitler naturally saw nothing in such an argument, having
absolutely no use for many-sided discussions, feeling, no doubt,
that he was ill-equipped to engage in the diplomatic interplay
which they involve.   Hitler could dictate; he could not negotiate.
His mental rigidity made it impossible for him to reach a
compromise, and it was his uncompromising nature, of which
he always boasted, which finally proved his downfall.

Three weeks after this Munich Conference I again went to
Rome with Göring.   The Axis position in North Africa seemed
serious, and Göring was trying to stimulate the Italians to
greater activity.   At the sessions with Italian officers, he ranted
and threatened.   He showed very little psychological insight,
for he alienated all the Italians by his crude insensitive behaviour
and my impression was that he left them still less inclined to
make an effort than they had been before.

On this same problem of the defence of North Africa, I
later interpreted at a conversation between Göring and the
French General Juin in Berlin.   Juin offered to defend the
Italo-Tunis boundary at the Mareth line with French troops
against the British who were pursuing Rommel from the east, but
he declined to carry out his defence jointly with the Germans.
"As long as there are still French prisoners of war in Germany,"
he said to Göring, "I cannot ask my officers to fight with the
German Army."

Towards the end of December 1942, there was another
Three-Power discussion between Hitler, Ribbentrop, Göring,
Ciano and Laval, this time at the forest camp in East Prussia.
Laval was again treated very harshly.   The interesting feature
of this discussion was Ciano's urging that peace be made with
the Soviet Union.   "At least we could give up any offensive
operations in Russia," he said, obviously on Mussolini's instructions.   "We could build up a defensive line which could be
held with relatively small forces."   All the Axis forces, he said,
must be available for the battle in the West, particularly, of
course, in North Africa.   Hitler ignored these arguments and
confined himself to reproaching Ciano for the conduct of the
Italian troops on the Eastern front, saying that it was their
lack of staying power that had made the Russian break-through

near Stalingrad possible. I need hardly say that the whole list of France's misdemeanours was once more recited to Laval. More fantasy in the dark wood at Rastenburg!

Just a month later Roosevelt and Churchill met at Casablanca. We had had a report from Spain some time before on the pending conference, and in translating the Spanish text too literally the Languages Service had made a dreadful howler. They had not realised that Casablanca was a place name, and rendered it, correctly but erroneously, as the White House. Our Foreign Office spokesman thereupon boasted to a Press conference that we had certain knowledge that Roosevelt and Churchill were very soon to meet in Washington. It was an unpleasant surprise for our Press Chief when the Conference took place a few days later in North Africa.

I was filled with dismay when I translated the fateful declaration about unconditional surrender announced at that Conference. I immediately realised how immensely it would strengthen Hitler's position at home and abroad, and how it would weaken much of the opposition to his policy, such as I had recently heard expressed by Ciano. It was quite clear to me that internal opposition to Hitler received a very severe blow by the demand that Germany must capitulate unconditionally. At that time, of course, I did not know that considerable criticism of this demand was also expressed among the Allies.

Cordell Hull writes in the chapter of his Memoirs exclusively devoted to the demand for unconditional surrender, that he had been just as surprised as Churchill when, for the first time, the President, in the Prime Minister's presence, stated it suddenly to a Press Conference during the Casablanca Conference in January 1943. He says he was told that the Prime Minister was dumbfounded. So Roosevelt had also surprised his Foreign Minister. Cordell Hull says he was basically opposed to the principle for two reasons, as were his associates. One was that it might prolong the war by solidifying Axis resistance into a battle of sheer desperation. The second was that the principle logically required the victor nations to be ready to take over the defeated enemy's national and governmental activities and properties. In his view, the Americans and their

Allies were in no way prepared to undertake that vast operation.

During an interesting debate in the House of Commons on July 21st, 1949, Mr. Churchill stated that he heard the formula of unconditional surrender for the first time when the President announced it. "The statement was made by President Roosevelt without consultation with me," he said. "I have not the slightest doubt that, if the British Cabinet had considered that phrase, it is likely that they would have advised against it, but, working with a great alliance and with great, loyal and powerful friends from across the ocean, we had to accommodate ourselves."

We learn from Cordell Hull that not only were the American Secretary of State and the State Department in agreement with Mr. Churchill and Mr. Eden in their disapproval of the formula (which Roosevelt, as he stated, took from the American Civil War), but also General Eisenhower's advisers and even Stalin disapproved of it. In December, 1943, Stalin stated at the Teheran Conference that the principle of unconditional surrender was "bad tactics in the case of Germany."

But in spite of all the objections put forward, Roosevelt refused to retract; over this question he was just as uncompromising with his Allies as I had found Hitler to be in his discussions with the Axis partners.

"You can see for yourselves," I was often to translate for Hitler, when the Italians or Antonescu advised him to conclude peace with the Western Powers or with Russia, "that we would get nothing but a demand for unconditional surrender if we tried to come to terms with one of our opponents." To Ribbentrop, Keitel and others of his entourage I often heard Hitler say: "Now that the enemy threatens us with unconditional surrender the German people will follow me with all the more resolute determination to final victory."

Shortly after the Casablanca Conference I went with Ribbentrop to Rome to explain away the Stalingrad disaster. Then came the Salzburg Season in April, which I have already described, and in May there were more empty conversations between Hitler, Laval and Ciano's successor, Bastianini.

The last meeting between Hitler and Mussolini before the collapse of Fascist Italy was a memorable one. It was held at a small country house near Belluno, in Northern Italy. Mussolini was taken severely to task by Hitler before the assembled Italian Generals. During the session, moreover, exaggerated reports were received of the first big air-raid on Rome, which the city suffered that very afternoon. This meeting of July 20th, 1943, was one of the most depressing in which I have ever taken part. Mussolini himself was so overwrought that on his return to Rome he asked urgently for my report: we were told that he had not been able to follow the conversation, and could therefore only consider the defensive measures agreed upon when he had my text before him. After Hitler had gone through the report in East Prussia, it was despatched to the Duce by special plane.

One of the most remarkable meetings at which I was ever present was that between Ribbentrop and the new Foreign Minister of the Government Badoglio had formed after the fall of Mussolini. They met in August at the Italian frontier town of Tarvisio. There were not many people in Germany at that time who knew that Ribbentrop was actually prepared to negotiate with an envoy of "the rogue Badoglio," as the new head of the Italian Government was called by the Gœbbels Press.

"We must leave all our secret papers and cipher keys on German soil," Ribbentrop said when we left by special train for this discussion. "It's by no means impossible that these brigands intend, on British and American instructions, to kidnap us on Italian territory." For this reason, in addition to myself there was only a very small staff. A few SS men sat by us in the train with loaded tommy-guns, and when we arrived at Tarvisio they immediately threw a protective cordon round Ribbentrop's saloon coach in which the negotiations were carried on.

The Foreign Minister, Guariglia, who had recently been Ambassador at Ankara, asserted that Italy would continue the war; at the same time Ambrosio, the new Chief of the Italian General Staff, aroused our suspicions by endeavouring to restrict the transport of German troops over the Brenner. Ribbentrop stated that we were sending these troops "for Italy's protection." After two hours of futile discussion, in which both parties seemed to be out-lying each other, this fantasy also came to an end.

We were not kidnapped, but when our train left the station our Italian Foreign Office colleagues, who had bade us farewell on many a triumphant occasion with the Fascist salute, just stood at attention by our coach, wearing embarrassed smiles. This final act brought home to us more than anything else that the Fascist regime in Italy was ended. That moment revealed to us the menacing background to the fantasies that had been enacted on the political stage during the last two years. The unlifted arms of these Italians at that little frontier station constituted a *mene tekel* presaging Italy's secession.

This secession indeed followed shortly afterwards, on September 8th, 1943. It came as another heavy blow, after a succession of catastrophes: the capitulation at Stalingrad on February 3rd; the Tunisian collapse in early May; the British landing in Sicily on July 9th and the fall of Mussolini on July 25th, only a few days after the Feltre meeting. Whilst the storm clouds massed ever thicker over the military sky, the conversations that I had to interpret had been carried on in tones that sounded ever more hollow.

CHAPTER IX
(1944-1945)

A week after the capitulation of Italy, so clearly foreshadowed in Ribbentrop's remarkable conversation with Guariglia, one of those unexpected switches occurred that characterised foreign policy under Hitler's regime. On September 15th, 1943, Mussolini was freed and proclaimed Leader of the Fascist Republic. A year after the Feltre conversation, which I had thought would be the last between the two dictators, I was again present at a meeting between Mussolini and Hitler. This took place only a few hours after the attempted assassination of Hitler on July 20th, 1944, in the camp near Rastenburg.

During the autumn of 1944 whilst I was in the East Prussian camp I saw the culmination of the political drama in a form which could not have been more typical of Hitler's self-delusion. When I had to translate parts of the notorious Morgenthau Plan I realised that even in the Allied ranks there existed deluded fanatics devoting themselves to destructive projects. The Plan was initialled by Roosevelt and Churchill in September 1944, at the second Quebec Conference. The details, as I translated them, seemed to me exactly on a par with Hitler's destructive mania. I know now, as I did not then, that the U.S. Foreign Secretary—how different from his German opposite number!—brought all his influence to bear against the adoption of this ruinous plan. He appropriately called it "the goat pasture plan," because the intention was to rob Germany of her entire heavy industry and turn her into a pasture-land. Cordell Hull was more successful over this than he had been over opposing the unconditional surrender formula, and the Plan was finally dropped, although the Morgenthau spirit persisted for quite a time. Cordell Hull has devoted a whole chapter of his book to the departmental wrangles about the Plan. Even Roosevelt finally decided against it. Cordell Hull says:

"Stimson informed me that the President was obviously horrified when I read him these sentences (from the Morgenthau Memorandum) and declared he could not imagine how he had come to initial that Memorandum; he must have done so without much reflection."

Mr. Churchill told a more than usually attentive House of Commons afterwards: "Anyhow, if the document (the Morgenthau Plan) is ever brought up to me I shall certainly say 'I do not agree to that, and I am sorry that I put my initials to it.' "

Throughout the time I interpreted for Hitler I never once heard him make a similar admission of error, even to his closest friends. This seems to me to be a noteworthy difference between Hitler and the statesmen of the West.

In 1944 the fantasies produced by Hitler's self-delusion continued on their routine course. I still made frequent trips to collect Hitler's visitors from the frontier, and then conducted them back again. I liked this occupation, not only because one could sleep better in a train than at home, but also because the journey from Headquarters to the frontier and then back to Berlin gave me an excellent opportunity to dictate my accounts of the conversations in peace and quiet. Conditions in Germany were already such that fairly continuous work was only possible in an office on wheels; at the end of such a journey I always left with regret the sleeping compartment in which I had lived and worked undisturbed by sirens for about a week.

It was in the course of these duties that, towards the end of October, 1943, I awaited Prince Cyril and members of the Bulgarian Regency Council at the German-Hungarian frontier. As host, I sat twice daily opposite the Prince in our banqueting saloon, so I had ample opportunity of talking to him. Especially in his manner of speaking, he reminded me very much of his brother, King Boris, who had died in such strange circumstances, and who had frequently met Hitler. I was not usually present during the lengthy political conversations between the King and the Führer, as Boris spoke fluent German, and Hitler did not seem to want a record of these conversations. But I had happened to be there sometimes when they met, and had noticed that Boris, a skilful diplomat, knew how to handle

Hitler. Without any sign of the uncertainty, if not shyness, that I had remarked in other crowned heads,—for example, Victor Emanuel and Leopold of Belgium—King Boris was quite unconstrained with Hitler, speaking without hesitation about the most delicate matters as though it were the most natural thing in the world. This unassuming ease was indeed his great strength. When he travelled in the special train Boris sometimes rather embarrassed the Foreign Office representatives who accompanied him by saying that for an hour he did not wish to be a State Visitor. "I'll look up my colleague on the engine," he would say—for he had passed the express-train engine driver's test in Germany. He would go off, turning up some time later, to the relief of his German escort, somewhat sooty and with a pleased smile.

His unassuming manner made a good impression on Hitler and his entourage. While confidence in the "sly fox" was not unqualified, Boris was congenial, at any rate for a monarch. In his negotiations with Hitler this King had achieved a short-term success of an unusual kind—realising Bulgaria's territorial ambitions without a shot being fired. He was promised Macedonia, and his boundary extended to the Aegean Sea. He might perhaps even have got Salonica. But a Soviet Minister remained accredited to him during the whole war, and when Hitler sounded him about coming into the war he had always replied: "The Bulgarian people would never go to war against Russia, whom they regard as their liberator from the Turkish yoke." As events have turned out, his policy, had he lived, could have brought him no more than a short-lived, if brilliant, success.

Prince Cyril was given the usual pep talk, like the ones I had translated dozens of times. I always felt that Hitler himself believed what he told his foreign visitors. He seemed to apply a sort of auto-suggestive Coué system to himself and to his visitors, only he spun out Coué's brief statement: "Every day and in every way I get better and better" into an interminable monologue adorned with a wealth of technical detail. I noticed that Hitler based his argument on certain false premises that fitted in with his wishful thinking, and that on these he erected a completely logical structure, quite convincing to those who did

not see that the premises were false, but which naturally
collapsed like a house of cards when their falsity was perceived.
Cyril, like many visitors before and after him, seemed to fall a
prey to Hitler's illusions. But he, too, found that the edifice began
to crumble when he examined its foundations on his return
journey, and to fall completely in ruins when he got home and
learnt the true facts in all their bleak reality.

I never saw the collapse of this capacity for self-deception
in Hitler. I last saw him personally in December, 1944, when he
and Szalasi, the head of the new Hungarian Puppet Government had, to quote the official communiqué: "a long conversation on all questions affecting the political, military and
economic collaboration of Germany and the Hungarian nation
united under the revolutionary Hungarian movement." The
phrases "firm determination of the German and Hungarian
peoples to continue the defensive war by every means" and "the
old, traditional and proven comradeship in arms and friendship
of the two peoples" were typical examples of such self-deception.
Hitler's Coué mentality had not changed, although the enemy
had already advanced far into Reich territory. Moreover,
in this last conversation a few months before the collapse,
I saw no sign that Hitler had lost any of his facility in argument.

After the war I was told, by acquaintances who were near
him up to the last, that Hitler's illusions were shattered only
just before the end, when he suddenly realised that he was giving
orders to an army which no longer existed. He sat for two
hours in complete silence in the Chancellery bunker, his map
spread before him, gazing into vacancy. Then, like a bad
captain, he left the sinking ship, abandoning the passengers to
their fate.

Auto-suggestive treatment was tried once more at the "Salzburg Season" of 1944, but by now some of the patients had begun
to rebel. Antonescu's remarks had for some time been more and
more critical and challenging. This old pupil of the French
Staff College ruthlessly laid bare the weakness and errors of

Hitler's strategy. Fine words no longer availed with him, and I was interested to observe that Hitler gave up any attempt to conduct a conversation with him on Coué lines. With astonishment I saw that the overbearing dictator was modestly consulting the Rumanian Marshal. "I do not know whether I should evacuate the Crimea or defend it. What would you advise, Marshal?" he asked. I had never had to translate such a sentence for Hitler.

"Before I answer your question," said Antonescu rather condescendingly, "you must tell me whether you have finally given up the Ukraine."

"Whatever else happens I shall recapture the Ukraine next year," said Hitler, referring to 1945, "as the raw materials there are indispensable to us for carrying on the war."

"Then the Crimea must be held," was Antonescu's verdict.

Another miracle occurred. "I suggest a compromise," said Hitler, who would have liked to evacuate the Crimea. "We will draw up two plans, a plan for its defence and a plan for its evacuation."

"Agreed," said Antonescu in a brusque military tone.

Hitler took it all quite calmly. Indeed, on this and on future occasions he was more friendly to Antonescu than to any of his other visitors. Perhaps the Rumanian Marshal had found the right technique for dealing with dictators.

Hitler was less amenable over important political questions. Antonescu was constantly, and more especially in the spring of 1944, advocating coming to terms with the Western Powers, but Hitler would have nothing to do with this. He would perhaps more readily have considered an understanding with Stalin, and although he refused any hint of this possibility made to him in my presence, I was struck by the fact that he did not turn down the idea with anything like the fanatical emphasis he showed when speaking of the "plutocrats."

I was very interested to see Hitler's reaction to the peace feelers put out by Russia at this time, of which we were informed by our Stockholm Legation. I happened to overhear a conversation between Hitler and Ribbentrop in which Hitler decided against going any further into this matter because the confidential agent in touch with our Legation was a Jew, and "because

Stalin is certainly not in earnest, but hopes by such a manœuvre to incite his Western Allies to open up the second front."

Towards the end of 1944 and early in 1945 the Germans themselves put out peace feelers to the Western Allies through their Embassies or Legations in Sweden, Switzerland and Spain. At first Hitler was against this, but he finally permitted Ribbentrop to launch this inefficient peace offensive. "Nothing will come of it," he told Ribbentrop, "but if your mind is set on it, you can make the attempt."

"A preliminary condition for any peace talks is that the Führer confines himself to his position as Head of the State, and hands over the Government to a Mr. X," I read in a telegram from Madrid.

"I would also lose my post," I heard Ribbentrop say when the telegram was brought to him. "There can be no question of that."

Not a word was heard from Berne or Stockholm.

* * *

I also escorted Horthy to Salzburg in the Spring of 1944. He was becoming more and more fractious. Once again I was dismissed when Horthy arrived, and so I do not know the details of his discussion with Hitler.

Having nothing to do, I was chatting to some colleagues in the hall of the great castle, when suddenly the door of the conference room flew open, and to our surprise the aged Horthy came rushing out, very red in the face, and began to climb the stairs to the first floor. Hitler, looking angry and embarrassed, came running after him and tried to call his guest back. Showing great presence of mind, the tall *chef de protocole* Freiherr von Dörnberg threw himself in the path of the runaway Hungarian Regent, entangling him in conversation until the other runner in the race, Hitler, could catch up and accompany his guest to his room. He then came downstairs again angrily, and disappeared with Ribbentrop in the council chamber.

We soon discovered what had happened. Hitler, alleging the unreliability of the Hungarian Government, had put demands that amounted to the institution of something like a German Protectorate over Hungary.   Horthy had jumped up and, with an excitement unusual in a man generally so quiet, had exclaimed: "If everything has been decided already, there is no point in my staying any longer.   I shall leave at once!" With these words he had left the room.

The castle now became as active as a disturbed beehive. Horthy sent for his special train (there was a special station near the castle for guests of honour), Ribbentrop contacted the Hungarian Minister in Berlin, a most convincing fake air-raid was staged, which even included a smoke screen over the castle, as an excuse for preventing Horthy's special train from leaving, and the telephone line to Budapest turned out to be "badly hit," so that the Regent was cut off from the outside world. By the use of these diplomatic and military devices, another conversation between Horthy and Hitler was finally arranged.

"If Horthy does not give way," Ribbentrop informed me, "you will not accompany him back to the frontier. He will have no guard of honour, but will travel as a prisoner."

I did conduct Horthy back to the Hungarian frontier that evening with full honours, for he had said he was willing to replace the "unreliable Government," of whose contacts with the Western Powers we had been informed, with a new government under Stojai.   I was much struck by the contrast with Antonescu's behaviour in similar circumstances; Hitler had shown him documents from which it appeared that his Foreign Minister, Mihai Antonescu, was in touch with the Western Powers.   But the Rumanian Marshal had categorically refused to dismiss Mihai Antonescu—who, by the way, was not related to him.

On the return journey we were invited to dine with Horthy in his coach.   In spite of his troubled day the old gentleman was once again a grand seigneur of the old double monarchy, and as such I had always found him very congenial.   He made no reference to the painful scenes of the day but entertained us with delightful stories of the old Austria-Hungary, memories of the first world war, and the time when he commanded the Austro-Hungarian fleet in the Mediterranean.   Later I found it particularly painful to recall that delightful evening, for Hitler vented his proletarian spleen on the old aristocrat.

He had had him brought to Germany in captivity after Horthy's son had been kidnapped rolled up in a carpet as a means of bringing pressure to bear on his father.

***

I returned to Salzburg from the Hungarian frontier as further visits were in prospect. Before these occurred, I paid a visit to the Berghof when Hitler's future wife Eva Braun was staying there.

I had heard rumours linking Eva Braun's name with Hitler's, but had not thought there was much in them, since Hitler seemed to me to take no interest in women. I knew better when I saw them holding hands by the fireside one evening in the large hall of the Berghof. At dinner I was able to observe Eva Braun, who was sitting next to Hitler, more closely. Tall, slim and goodlooking, her dress and general style were typical of Berlin's West End; not at all the type of German womanhood featured as the ideal of National Socialism. She was very well made up and wore valuable jewellery, but somehow she did not seem to me to feel quite at ease in her rôle. I did not get to know her well, as I did not form part of the intimate circle at Obersalzberg. Her presence there was carefully concealed from outsiders; Hitler's permission was obtained before I was admitted on that occasion.

The next visitor whom I was sent to collect was Mussolini, who then ruled the Fascist Republic of North Italy from Milan. His daughter, whom we had liberated as we had Mussolini's wife and children, remained in Germany.

I twice interpreted conversations between Countess Edda Ciano and Hitler. On each occasion the tall, elegant daughter of the Italian dictator raised political questions with Hitler, and did not hesitate to express views opposite to his own vehemently and with great ability. "You can't punish someone just because his grandmother is a Jewess," she once said, her large brown eyes flashing like her father's. She warmly advocated more humanity in the treatment of the Jews. At her second visit, which occurred after Mussolini's downfall, she put forward forcefully a long series of complaints about the treatment of Italian prisoners of war in Germany. Hitler was obviously impressed by the force with which Edda Ciano expressed her views. He tolerated her saying things which he would have taken ill from a man criticising his policy. But he remained obdurate on the question of Ciano and his wife going to Spain.

"I fear you would only have unpleasantness there," Hitler said. "You are better off with us in Germany." This refusal cost Ciano his life.

As I have said, I was meant to fetch the temperamental Edda's father from the Italo-German frontier at the end of April, 1944, as he too had been invited to Salzburg. But fate decreed otherwise.

The Head of the Fascist Republic naturally no longer possessed a special train, to which, in the ordinary way, my two coaches would have been attached at the frontier, and so I was entrusted with most of the coaches of Hitler's train, which was to go to Milan to collect Mussolini. When I was leaving, Dornberg said: "Now don't please make yourself too comfortable and stay in the train until Milan. The guard of honour only takes over at the German frontier, and if the Italians, in their present sensitive mood, hear that you travelled on to Milan they will start saying that the German Foreign Office has now extended the Reich frontier up to Milan!"

I arrived at Lienz on the River Drau in the Fuhrer's special train at three o'clock in the afternoon. Here the guard of honour left the train, with the intention of rejoining it at three the following morning for the journey back. But when the train came in next morning not one of the guard of honour was there—they were all in Lienz hospital suffering from concussion and fractures. A District Officer better qualified to control men than a car, when driving us to Heiligenblut, had swerved to the side of the road as a result of a puncture, the car had crashed down the bank, toppled over, and we had all been thrown into the Drau.

For the time being there was to be no more travelling or interpreting for me. When I was discharged from hospital, the Foreign Office sent me to Baden-Baden to convalesce. I stayed in an attractive suite of rooms at Brenners Hotel, which an interned American diplomat had occupied before me. Later, when I was interned by the Americans, I was interested in comparing American and German hospitality to interned diplomats.

At Baden-Baden I had my treasured wireless set by my bedside; it had enabled me to listen to Churchill and Roosevelt throughout the war. It was always a literary delight to hear Churchill, even though I by no means always agreed with what he said. My wireless was largely responsible for my battle vocabulary, whose extent often surprised my listeners when I expounded on the situation at the front. "The longer the war lasts, the easier translating gets," I once told a colleague; by carefully listening to and comparing the texts of both sides I observed that each combatant said very much the same thing in a similar situation. This parallel was especially marked in the appeals made in Germany in connection with the formation of the *Volkssturm* towards the end of the war: I told the Languages Service when they translated these appeals to use the texts of the English broadcasts made when the Home Guard was raised in 1940; with these texts beside them they would find the translation much easier. That was not by any means the only occasion on which the Languages Service went to their opponents for valuable assistance.

* *
*

Much has already been written about the unsuccessful attempt to kill Hitler on July 20th, 1944, but scarcely any mention has been made of the fact that only two hours after the attempt Hitler met Mussolini for a political discussion at the scene of the explosion.

"No! Not even you can go to Headquarters today," a guard mounted at a barrier told me.

"I have been summoned to a conference between Hitler and Mussolini. You must let me through!"

"The conversation will not take place," the guard said.

"Why not?"

"Because of what's happened."

This laconic answer was the first intimation I had of the attempt of July 20th.

There was an auxiliary railway station with the code name of Görlitz just by Hitler's quarters. I did finally succeed in getting past the sentries, and reached this station, where I was to meet Mussolini on his arrival early in the afternoon. At the station I heard what had actually happened from Hitler's physician, Professor Morell, who had not himself fully recovered from the shock of the explosion. He told me that Hitler had, miraculously, escaped practically unhurt, whereas other people in the room had been severely wounded. He expressed great admiration for Hitler's complete calm; he had found his pulse quite normal when examining him for injuries.

While the doctor was telling me this, Hitler himself suddenly appeared on the platform to welcome Mussolini. There was no evidence of what had happened, except that his right arm was rather stiff. When the train came in, I noticed that he held out his left hand to Mussolini, and that he moved much more slowly than usual; it was as though one were watching him in a slow-motion film. During the three-minute drive to his quarters Hitler told Mussolini what had just happened, quietly and almost in a monotone as though he had had no part in it. Mussolini's naturally prominent eyes seemed to start out of his head with horror.

We went straight to the conference room, which looked like a bombed house after an air-raid. For a while the two men looked round in silence, and then Hitler related some of the details. He showed Mussolini how he had been bending over the table to see something on the map, and was leaning on his right elbow, when the explosion occurred, almost exactly beneath his arm. The top of the table had been blown off and it was this which had hurt his right arm. In a corner of the room was the uniform which Hitler had been wearing that morning, and he showed Mussolini the tattered trousers and the slightly torn tunic, and also showed the back of his head, where his hair was singed.

Mussolini was absolutely horrified; he could not understand how such a thing could happen at Headquarters; his face expressed utter dismay. In the ruins of this office, the nerve centre of the Italo-German partnership, he must have seen the ruins of the whole political structure of the Rome-Berlin Axis.

At first he could only think of the event as a bad omen, and some time elapsed before he pulled himself together enough to congratulate Hitler on his escape.

Hitler's reaction was completely different.

"I was standing here by this table; the bomb went off just in front of my feet. Over there in the corner of the room colleagues of mine were severely injured; just opposite me an officer was literally blown through the window and lay outside severely injured. Look at my uniform! Look at my burns! When I reflect on all this I must say that to me it is obvious that nothing is going to happen to me; undoubtedly it is my fate to continue on my way and to bring my task to completion. It is not the first time that I have escaped death miraculously. First there were times in the first war, and then during my political career there were a series of marvellous escapes. What happened here today is the climax! And having now escaped death in such an extraordinary way I am more than ever convinced that the great cause which I serve will be brought through its present perils and that everything can be brought to a good end."

Hitler had talked himself with these words into a state of fine enthusiasm, as he was always able to do; he had passed from the quiet reporting tone in which he had related the details of the event, into that kind of rhetoric which seldom failed of its effect on the man to whom he was talking. It was something quite different from the raging and ranting of his public speeches. Outbursts of rage like those which occurred in the speeches, which he has often been credited with in private conversations, never took place at any conversation where I was present as interpreter.

Mussolini was obviously heartened by Hitler, who had once more produced one of those remarkable effects I have noted. On such occasions Hitler always seemed somehow to be convincing. Mussolini began to look cheerful; he seemed to have forgotten his anxiety.

"I must say you are right, Führer," he replied emphatically. "No one who has seen the wreckage in this room, and sees you standing there almost unhurt, and hears you talk, can dispute the fact that heaven has held its protective hand over you. Our position is bad, one might almost say desperate, but what has happened here today gives me new courage. After the miracle that has occurred here in this room today it is inconceivable that our cause should meet with misfortune."

After some time we sought a more comfortable place in which to discuss the various matters on the agenda; but it was natural that in the excitement of the recent event nothing else was seriously discussed. The prevailing feeling was summed up in both the dictators' comments amidst the ruins—our position is desperate but we hope for a miracle, or, to put it more accurately, after today we know that a miracle will happen, just as one happened here, and we must not let ourselves be discouraged. It was the last time Hitler and Mussolini met.

Hitler now believed more firmly than ever in his Destiny. His vengeance was inhuman.

One of the most remarkable examples of Hitler's complete lack of touch with reality following on this providential interference was the negotiations conducted at the same Headquarters for a week in October, 1944.

I refer to Hitler's attempt to form, in particularly fantastic circumstances, a new French Government. The head of this Government was to be a French ex-communist, Jacques Doriot, who had founded a party of the extreme Right in France. The France this new Government was to represent was already almost entirely in the hands of the Allies, so it was proposed that the seat of Government should be at Sigmaringen, in southern Germany, whose Gauleiter protested against flying the tricolor.

The negotiations between the prospective French Ministers reminded one of the pre-war French film *Les Nouveaux Messieurs*. Personal rivalries were much in evidence, and "Prime Minister" Doriot was so much disliked by the other Frenchmen that he lived instead with us in the Sports Hotel, so that I had many opportunities of talking to him. Doriot was a highly intelligent man who seemed to know exactly what he wanted. When he had been a communist he had been received by Stalin, and he knew the East, particularly China, very well. He dominated the other Frenchmen of the "Government delegation," and was far superior as a negotiator to Ribbentrop.

After a semblance of unity had been achieved by super-human

efforts, Hitler received the new French Government, discoursed to them on Calais and Dunkirk, and gave them his paternal blessing. The sound of Russian gunfire in the background heightened the unreality of the scene.

That was the last time that I saw Hitler. On April 14th, 1945, I received my last instructions from Ribbentrop. I was to proceed to Garmisch, where the Ministries were then situated. I did not get further than Salzburg, where the end of the war found me.

* *

Thus ended my work as an interpreter. It had begun on August 1st, 1923, and had caused me to play for almost a quarter of a century a modest but not unimportant part, closely associated with political events in Europe and the rise and fall of my own country. My experience led me to the conviction that certain principles hold good for all peoples, and determine events regardless of the will of any individual, however powerful.

I refer in particular to the moral laws inculcated by parents and teachers in everyone of my generation: respect for the individual, his life, thought, and property; and the respect deriving from it, respect for the people's natural rights to independence, to a standard of living in keeping with their industry and the standards of their neighbours, and to social and political justice. In my work I have seen that departure from these principles has in the end brought ruin to statesmen and peoples, however apparently successful initially. This is the lesson which I, as a German, have learnt from my experiences, and which I also consider gives hope for our people in their present plight. The basically Christian ethics which activated most European statesmen in the 'twenties and early 'thirties, however vigorously they represented the interests of their countries, resulted in the progress which I saw achieved year by year at successive conferences in those days.

Thereafter I witnessed the mighty struggle between the eternal principles of Christianity and the exponents of a new attitude towards human rights contrary to all accepted ideas.

I saw the apparent triumph of this new attitude, but, being closely associated with events, I perceived with increasing clarity on which side strength essentially lay. The outbreak of war in 1939 was the beginning of the end for this new force, at first victorious, but whose accelerating decline, culminating in the greatest catastrophe of all time, I also followed closely in all its phases, year by year.

As well as the ineluctable rule of these moral laws in the lives of peoples, I became aware in my quarter century of conference rooms of another determining factor: the irresistible power of the laws of economics. How different would have been the history of the last decades had statesmen and peoples conformed to the principles advocated by sober economists during those years, and which I welcomed so hopefully in Geneva, and in many other European conferences from 1927 onwards. The people and their political leaders, with short-sighted selfishness, ignored the advice of the economic experts; actuated by emotional political motives they ignored those laws of economic cooperation, increasingly decisive in our era of technical progress, and drove the impoverished masses into the arms of fanatics. They brought down the avalanche which overwhelmed the peaceful homesteads of the people of Europe.

Having stood as a mute on the diplomatic stage for twenty-five years, I find no difficulty in perceiving what is going on behind the scenes from the gallery. I have followed the diplomatic drama of the post-war period as a spectator since 1945, and I believe that from my humble position I can see the great moral and economic laws in operation, even though the costumes and properties on the stage have changed.

My work in the Foreign Office was terminated with the unconditional surrender of May 8th, 1945, but my activities as an interpreter and translator were to continue.

POSTSCRIPT

(1945-1949)

SOON after Whitsun, 1945, I drove past the scene of the "Salzburg Fantasies" once more. I was in a crowded lorry guarded by two American soldiers with their rifles at the ready. The last time I had seen lorries full of civilians under armed guards was in 1934 after the Rohm *putsch*, when Hitler had everyone who was suspected of hostility to his regime arrested and transported to the concentration camps at Lichterfelde or Oranienburg. These scenes were constantly in my thoughts as we drove past Munich to the internment camp at Augsberg.

I had been arrested by the U.S.A. Counter-Intelligence Corps, and for the first time I heard the heavy door of a prison cell slam behind me. I was treated correctly, and sometimes with friendly consideration, by the Americans, but that slamming door opened up a new chapter in my eventful life.

In the next few years I had a unique observation post and could follow the liquidation of the past and become acquainted with those who dealt with this work on the Allied side.

Escorted by a very obliging French officer, I drove to Paris in August, 1945, in what had been von Rundstedt's car. We passed through Verdun just as the verdict on Pétain was announced there, so that I was too late to give evidence at his trial, as had been originally intended. The associates of de Gaulle, who was then head of the French Government, were much interested in other matters of which I had knowledge, particularly in the conversations between Molotov and Hitler.

Coming from an internment camp in devastated Germany I felt as though I was dreaming when I walked, practically at liberty, along the boulevards in Paris, where I did not see a broken window pane. With my escort, a friendly police inspector, I sat on the café terraces I knew so well, or walked up and down the Boulevard Saint-Michel. Once I dined at Fouquet's. This dream lasted ten days, and then I returned to the internment camp near Mannheim.

The next three years were spent in this alternation—between individual arrest and lodging in a villa; between a witnesses, prison at Nuremberg and nominal house arrest at Tegernsee; and, to complete the experience, I spent three months at the notorious concentration camp of Dachau, under very strange circumstances.

My experiences during this period were little inferior in historical and human drama to those of earlier years. I not only appeared as witness for the defence and for the prosecution at the main trials at Nuremberg, but I also worked as interpreter and language maid-of-all-work in the Nuremberg "witnesses' prison," an arrangement typical of the period after the conclusion of hostilities. For a short time I was employed in the American languages service, the Language Division, and made some tragic and also some highly comic contacts under the occupation regime as official court interpreter in court-martial trials of American members of the Wehrmacht. The night when those convicted in the main trial were executed, I was staying in a wing about fifty yards from the gymnasium where, the last few nights, I had heard the dull blows as the gallows were erected. I interpreted for the American psychiatrists, accompanying them on their visits in the Nuremberg prison, and witnessed human dramas of deep tragedy.

In my professional capacity, I took part not only in the liquidation of the past, but also in the political, and more especially the economic, developments of the immediate future. I had to translate many a memorandum by German officials for the Allies. The problems and their phrasing often bore a striking resemblance to papers I had worked on in the 'twenties, and my old vocabulary of the period of reparations conferences and trade negotiations stood me in good stead. I started again from the beginning as a one-man languages service, translating as I had in 1923 about trade balances, levels of trade and industry, pressure of taxation and unemployment. A rather inferior portable wireless, successor to my old friend, kept me up to date with the vocabulary of the post-war period—the distress of refugees, the iron curtain, dismantling and the air lift.

My experiences during this post-war period were no less varied than during diplomatic events from 1923 to 1945. They were, however, no longer concerned with the diplomatic stage, although the work was similar, and I had been relegated from the stage to the auditorium, so they do not come within the scope of this book.

INDEX